CARING

CARING

An Essay in the Philosophy of Ethics

Stan van Hooft

Foreword by Jean Watson

UNIVERSITY PRESS OF COLORADO

Published by the University Press of Colorado
P.O. Box 849, Niwot, Colorado 80544

The University Press of Colorado is a cooperative publishing enterprise supported,
in part, by Adams State College, Colorado State University, Fort Lewis College,
Mesa State College, Metropolitan State College of Denver, University of Colorado,
University of Northern Colorado, University of Southern Colorado,
and Western State College of Colorado.

The paper used in this publication meets the minimum requirements
of the American National Standard for Information Sciences—Permanence of
Paper for Printed Library Materials. ANSI Z39.48–1984

∞

Library of Congress Cataloging-in-Publication Data

van Hooft, Stan, 1945–
    Caring: an essay in the philosophy of ethics / Stan van Hooft.
        p.   cm.
    Includes bibliographical references and index.
    ISBN 0-87081-361-7
    1. Ethics. 2. Caring. I. Title.
    BJ1012.H66   1995
    171'.8–dc20
                                                            94-38973
                                                            CIP

10   9   8   7   6   5   4   3   2   1

CONTENTS

Introduction   *1*

1. Commitment   *13*

2. Caring   *29*
Caring as Motivational Structure
Deep Caring

3. On Being Human   *48*
A Model for Exploring Humanity
The Biological Level
The Perceptual and Reactive Level
The Evaluative and Proactive Level
The Spiritual Level

4. Caring-About-Others   *75*
The Biological Level
The Perceptual and Reactive Level
The Evaluative and Proactive Level
The Spiritual Level

5. Communication   *96*
The Biological Level
The Perceptual-Reactive and
    Evaluative-Proactive Levels
The Spiritual Level

6. Prereflexive Ethics   *119*
The Biological Level
The Perceptual and Reactive Level

7. Ethics and Prudence   *140*

    The Evaluative and Proactive Level
    The Nature of Ethics
    Ethical Discourse and Caring

8. Morality and Integrity   *164*

    Morality and the Fourth Level of Our Being
    Freedom and Integrity

Notes   *193*

Bibliography   *203*

Index   *209*

Fellow-feeling may vary in level and in degree of penetration into its object; it may extend to peripheral conditions, or to the inmost depths of personality, and with feelings of a sensory, vital or spiritual kind; but this is entirely dependent on the antecedent category of the love which underlies it — i.e., according to how love is directed upon that particular level.

— Max Scheler, *The Nature of Sympathy*

FOREWORD

Though the roots of civilization and modern medicine were founded upon caring as a means for both survival and treatment, there is increasing uncertainty as to whether logic, moral reason, or science can relieve us of the dilemmas our world now faces. Indeed, there is concern over whether the field of medical ethics, as constructed by current thinking, can progress much further in solving the issues of caring in society than science can. As it has happened, some contemporary versions of moral realism and moral rationalism have attempted to import the methodology of science to ethics — unsuccessfully, I might add.

Stan van Hooft's major work *Caring: An Essay in the Philosophy of Ethics* is an antidote to the intellectual discourse in medicine, science, and ethics, which has not known how to handle human caring as a guiding principle, an ethic, or a condition of being human. The overriding strength of this important work on caring and ethics is the fact that caring is given its own ontological status in moral theory and in life itself. Thus van Hooft's starting point, moral theory in crisis, is unraveled. He then lays out a framework for explicating a philosophy and ethic of caring that is made more explicit than contemporary moral discourse (except for the contemporary field of feminist ethics and caring).

This work then becomes a theory on deep caring as the ultimate foundation for being human, which grounds ethics and must be included in any philosophical system of ethics. This work seeks to take the reader, student, colleague "all the way down" to the depths of caring for self and for others, caring which permeates and motivates self-expression in all aspects of human existence, including the basic biological, environmental, perceptual, reactive levels from which we orient ourselves to the world and find our being in it. Further, this work unifies multiple levels of our being, from the biological to the spiritual, whereby we are called to live out our highest hopes, loves, and faiths. Finally, this deep exploration uncovers a living ethic of a caring being and our being as care.

Though Heidegger posited such notions of caring as ontology earlier this century, it seems that van Hooft has uncovered the same wisdom from his own explorations of the human condition with respect to moral theory and philosophy of ethics. The deep caring which has been uncovered in this work holds forth new ways of thinking, being, and knowing. Yes, moral theory is in crisis, and so is moral action; this work offers new ways of considering both our life and our ethics, positing caring as primal and primary to all theory and action. Now it must be brought front and center in our discourse and any further developments in theory and practice of ethics and morality in medicine, in science, in philosophy, in life.

— Jean Watson, R.N., Ph.D., FAAN
Director, Center for Nursing Health Sciences Center, Denver

Acknowledgments

I began thinking about the issues in this book while lecturing to first-year nursing students at Deakin University in Australia. Many of the ideas were initially tested out on my students in various philosophy courses and on my philosophical colleagues in various seminars and meetings. I am beholden to all of these people for their feedback, to an anonymous reviewer of an earlier draft, and especially to Dr. Graeme Marshall of the University of Melbourne for his continued encouragement. Thanks are due also to my wife, Lynne, and my children for putting up with my obsessiveness.

CARING

INTRODUCTION

Moral theory is in crisis. Many[1] have impugned the assumption of traditional moral theory that it can offer a rationally grounded guidance for action or identify our bjective obligations. The various versions of consequentialism and utilitarianism wallow in sophistry as they seek vainly for a clear moral objective in light of which actions might be justified. The notions of virtue and honour which might once have constituted the guiding spirit of practical affairs are now thought to be anachronistic irrelevancies. Outside of the academy, moral convictions are taken to be merely personal preferences regarding policies for action which are distinguished from other such policies only by their greater felt stringency. The origin of this stringency is seldom inquired into, but when it is, it is identified merely as upbringing or peer group pressure.

In an age when "God is dead," moral scepticism seems to be unavoidable. Given that neither Divine Law nor any of its Kantian substitutes grounded in the transcendental laws of reason seem to have any hold on the modern secular mind, the recent arguments of several philosophers[2] to the effect that relativism or even amoralism is incoherent seem somehow to miss the point. If even the authority of reason is under challenge, then an incoherently solipsistic subjectivism in moral thinking cannot be prevented from growing in the rich soil of secular nihilism.

Still seeking to avoid this outcome, some philosophers[3] suggest that an ethical point of view can be rationally chosen. But such a choice would be rational only in the sense that it is justifiable. It would not be rational in the sense that the arguments for it would be so compelling as to force anyone who hears them to accede to them. That one should be able to make one's choice rationally comprehensible, even if only after one has made it, may be all the scope that reason has available to it in an age when the shared traditions upon which rational agreement might have been established are no longer available.

INTRODUCTION

The most frequently heard modern symptom of this condition of our moral culture is the dictum that in the face of difficult moral choices, we must do what feels right for us. This dictum may have a range of meanings. It may be a suggestion that we appeal to our conscience, a suggestion based on the confidence that were we to do so, we would find there the traditional values which, having been internalised through our socialization, continue to hold us within the accepted moral bounds that make social life possible. Or it may be a suggestion that we should appeal to our most deeply felt wants and needs, a suggestion based on the view that we have within us a real being whose authentic desires have been distorted or hidden by our socialization, so that if we were only able to let this real self within us express itself, then we would act rightly and achieve self-fulfillment. Of course, it may also indicate an outright hedonism in which we are simply urged to do whatever we feel like for the simple reason that we feel like it. Insofar as this view is supported by any theory, it might be one that adopts the model of the pressure cooker and suggests that pathological outcomes will ensue unless we are able to fulfill our desires. Or it may be the quite credible thesis of some feminist writers that affection and concern for relationships should play a stronger role in our ethical lives, as they have always done for women.[4]

This turn towards feeling in response to our disillusionment with reason has point. I believe that much wisdom is still to be found in Aristotle. His dictum that to act well we must not only reason truly but also desire rightly[5] points to a motivational basis for ethical behaviour other than simple preference and other than the purely rationally grounded principles so beloved of the Kantian tradition. Desiring rightly is an appropriate motivational response to a particular situation linked to an appropriate way of understanding that situation in practical terms. It is my view that desiring or feeling rightly in a given practical situation depends upon our caring about relevant aspects of that situation, and that the basis for this caring lies deeply within us. Moreover, I believe that our caring can issue in settled ethical convictions which I call commitments. Further, our caring can come to expression in ethical discourse. Achieving some clarity about the concepts of caring and commitment will lead us towards a new way of conceptualising our ethical convictions and their felt stringency without requiring us to return to discredited moral theories.

* * *

Our contemporary understanding of morality derives from a tradition that extends back at least as far as Plato and includes as its preeminent theorist Kant. We see in Kant all the hallmarks of the modern discourse of morality: moral realism, rationalism, universalism, deontology, and the metaphysical bifurcation of human being, and all this postulated in order to give morality a single ultimate foundation. His theory of morality encourages the belief that there are rules or principles that should be followed for their own sake, irrespective of the agent's inclinations and caring. As a result of Kant's influence, the key terms in understanding modern moral psychology are *moral obligation* and *duty*. This notion of obligation seeks to distinguish itself strongly from prudential reason and suggests the transcendent existence of objective external reasons for acting. As such, it leaves no room for such personal and particular motivational aspects of our being as caring.

No one has done more to counter this modern view of morality than Bernard Williams. Central to his critique is his alternative account of moral obligation, which he takes to be an example of a more general phenomenon called *practical necessity*.[6] Whether they are a part of the daily routine or felt to be important in a unique way, our projects typically involve tasks which I feel I "must" perform. This experience of practical necessity, of the feeling that I "must" do something whether I feel inclined to do it or not, has been taken by many to be the defining mark of obligation and therefore of the moral.

Against this, Williams argues that this feeling is not unique to the moral sphere. A stamp collector might feel that he or she "must" do what is required to obtain a rare stamp. This shows that practical necessity is an experience that arises in a range of contexts wider than those characterizable as moral. Williams analyses it as involving two features. Firstly, the agent must consider the matter at hand to be important, and secondly, the agent must give it deliberative priority. The motivational force of practical necessity must be understood as arising from the agent's concerns and commitments rather than from external imposition or moral duty. But is this enough? If a stamp collector can feel that he or she "must" acquire a certain stamp, and if I can feel that I "must" hurry to catch a train, am I really describing the kind of stringent practical necessity which leads some to undergo great suffering and hardship and even the loss of life itself?

In thinking morally, we are responding to the question of what we should do in a given circumstance, where that circumstance appears to be of great moment. Some sort of ultimacy seems to attach to these situations. Things or people in such situations seem to call out to me in pressing ways. There may be a continuum of cases ranging from a rare stamp "calling out" to a collector such that the latter feels he must buy it, to someone's father calling out from a burning building to his son that he might save him. But the latter case seems to differ at least in degree of importance from the former. It does seem true that we often feel ourselves duty bound to act in a certain way rather than pressed by mere urgency or interest.

Williams suggests that the key element that marks the difference we are looking for is that in the cases we are apt to describe as moral, the matter at hand is important. However, this begs the question of whether there is any objective, rational, universal, or transcendent criterion for whether anything is important.[7] Williams's answer to this problem is to suggest that the typical collector's interest in stamps does not go "all the way down" into the character of the person[8] in the way that concerns about matters of genuine import do. We give deliberative priority only to matters which concern us deeply. It is our concerns rather than objective moral facts that determine what will be important. Williams does not explicate the suggestive phrase "all the way down." It is clearly intended to point towards our most fundamental motivations. My book will explore this phrase and present a theory to explicate it. I will argue that deeming something important is an interpretation grounded in the commitments of agents or in what agents care about. I will argue that it is our caring which grounds the feeling that we "must" do something.

In order to theorise this argument, I propose a model of what it is to be human drawn largely from the Continental European philosophical tradition and reminiscent of Aristotle's view of the soul, in which caring and commitments can be seen to express a primordial motivational field which I call *deep caring*. Deep caring is a motivational comportment which defines the self even as it relates that self to others and to the world around it. Accordingly, I analyse it as comprising two aspects: caring as self-project and caring as caring-about-others. Further, this motivational comportment will express itself in all aspects of our lives. I classify aspects of our lives, or forms of human living, as occurring on four levels, so that our deep caring expresses itself on these four levels. Existing as a human being comprises a biological level of interaction with the physical environment; a perceptual and reactive level in which we cognitively orient ourselves to the world and find our place in it; an evaluative and proactive level in which we define ourselves as reflective, purposive, and active beings in a world we appropriate as our own; and a spiritual level in which we live out our highest hopes, loves, and faiths so as to make the whole meaningful and in which we express our prereflexive solidarity with, and acknowledgments of, the other through such phenomena as moral discourse. These four levels are unified in that they jointly constitute the basis of the attitudes and commitments which are differing expressions of our being as deep caring in the twin forms of self-project and caring-about-others.

My elaboration of what it is for our motivations to go "all the way down" is not intended only to fill out Williams's sketch for an alternative theory of what the tradition identifies as moral obligation. It is also intended to justify my claim that ethics and morality are to be understood as expressions of our deep caring. The key premises in my argument will be the idea that ethics has a communicative dimension and that this links with the communicative dimension of our being as care. In this way ethics becomes an expression of our wish to maintain communicative links with others.

The only demarcation that this theory provides between those things we judge to be important because they accord with interests of ours which most others do not share — such as an interest in collecting stamps — and those things our moral tradition has judged to be important in themselves is that the latter are apt to be part of the ethos of our society in which I have my formation as a person. This is not a matter of saying that stamp collecting is only a minority interest and therefore less likely to be deemed universally important, whereas certain norms of behaviour and character are much more widely held to be important and thereby approach the standing of a universal requirement. Morality is not established by plebiscite. Rather, my claim is that I will judge or find certain behaviours to be important in a deeper way than others because these accord with my being as a self-project and a caring-about-others as this being is historically formed in a given society. Mature persons should be able to let go of their interest in such things as stamps to a degree that they cannot let go of their commitment to ethical values, because the stringency of ethical values is a function of the cultural formation given to my deep caring as self-project and caring-about-others.

Once we understand ethics as an expression of our deep caring, we will be led to a new view of the meaning of traditional morality and of our freedom as ethical agents.

* * *

Before arguing my points, I should make a few methodological remarks. The analysis that I offer is to be distinguished from the form of description which is characteristic of science and which is marked by a dependence on causal explanation offered in terms of observable or hypothetical entities. When science approaches human reality, it does so from the outside. It observes, describes, and explains. In contrast, my approach is phenomenological. We who ask the question of what it is to be a human being are the human beings in question. In seeking an answer, we can reflect on our own experience. Of course, the only experiences that I can reflect on directly are my own. Can I generalise from this without relying on observation and hypotheses?

There are two solutions to this problem. Firstly, our understanding of what it is to be a human being should be informed by and consistent with relevant biological, psychological, and anthropological knowledge, although this knowledge must be interpreted and applied sensitively. The best test for whether this has been achieved is whether the resultant findings are true to my own experience. Secondly, my own experience, like everyone else's, is structured by shared cultural understandings. It follows that my reflection on what it is for me myself to be a human being is not confined to my own case. My experience is articulated through the understandings that I share with others. Accordingly, I can reflect on what others tell me, on my reactions to that, and on what such communication discloses about the worldview that we share.

The history of human culture is the history of such communication and of reflection upon it. Along with the many functional exchanges that people use language for, as when we go to the grocer and ask for a tin of baked beans, there are personal, literary, and scientific exchanges in which people's understandings of each other, of life, and of the world around them come to articulation. Reflection on these matters becomes a reflection on the vast amounts of thought, aspiration, and discovery that are part of the human condition. The question of what it is to be a human being will involve not only a reflection on my own experience but also on the collective experience of many other people as transmitted in the languages and cultures of which I am a part and with which I have contact.

A second methodological point is that when I describe human being, I prefer to use verbs rather than nouns that seem to name mysterious metaphysical entities. For example, I prefer to speak of us as acting freely, rather than as having freedom. The metaphysical approach is epitomised by the postulation of *free will*, understood as a faculty unique to those beings who are said to be free in the relevant sense. Aspects of experience cannot be explained without circularity by postulating metaphysical entities which will serve as faculties which generate those experiences. The difficulty of reconciling the existence of an entity called free will with a universe in which all phenomena are to be understood in terms of causes and effects is well known. In a similar way, I deal with such nouns as *life, soul,* and *mind* by turning them into verbs. I speak of living and being conscious instead.

My model is not a picture of an archetypal static entity called a human being but a description of the activity of being human. *Being* is a verb. But do we really engage in an activity called "being a human being"? We engage in such activities as eating a meal, going to the grocer, helping a friend, caring for a patient, being with a lover, worshipping our God, and so forth. Is there an activity called being a human being over and above all these particular activities? Surely not. These particular activities, along with many others, are the sorts of activities that add up to being a human being.

Yet it is not true either that being a human being is simply the sum of these various activities. This is because, insofar as these activities are engaged in by human beings, they are engaged in in a humanly meaningful way. Being a human being is realised in the way we do things, as well as in what we do. The meanings which our activities have are, in their turn, derived largely from our cultures. In this way our cultures make it possible for us to be human in the way that we are. Human being involves a range of behaviours, mental activities, states, and dispositions which have culturally constructed human meanings.

This raises a third methodological point. I assume that cultures form, but do not determine, what it is to be human. The relations between human beings and their cultures are dialectical. Not only do human beings require the formation given them by their cultures, but they also actively contribute to those cultures as they live in a creative way. Individual persons cannot live as human beings, with all the experiences, aspirations, and projects which that entails, unless they are formed within their culture. Further, their pursuing their plans and projects adds to and sometimes changes culture and society, albeit that such change usually occurs in a gradual way. To be a human being, or to be in a human way, is both to exist and act in relation to cultural and social realities which define one's identity, and to contribute to that context. Accordingly, a description of our being is a description of the various dynamic interrelationships which we participate in at the four levels of our being and which we are motivated to enter into by our caring. These range from biological processes of interaction to the intimate and ethical intersubjective dialectic which springs from our comportment towards others and from their responses to us.

A fourth methodological point flows from this. Thinking about human phenomena involves thinking in a hermeneutical manner. I reject empiricist observation, causal explanation, and the postulation of metaphysical entities. What is left to aid our understanding? Given that culture and language structure all our thinking, we can develop concepts which refer to phenomenological experience and which will provide a horizon against which we can understand the phenomenon in question.

My notion of deep caring is a case in point. I will argue that deep caring is preconscious and thus without phenomenology. However, ordinary caring is experienced by us, and this experience can then provide the conceptual content of the notion of deep caring. In its turn, the notion of deep caring can provide the horizon against which particular caring (including moral concerns) can be understood. When I speak of deep caring as being foundational to our particular concerns or commitments, I do not mean that deep caring can provide a causal explanation for commitments or that deep caring is a metaphysical faculty which is postulated to account for commitments. Rather, I mean that we can understand the place of our particular caring and commitments in the structure of our lives against the interpretative horizon of our deep caring.

But this will only advance our understanding if we note a final methodological point. In describing a deep form of caring and four levels of our existence, we are engaging in ontology. This means that we are describing the mode of being which we enjoy as human beings. We do not exist as things do. Our mode of being is the key to understanding all human phenomena. If we existed as physical objects, then all understanding of our existence would be summed up in physics. If we existed as plants or animals, then all understanding of our existence would be summed up in biology. If we existed as cogs in a social and productive machine, then all understanding of our existence would be summed up in sociology and economics. If we existed as pure thought, then all understanding of our existence would be summed up in Kantian philosophy. But we exist as human beings. Understanding what that means requires that we engage in ontology. We understand ourselves when we understand what we do, feel, and say as an expression of the kind of being that we enjoy: namely, being as caring.

* * *

INTRODUCTION

Jeffrey Blustein's book *Caring and Commitment*[9] came to my attention after I had almost finished drafting this book. There is some overlap between my first two chapters and his work in that he describes more eloquently than I ever could the place of caring and commitment in our moral psychology. However, where Blustein goes on to develop the implications of his descriptions for such questions as whether intimate relationships should override the impartiality required by the moral point of view, I seek to offer a theoretical grounding of the place that caring and commitment have in our motivational lives. Blustein offers excellent descriptions and conceptual analyses of such key concepts as commitment, caring, and integrity. True to the methods of linguistic analysis, Blustein unpacks the implications of how these words are used in everyday speech, including our moral discourse. In contrast, my own concept of deep caring is a theoretical construction offered as a means of understanding our inner lives. It goes beyond ordinary language and seeks to revise how we understand ethics.

An example of where this distinction between us matters occurs when Blustein concludes his discussion of integrity and self-transformation.[10] He says that integrity should allow for change, meaning that it is part of the meaning of the word *integrity* that persons so described are not inflexible or fanatical. This is true, but it leaves us wondering what the basis can be of such a change and how we would distinguish authentic changes from instances of weak will. One can answer this question by positing a deeper level in the self which can find expression both in actions which are consistent with commitments and in actions which are not but which still preserve the agent's integrity. One needs to posit a level of caring to account for self-transformations which are not simply instances of fickleness.

Again, Blustein says that "if the individual has a plurality of identity-conferring commitments, integrity requires that these too be ordered or integrated in some way."[11] But in what sense does integrity require anything? The answer, of course, is that this is a conceptual requirement. It is part of the meaning of the term *integrity* that the agent's commitments be ordered. My alternative account would be that the requirement arises from the existential self-projects of agents. People demand it of themselves that they order their commitments so as to achieve integrity. We all strive to live our lives in a coherent way, and we display integrity to the extent that we succeed. By positing a deep level of caring, rather than simply unpacking the meaning of the relevant words, I am able to interpret integrity as the aim of our striving for selfhood, rather than merely a term used for ascriptions.

Similarly, consider the definition of the self which Blustein offers: "With respect to personal integrity, the person is a unified whole in terms of commitments."[12] What this means is that a person achieves selfhood, or becomes a unified whole, only if his or her commitments are coherent. The question that this raises is what the origin of this wholeness can then be. If the coherent self is the product of cohesion, then who is the subject of the commitments which are supposed to cohere? Again, we need to uncover a deeper level of our being in order to answer this question. A way out of the conceptual circularity which defines selfhood in terms of coherent commitments, and coherent commitments as the result of selfhood, is to open a new hermeneutic level of description.

Moreover, I believe that there are some quandaries in Blustein's thesis which my theoretical grounding would help to overcome. For example, Blustein makes a distinction between "deep-seated or serious caring" which is "capable of endowing our lives with meaning," and "peripheral care," the objects of which "are not positively endorsed."[13] Although this distinction resembles my own between deep caring and particular caring, it differs in that the basis of Blustein's distinction is that the object of serious caring must be deemed to have impersonal value by the agent, whereas the object of peripheral caring has personal value only. It seems that Blustein is committed to one of these two theses: firstly, that there is such a thing as objective impersonal value which agents recognise and adhere to, or secondly, that impersonal value is something that agents deem to be real as a function of their serious caring. But if the latter is right, then the distinction between serious and peripheral caring breaks down, because the importance of what agents care about is a function of caring in either case.

A further way in which Blustein makes the distinction is by saying that "a notion of impersonal value is not only needed to explain what is involved in viewing one's *life* as meaningful, but is also implicated in ascriptions to *oneself* of integrity."[14] This alludes to Blustein's important point that one invests oneself in what one cares about — a point which I express by saying that one of the forms of deep caring is our self-project. But this still begs the question of whether the importance of what one cares about is a function of that caring or of some impersonal value. Blustein hedges his bets by saying that agents must believe the objects of their serious caring to have impersonal value, but also that they need not believe that everyone ought to care for the same things.[15]

There is evidence that Blustein is, nevertheless, wedded to the first of these theses: namely, an objectivist account of impersonal value. In the course of his defence of utilitarianism against the charge that the impartial standpoint of this calculative moral theory demands that we stand aside from our commitments and thereby jeopardise our integrity, Blustein makes the remark that "even if persons do not naturally act in accordance with the impersonal standpoint of utilitarianism, what is 'natural' may not be appropriate, rational, or something we should cultivate or encourage."[16] This clearly suggests that there are impersonal values or external reasons which should override our natural caring.

Again, in the course of his discussion of integrity, Blustein distinguishes moral integrity from personal integrity.[17] Moral integrity is not simply perspicuous commitment to the agent's own ideals. This would not distinguish it from personal integrity. Nor does the ascription of moral integrity require that the ascriber agree with the moral norms of the agent. Rather the ascription seems to refer to traits of character such as "honesty, fairness, truthfulness and being a person of one's word."[18] But what this makes clear is that the real distinction between personal integrity and moral integrity is that the latter is an ascription, whereas the former is the object or achievement of an existential quest.

Personal integrity is the aim of our caring and the product of our adherence to our commitments, whereas moral integrity is a description of personal integrity offered from a third-person perspective. And this third-person perspective is motivated by social needs. Because personal integrity has social utility in certain contexts, it is praised by being called moral integrity. If there is anything more to the distinction than that, Blustein must be committed to an objectivist understanding of morality. And that Blustein is so committed is clear: "The reliability of conscience is not self-certifying; support is needed from some source external to conscience itself."[19] It is in relation to this unquestioned acceptance of a traditional view of morality that I differ most from Blustein.

1

COMMITMENT

Commitment is a stance towards the world or towards others on the part of an individual or group which defines what is important or imperative for that individual or group. Moral nihilism can be countered by commitment. Commitment is a basis for making decisions in both moral and other spheres which, though not being grounded in supernatural or transcendental realities of the sort which our secular culture can no longer accept, nevertheless transcends the immediate wants and wishes of the individual agent or group because it arises from a deeper level of our being than reason. Rather than being grounded in reason, commitment provides a matrix within which reason operates. If it is amenable to the critical scrutiny of reason, it must be because other commitments motivate such critical reasoning.

This view of commitment is supported by the remarks of several philosophers. Kai Nielsen, in the context of a discussion of the question, Why be moral?, admits that "a complete justification of any practical claim necessarily involves making a choice or decision" concerning the principles in light of which practical considerations will be taken seriously.[1] He further insists that there must be a proper way of choosing these ultimate principles, even if no objective criteria are available. It may be that common-sense attitudes about what makes life worth living or sensitivity to shared human needs are the sorts of bases that are available for making these ultimate decisions, but no such basis can completely determine the choice. Nielsen uses the term *commitment* to refer to these ultimate decisions or choices and encourages the view that practical reason operates within the context of commitment rather than being able to ground it.

The notion of commitment as a fundamental choice which grounds both practical reason and moral imperatives is also developed by Leszek Kolakowski in his book *Religion*.[2] Kolakowski argues that religion, being "not a set of propositions but a way of life in which understanding, believing and commitment emerge together in a single act" cannot be grounded rationally. It emerges, rather, in the life of people "as a result of their actual initiation into worship."[3] It is, in short, a way of life which contrasts with an atheistic way of life. Each of these ways of life can be internally coherent in relation to beliefs, practices, and norms of action. When we become reflexively conscious of the possibility of doing so, we must choose between them in a way that carries implications for what we will then find it rational to believe and do and what we will take to be required of us morally. Further, we will be able to argue about such matters on the basis of what is already recognised as being implicated in the way of life we have chosen. Practical reason will seek to uncover what it is rational and therefore imperative for us to do given our originary choice. The choice itself, however, cannot be grounded in reason.

Stuart Hampshire, in an article critical of calculative reason in moral thought, discusses the problem not only of whether rationality might be a basis for morality, but whether it may be used to adjudicate between conflicting inclinations in situations of difficult moral choice or dilemma. He argues that "no sufficient reason of any kind is on occasion available to explain a decision made after careful reflection in a situation of moral conflict"[4] but applauds this fact as providing humanity with the opportunity for moral experimentation and progress. As for what does ground moral choices, if not reason, Hampshire suggests that a person's "imagination of possibilities has its part, and so do intuitions that he cannot fully explain, arising from experience."

Discussing the case where a person allows no compromise of his or her moral preferences, a case he describes as one in which the agent has a "mission," Hampshire says: "For him there is an ultimate choice focused on this occasion between two ways of life, and he cannot refer this conflict of moral claims to an order of priority among the virtues constituting his ideal way of life." Such persons, says Hampshire, "will be guided by intuition, which entails reflecting on the two possibilities as fully as possible and then coming to a conclusion for reasons which they cannot arrange in a conclusive argument."[5] This ultimate choice, which Hampshire also calls a commitment, is a perimeter beyond which practical reason is not able to reach.

Whether such a choice must also be inexplicable in terms of the agent's character is a question that Hampshire does not discuss very fully, though he does hint at a negative answer when he says that such a fundamental choice or commitment "arises from dense personal experience, and as a consequence of a man's particular conditions of life, and of his philosophical beliefs. No more can be said in general terms, except that morality does unalterably have this aspect of commitment to a way of life, even though many persons may never consciously confront such an ultimate choice."[6] Here there is a hint that the relation between agents' characters and their basic choices or commitments may not be contingent or accidental. The nature of this relation is indicated by Hampshire's mention of experience. The accretion of moral experience goes into the making of a moral character, and that character then becomes, by way of its intuitions, the basis upon which subsequent decisions are made. If we add to Hampshire's account the point that moral choices made in early life might have been made on the basis of upbringing and socialisation, it becomes clear that agents are at no point completely without a basis for making moral choices, even if they might be without a foundational moral theory to ground their thinking. The mention of character and of the moral intuitions to which it might give rise encourages me to ask whether the foundations of character might not include, along with such causal factors as upbringing and socialisation and such biographical factors as previous experience, existential factors such as commitment and caring.

Gabriele Taylor, in a discussion of integrity, highlights this point. She argues that practical reason operates within the matrix of commitment. Further, unless this commitment is grounded fully in the agent's character, it would not constitute the basis of the moral imperative which attaches to the decisions arrived at by practical reason. By itself, practical reason can only tell us what is the best thing to do in a given situation. That we should also feel called upon to do that which is best needs further explanation.

Taylor finds this explanation in the need for persons to hold all of the aspects of their personalities or characters together in a coherently lived life. Taylor calls this *integrity*. Persons must act as practical reason indicates, lest they fall apart. "There is to the 'must' or 'cannot' a background consisting of the various implications of some one commitment or of interrelated commitments."[7] Given that a commitment, for Taylor, constitutes a moral worldview, and given that a moral worldview is not a function solely of an intellectual position, but of the various other aspects of character and experience which we have already alluded to, it emerges that commitment has a crucial and originary function in the moral life of persons. Integrity involves holding all of these various aspects of the person together and acting consistently with them. Commitment provides the basis and background for this unification of life and is thus situated at a crucial and fundamental position in the existential map of our ethical lives.

The notion of a vocation or a profession captures something of what a commitment is. In the classical sense of the term, when one professes something, one announces one's dedication to it. One professes a religious faith. One professes a life of work dedicated to a particular end. For example, a medical doctor professes a life given over to healing. A lawyer professes a life given over to justice, and so on. However debased these notions might have become in our own cynical age, the classical meaning of the notion of profession is a central part of the notion of commitment which I am developing. Although the worth of healing and justice is clear and unarguable, the major connotative force in the word *profession*, made especially clear when we concentrate on the verb *to profess*, points towards the subject. The person who professes declares a dedication. This is more than an acceptance of the value or goal inherent in the life being chosen. It is a choice that that particular value become the ruling value of that person's life.

In contrast, the notion of *vocation* points a little more towards the object. A vocation is a calling. In the religious tradition, the call is said to come from God and is therefore quite literally a call. In a more secular sense, however, the call may be metaphorical and might consist of the innate attractiveness, to the responsive spirit, of the life of healing or the pursuit of justice, or it may simply consist of another's need in a specific situation. In either case a vocation is a call to respond to something outside the agent which is apprehended as valuable or as being in need. My suggestion is that the notion of commitment combines both the more subjective connotation of *to profess* and the objective connotation of *vocation*.

Commitment is a two-way dynamic relationship between a subjective state and an intentional object. Commitment is intentional in the sense of being directed upon an object. One is committed to something or to someone. One cannot simply be committed in the sense of taking a generalised subjective stance without holding something before one as the object of that commitment, although that object may be vague or ill-defined. Indeed, there are two ways of understanding this intentionality. On the one hand, the intentional object seems to attract or solicit the commitment which is extended to it. On the other, there are aspects of the agent's character to which this object is attractive or solicitous so that the agent responds by taking a committed stance. In this way, commitment seems to arise both from that to which one is dedicated or devoted and from the aspects of personality or character which are engaged by those objects. The intentional object which attracts our commitment must seem worthy of our dedication or devotion. However, it must appeal to a state of my being which, I will argue, can be described as my caring about that object. Commitment is a relationship which can only be fully understood by understanding both the objective and subjective terms of that relationship. In Chapter 2, I will seek to understand the subjective term by exploring the notion of caring. For now, I will seek to understand the intentional objects of commitment.

To describe those things that might be objects of commitment, let us borrow an example that Stuart Hampshire mentions briefly in his paper "Morality and Pessimism."[8] In this paper Hampshire challenges utilitarianism and its corrosive effect on the values of the traditional conscience. He argues for the legitimacy of standards of behaviour even where a full rationale for those standards is not available. Agents may simply feel that what they are called upon to do is inescapably something that they will not permit themselves to do.

Hampshire's example involves the torture of military prisoners to obtain secrets the disclosure of which would save many lives. The utilitarian challenge to overcome one's scruples against torture here is obvious, but Hampshire makes the point that it is perfectly correct to stand by one's scruples rather than be swayed from them by the logic of utilitarianism. The would-be torturer senses a moral line that cannot be crossed. Hampshire describes this as a commitment to standards of behaviour which arises from a yet deeper commitment: namely, a commitment to a way of life of which these standards of behaviour are a part. Just how the various standards and prohibitions of behaviour are integral to a way of life is not spelled out by Hampshire, and perhaps it cannot be spelled out, except by reference to the ethical discourse of the relevant moral community. The central point is that the fundamental commitment that the would-be torturer expresses in refusing is a commitment to a way of life.

One way of understanding what a commitment to a way of life might involve would be to state what it is about a way of life as a whole that attracts our moral allegiance. But this would be an analysis of making a commitment rather than of having a commitment. This is presumably what lies behind Nielsen's suggestion that our commitments are grounded in common-sense attitudes to what is needed for a meaningful life.[9] In his view, we would make a commitment to a given way of life when we judged or felt that our need for meaning would be satisfied in such a life. And we could do this by making a new commitment or by reflexively confirming or remaking a commitment that we already have.

Making a commitment in either of these senses is an originary choice which founds our adherence to a way of life and to the norms of practical reason which attach to it. But the word *choice* introduces some problems. Choice is frequently understood as a free act arising out of an existential void, whereas I think of commitment as having a basis in the character of the agent. I believe it is the more common experience that the way of life which is the object of a commitment is simply found to be attractive or "natural" to given agents rather than offering itself to them for consideration. We have commitments but make them only rarely. It seems a more apt analysis of Hampshire's soldier to say that agents typically find themselves caring about a way of life and the objects and norms of behaviour that belong to it. Moreover, they generally make this reflexive discovery when some immediate situation creates a moral crisis or dilemma for them rather than in everyday, routine circumstances. It would therefore seem inappropriate to say that we typically make or have commitments to ways of life in any self-conscious sense. It is more likely that we simply have commitments to given ways of life and that further and more self-conscious commitments to specific persons or things are based on the way of life with which we find ourselves.

Indeed, we might say that a commitment to a way of life is so basic as to form part of one's historical and social identity as a person. For most people there is no break between what they are as persons and the way of life to which they are committed. It would seem to follow that commitment to a way of life is an aspect of character. It is out of what we are, as described by the way of life to which we are committed, that our more focused and specific commitments arise. For Hampshire, these more focused commitments include a commitment to standards of behaviour.

However, these suggestions of Hampshire's have an inescapably reflexive element to them. A commitment to a way of life and a consequent commitment to standards of behaviour all have an air of self-reference and self-preservation about them. A way of life is an expression of one's character and upbringing, and thus a commitment to a way of life is foundationally a commitment to one's own identity or self-image. But this seems to counter the frequent moral intuition that the moral value of a commitment arises from its being a commitment to other persons. The moral prejudice of our age prefers other-directedness to self-directedness. I will return to this matter in later chapters. For the moment, I do not want to prefer one of these analyses over the other without first exploring the relationship between a commitment and its objects in the case of commitment to persons.

Let us use Hampshire's example in a slightly different way. Imagine that you are the prisoner rather than the would-be torturer. Your resistance to the torture you anticipate undergoing might be motivated by a concern for your comrades-at-arms, who would surely be killed if you divulged the information, rather than by a way of life such as blind militaristic nationalism, for example. Your fear of the torture is not greater than your determination not to betray your companions. This would be a case of commitment of a deep kind. Whereas in Hampshire's analysis such a commitment is to standards of behaviour, in mine it is to persons. Of course, the distinction is not sharp. One might argue that the commitment, in the second case, is to not betraying one's comrades, where in the first, it is to not treating persons as mere means (if I might be permitted so Kantian a formulation), so that this first case, too, might be considered in general terms as a commitment to persons.

However, I do think that an important distinction is being marked when we note the difference between a commitment to persons in general and a commitment to particular persons with whom one has a relationship. The prisoner who demonstrates the latter commitment offers a better illustration of the phenomenology of commitment than the earlier case, which constitutes that general kind of moral stance towards persons and to standards of behaviour which our postmodern age has rendered problematic.

Commitments to ways of life are similarly general and vague. Perhaps my suggestion that commitments to standards of behaviour are the determinate form of the more inchoate commitments to ways of life should now be modified. Perhaps our standards of behaviour; our image of ourselves as moral agents; our general concern for people, for the environment, and for other living things are all examples of nondeterminate commitments which constitute character and which find expression and form in specific commitments such as those to particular persons, particular causes, or particular actions. Perhaps commitment, seen as a function of subjectivity, is always underdetermined but becomes focused and determined just to the degree that its intentional object is focused and determined.

Marriage might be an illustration of a commitment to persons where the focus of that commitment is sharp, being centred on the spouse and children. It is interesting to note that in this case the commitment, for all its being focused on particular persons, is nevertheless general in the sense that the range of actions to which one is committed is not specified in advance. One is not committed to any particular course of action, but to whatever actions are necessary to secure the well-being of one's spouse and children.

This marks a difference between this kind of commitment to persons and that of our prisoner. The commitment that our prisoner demonstrates is to not betray his comrades. Outside of the situation in which he finds himself, the prisoner might not have any strong commitment to these particular persons. The commitment exists for as long as they are comrades and comes to the fore only because of the threat of torture which exists at a particular time.

When one utters marriage vows, on the other hand, one enters into a commitment and undertakes to live by it whatever the circumstances, although what is required to exercise that commitment in any particular case is not yet specifiable. In this sense, marriage is a commitment to persons in a more pure form, rather than a commitment to certain behaviours or standards of behaviour.

Of course, the traditional conscience frequently understands marriage as implying a commitment to at least some minimal standards of behaviour, especially regarding sexual fidelity. However, as the range of customs around the world shows, marriage may embrace a range of ways of life and norms of behaviour. Nevertheless, it will still have a person-centred commitment at its core. If there is a threat to this sense of commitment, it would be the frequency of divorce, which creates an ethos undermining the open-ended temporal scope inherent in the notion of commitment. One can hardly be said to have committed oneself in an authentic sense to a marriage partner if, in making the commitment, one keeps in the back of one's mind the possibility that if the relationship is no longer pleasing, one can terminate it. Of course, the commitment involved in marriage should not be equated with the marriage vows. When one utters marriage vows, one has usually made the commitment already. Indeed, the commitment which precedes the formal declaration of vows is the basis upon which the vow makes sense.

The commitment of marriage is an expression of love between intending partners. This is another sense in which marriage provides a good model for commitment. It is clearly relational and intentional. The commitment or love is elicited by something over and above the self — in this case, something lovable and attractive in the love partner — and it is a deep and caring aspect of one's own character or personality that is engaged by the partner to constitute the commitment. Further, the commitment is intentional in the sense that it has an object. It is a commitment to the partner. Again, the commitment is originary in the sense that the devotion of one partner to the other, the vows and promises that the partners make to one another, and all of the other spoken and unspoken obligations that arise within the relationship are based upon, fuelled, and made imperative by the commitment.

Being committed to ideals provides an example of a different kind of object of commitment. To clarify fully what an ideal is would take us too far afield, but insofar as it involves a vision of the good for human beings, whether it is attainable within history or not, one can think of commitment to an ideal as involving a commitment to persons in a generalised sense. It may also involve a commitment to certain political or social practices which respect certain standards of behaviour and value certain human objectives. Whatever the details a closer analysis might disclose, it would seem that a commitment to an ideal is not so different from the general and nondeterminate forms of commitment so far discussed. It seems to involve at least an indirect reference to persons and to a specifiable way of life. But it would require specific historical circumstances to create an occasion for such a general commitment to become a specific practical stance. One would be suspicious of avowedly idealistic persons who failed to act in pursuit of their ideals when occasion demanded it. But one would also be suspicious of avowedly idealistic persons who acted in pursuit of their ideals but at the cost of the well-being of specific persons, especially if the idealist had a relationship of affection or responsibility for those persons.

Given that I can now speak of commitment not only as a specific and particular practical stance, but also as a somewhat vague and deep practical orientation, it should not surprise us that in life as lived, a commitment will often remain implicit until some moment of dramatic choice brings it to the fore. One may not know what one is committed to until faced with a difficult choice and forced to consider options which may not, in the abstract, have presented themselves as real.

Even when a commitment is made publicly, as in a marriage, one may not know what that commitment entails or the degree to which one is committed until an occasion arises which tests it. It may not be until one is called upon to respond to the overtures of a sexually attractive alternative that one recognises the true nature of one's commitment to one's spouse. The celebrated example which Sartre develops in his essay "Existentialism Is a Humanism"[10] of the student who is torn between wanting to join the French Resistance during the Second World War and staying home to care for his mother is apposite. Sartre makes the point that in making that decision, it would be of no use for the student to reflexively seek to discover how much his patriotic feeling is stronger or weaker than his love for his mother. He must decide, and in deciding he will discover where his commitment lies and what he most strongly cares about.

Indeed, Sartre puts the point more emphatically. He says (without using the word *commitment*) that the commitment is constituted by the choice that the student makes. It does not exist in any form prior to that choice but comes into being because of it. For Sartre, therefore, the student will, in deciding, constitute a new commitment from that moment on. If he decides to join the Resistance, his commitment will then be such as to call on him to sacrifice his mother's needs to that of his nation. No matter how urgent her needs become, to attend to them would constitute for the student, after he has made his decision, a case of backsliding. Indeed, based on this sort of consideration, Sartre views commitment as entailing a diminution of freedom.

Sartre's view is based on a different notion from the one I seek to develop. Whereas I suggest that a commitment bears a noncontingent relationship to character, Sartre propounds a radical form of freedom in which there is no actual basis within the person for choice or commitment. A choice is simply made in utter freedom without any form of predetermination. To the extent that the choice is adhered to or the commitment honoured, the agent is less free.

A passage from Sartre's *The Age of Reason* to which Basil Mitchell draws attention[11] makes this point very well. Mathieu has just kissed the Russian girl Ivich in a taxi, and his internal monologue indicates that he now discovers himself to be committed to her. He is both surprised and dismayed that this act, which he performed spontaneously, has changed his life irrevocably. The kissing which constitutes the choice in that example is something which Mathieu finds himself doing rather than does deliberately, so that he finds himself, almost with a sense of surprise, committed to the girl in the taxi. This *acte gratuit* which carries a commitment in its train may indeed seem like a threat to freedom, but this is because of its spontaneous origin rather than its entailed consequence. One cannot acknowledge a spontaneous action as one's own.

The student who would join the Resistance provides a better example of the relation of commitment to freedom, because it seems psychologically implausible that no prior commitment or care exists in the student out of which the choice must be made. Why else would the choice be a difficult one if the student is not torn between an idealistic commitment to his country and a filial commitment to his mother? That is why I prefer to interpret his choice as disclosing the relative strengths of his deep commitments as well as radically constituting a new commitment. This is borne out by Mitchell, who remarks on the peculiar emptiness and heartlessness of Sartre's characters in his commentary on the Mathieu passage. They seem to be voids within. Thus it is understandable that any commitment would be experienced by such a person as a threat to freedom. If, on the other hand, we accept that a person already has affections, desires, cares, and hopes, then a commitment can be seen to be consistent with freedom to the extent that it expresses those aspects of character or personality.

Moreover, that freedom is not closed off by this choice is shown when we consider that the commitment, once made or discovered, does not prevent the possibility of backsliding. The student will need to remake his commitment whenever he hears of the needs of his mother. Although this remaking is not without predeterminations, it can be readily seen as an exercise of freedom in that the option to return to his mother is always real. Rather than seeing commitment and freedom as necessarily in conflict, therefore, we need to understand them as standing in a complex dialectical relation. The student both discovers and determines what he is committed to by making his choice. To this extent the choice is not radically free. But the commitment does not destroy other options or render them less available. Rather, it demands that the student recurrently recommit himself whenever other options become real. At no point is he actually prevented from pursuing those other options, though he owes it to himself to renew his commitment.

A problem remains, however. What do we mean when we say that he "owes it to himself"? What is the nature of this obligation which lies at the heart of commitment? The basis for the obligation that arises from a commitment is the very generosity or care or love of which the commitment is a disclosure and a determination. Indeed, it is questionable whether the notion of obligation is really appropriate here. It may be that the way in which people "owe it to themselves" to stay true to their commitments is the way they owe it to themselves to remain true to themselves. If the commitment is based on generosity of spirit or on care or on love for another person, then to remain true to that commitment is simply to express that generosity, care, or love in an ongoing way. It becomes simply a matter of integrity or authenticity.

Gabriele Taylor's paper on integrity makes the relevant and interesting point that commitment has a peculiar logical feature: namely, having a commitment entails being true to one's commitment.[12] That is to say, if you are not true to your commitment, then you were not committed in the first place. Moreover, you cannot be committed if you are merely pretending to be committed. A commitment is a decision made or a stance taken. It has an internal dimension of irrevocability. Nor can you be half-heartedly or weakly committed. One's intentions may not be firm enough to carry something through, or one may not care about something deeply enough, but one cannot describe this by saying that one was only half-committed. If one's determination is weak in this way, it shows that one is simply not committed at all. But this would make it hard to account for Sartre's student's choice. I suggested that he has an idealistic commitment to his country and a filial commitment to his mother between which he has to choose. But by Taylor's account, whichever one he chooses, that then shows he had no commitment to the other.

The difficulties of this position are apparent in the vexed question of weakness of will, which has, since the time of Socrates, occasioned deep quandaries.[13] I do not want to deny the manifest possibility of agents failing to do what they had decided to do, but there are at least two ways of understanding how this relates to commitment. On the one hand we could insist that such cases show that the agents in question were not committed to the person or way of life to which they believed themselves committed. If Sartre's student, having joined the Resistance, then deserts in order to return to his mother, it would show that his commitment had been to his mother all along. He may have thought that he was committed to France, but his actions disclose, even more strongly than his choices, where his real commitment lies.

There seems to be sense in ancient Socrates's claim that we cannot know what is right and not do it. Were we not to do it, it would show that we did not in a committed sense know that it was right. It is clear that Socrates's concept of knowledge as it applies to such objects as the Form of the Good, and as it issues in such things as morally assessable action, is more than just cognitive. One is attracted by the Form of Goodness so that one cares about it and becomes committed to it. This in turn will show itself in the moral quality of one's subsequent actions. If one's actions do not display moral goodness, that only shows that one could not have truly known, and therefore become committed to, the Form of the Good in the first place. And if we put in place of this last phrase any other which encapsulates persons and ways of life which have the power to attract our moral allegiance, the logical structure of commitment will be clearly illustrated. We have to care about something or be attracted to it if we are to be committed to it.

But commitment is more than caring. It is a decision that issues from that caring. Commitment is either total or it does not exist. The phenomenon of weakness of will indicates, therefore, a lack of commitment by those who experience themselves as failing to fulfill their demands upon themselves. This does not imply, however, that commitment is rare and saintly (or, perhaps, fanatical). It implies, rather, that commitment has to be remade when failures occur. A normal moral life might consist of commitments made, discovered, and remade.

On the other hand, we might want to argue that just as we disclose what our commitment is when we make a decision or perform an action, we might also disclose what our commitment is when we do something which offends against it and discover ourselves to have an uneasy conscience. The guilt we then feel will show that we were committed all the time. In this view, commitment would need to be seen as subsisting throughout the vagaries of our moral lives.

It seems that Socrates could not have accepted any notion of guilt. If we cannot knowingly do wrong, we would never have need to feel guilt. The fact that we do not always feel happy about what we have done, however, necessitates a standard against which we measure ourselves. We may not always be fully conscious of our deeper commitments. This hints at the possibility that our commitments may ground not only our choices and obligations as they constitute our way of life, but also our feelings of self-worth or guilt as they might arise from our moral successes or failures.

It would seem, then, that it is only against the background of commitment that weakness of will is possible. It cannot be the case that failures are to be explained by alleging the total absence of commitment. Rather, we must point to a deeper level of commitment. How can we still speak of commitment as necessarily total, therefore, in the sense that anything less than a total commitment is not a commitment at all, while allowing for weakness of will against a background of commitment?

We seem to be suffering from a terminological problem here. Weakness of will should be described as a failure in the executive virtues rather than as a lack of commitment to the relevant matters. The trouble is that this failure of executive determination is also frequently described in ordinary language as a lack of commitment. Perhaps Taylor's use of the term *commitment* has connotations of executive virtue, so that the person who fails to act can be said to have no commitment. But I seek to identify a motivational ground for action such that persons can be described as having such a ground — such a commitment — even when they fail to act. Perhaps we can preserve the insights of ordinary usage through a simple grammatical expedient: namely, the use of the article *a*. To have *a* commitment is to take a practical stance towards some suitable intentional object, whereas to have commitment is to feel and display determination in the service of that object. In this way we can say that the weak-willed person does not lack *a* commitment but lacks commitment in that he or she fails to meet the obligations that arise from the commitment that he or she has.

But commitments occupy a deeper stratum of our moral psychology than do moral obligations. Most moral obligations are said to be prima facie rather than absolute, in that a situation may call for a particular obligation to be overruled when a more pressing obligation is present. The classic example of not fulfilling one's promise to return a borrowed gun to a homicidal maniac illustrates this point. A commitment, on the other hand, because it grounds the way of life out of which our various obligations spring, cannot be overruled in this way. Indeed, the judgment required to see which obligations may need to be overruled in a specific case will be based upon the commitments that one has made. A commitment is the originary, basic, and often unconscious ground upon which such difficult moral discriminations must be made. What I think this shows about Hampshire's thesis in "Morality and Pessimism" is that when he talks about a moral prohibition which an agent will in no circumstance transgress, he is talking about commitments rather than obligations, as I understand that term. That he refers to a person's morality as having two parts bears this out.[14]

The quandaries concerning weakness of will which we have uncovered, therefore, can be resolved by noting that weakness of will relates to the obligations that arise from our commitments rather than to our commitments themselves. Our failure is to do what is required. That we should feel this as a failure requires that we should have, and continue to have, the commitment upon which that obligation is based. Were we not to have the commitment in the first place, our action would not produce a feeling of guilt or shame in us. We do not, therefore, conclude from the phenomenon of weakness of will that our commitment was not strong enough and was therefore nonexistent. Rather, the executive virtue required to put the commitment into effect was not strong enough. It is only in the case where no guilt is felt that we can say that there was no commitment, although the case of the person who fails constantly and feels guilt constantly would certainly lead us to think that there existed bad faith rather than commitment.

I can now return to the conflict between Taylor's claim that a commitment is an all-or-nothing factor in one's life and my way of describing Sartre's student. By my reading, the student's decision in favour of the Resistance would show the relative strengths of his commitments. His commitment to France is stronger than his commitment to his mother, whereas, in Taylor's view, we would have to say that his choice showed that he had no commitment to his mother at all. But if that were true, how would we explain his continuing concern for his mother? If the student felt no ongoing concern for his mother at all, we might deem his nationalist fervour to be single-minded to the point of fanaticism. Indeed, this is the reason why we are sometimes inclined to say that the student continues to have a commitment to his mother rather than that he simply continues to care for her. But, insofar as the student is fighting for France, and granted that he still feels a concern for his mother, it is certainly questionable whether *commitment* is the right word for his relation to his mother. Surely this relation could only be called a commitment if he were by her side.

The best test for commitment is action. However, it is not the only test. One may love someone even while being prevented by circumstances or by other commitments from expressing that love in action. One's feelings will then be the only measure. Perhaps the distinction we have already made between deep and nondetermined commitments on the one hand and specific and focused ones on the other will help here. The student's pre-existing commitments are of the first kind, whereas the commitment he has after he has made his choice is of the second.

We can make use of the notion of caring here. It would avoid terminological confusion if I referred to the student's deep, characterological commitments, the commitments that are a function of his subjectivity, as cases of *caring*, and to the focused, intentional forms of commitment as *commitments*. It is clear that the student continues to care about his mother even though his choice constitutes only one commitment. In this way I accede to Taylor's usage and speak of only one commitment when a choice is made, while also conveying the connotations of executive virtue and obligation to be true to one's commitment which attach to that choice. And I explain backsliding and regret by pointing to a characterological basis for these which persists even after the choice is made. The student makes a commitment to France and executes it with determination. He is committed. He is not committed to his mother, though he continues to care about her. Also, that there are a number of things he cares about will be the basis, along with less noble temptations, for any backsliding which might occur and any regrets that he might feel.

This model would suggest that people care about a variety of things at a deep level in their characters and that one or another of these cares comes to expression in commitment. Along with the many goals that one may adopt or find oneself with from time to time for a variety of purposes, and along with the many concerns and cares that one has, there will be goals and cares which are more basic and more stringent. If it were ever possible in a lived life to arrange one's various goals and purposes in an order that would show their relationship to a basic value or orientation towards life, then it is at this basic level that I would want to situate caring. Commitments would then be the expression, articulation, and specification of this deep caring. The authors I have cited, however, would see the commitment itself as basic while leaving its origin mysteriously grounded.

But there are two reasons why neither of these approaches will give us a very tidy conceptual picture. Firstly, a real life is not as coherent as the attempt to clearly distinguish commitment from caring would imply. We care about a great many different and conflicting things. Perhaps some non-pathological degree of plurality in respect to the fundamental structures of our characters should be allowed us. Too great a single-mindedness in respect to one's commitments might be a mark of obsession. The obsessive and the fanatic are a worry to us precisely because they seem capable of subsuming all of their projects under one dominating commitment. They may even behave insensitively towards others to whom they say they are committed. Secondly, our commitments not only express our deep caring, but they also ground what we come to find important and so what we come to care about in this new sense.

Sartre's claim that our choices constitute our caring rather than expressing it and that caring is a subsequent disposition resulting from commitment makes this plain. For him, the word *commitment* would identify the constitutive decision, and the word *caring* would be needed to identify the continuing solicitude that is felt as a result of the commitment. My notion of caring as identifying the deep and nondetermined basis for commitments threatens a degree of confusion which we will have to accept until we discuss the notion of caring more fully.

2

CARING

In Chapter 1, I spoke of commitments as being grounded in character or in such deep aspects of the self as a generosity of spirit, care, or love. In ordinary language we often use the words *commitment* and *care* interchangeably, as when I described Sartre's student variously as caring about his mother and being committed to her. I also suggested that our commitments ground our subsequent caring in that they are as often expressed in my feelings of solicitude and concern as they are expressed in our actions. It seems we will need to clarify these concepts before we can develop the thesis that deep caring is a mode of our being from which commitment springs.

Caring as Motivational Structure

The word *care* has many uses and meanings today. We are urged to care for our neighbours, our family, and ourselves. We are urged to care for our environment, for peace, and for social justice. And a significant criticism that can be levelled against persons is to say of them that they do not care about the things that we care about, or even that they do not care about anything. Caring is also a professional activity for health workers, teachers, social workers, and others. Caring, in opposition to duty, is cited by feminists as a basis for ethics. And the word *caring* is used to describe the relationships of friends and lovers. Is there a common thread that combines these usages?

As a noun, *care* refers to the cares that we have from time to time. In this sense, to have cares is to have burdens. Insofar as I will propose that caring can be understood as a fundamental motivational disposition, I suggest that the fact that the noun *care* can be used as a synonym for *burden* points to a link between being burdened by worries of this kind and my caring about the issues at hand. Perhaps it is because I care about paying my bills that the need to pay my bills is felt as a burden. This suggestion would lead us to conclude that caring as a motivational orientation is more fundamental than are cares as burdens, because the latter are a consequence of the former.

This motivational foundation might be designated by another noun usage in which *care* refers to something within us which we might display in our behaviour. When we are admonished to "take care," we are being urged to be careful. Being careful or taking care in this sense often involves adopting a caring motivation towards the project at hand. Though I might be able to display care by modifying my behaviour, as when I move more slowly and delicately, the best way to achieve what is being asked of me is to pay attention to what I am doing. But paying attention involves a motivational displacement. It involves concentrating on what I am doing, and I am most likely to do this when I care about it. The admonition assumes that there is a motivational reality lying beneath the descriptive notion of caring.

We notice this also when we consider the negative term *careless*. We apply this term to persons who are behaving in a way which might endanger themselves, their possessions, or their success. Perhaps they seem not to be concentrating sufficiently on the task at hand, or they might be performing it too quickly. We are right to warn these agents of the dangers of injury or failure to which they are subject. We might even be justified in castigating them for their carelessness. But if we castigate them or condemn them, it is likely that we are thinking not only that their behaviour is apt to be described as careless, but also that they do not seem to care enough about their task to be careful. It is the inadequacy of their motivational orientation which elicits our disapproval.

We can make this motivational imputation even more explicit with a different adjectival usage. When we say that a person has performed an action *in a caring way*, we are more obviously indicating something of the imputed motivation behind the action than when we describe the behaviour as *careful*. *Careful* might characterise the apparent way the action was performed, but when we describe the action as *caring*, we are very clearly imputing an attitude or motivation to the agent. To describe an action as caring is to say of it not only that it was carefully or gently performed, but also that it was done from a generous motivation or out of a concern for the recipient of the action.

We also use the adjective *caring* of persons. We describe persons as caring when we want to say that they typically act carefully or in caring ways. This makes it clear that we are imputing to these persons a characteristic set of motivations and concerns. Caring persons are those who are moved by what they care about to act with care or carefully in relation to those matters. There will be behavioural criteria for applying these descriptions, of course. Depending on what is appropriate to the matter at hand, caring persons might act a little more slowly when the work is delicate, or a little more quickly when it is urgent. When dealing with people, caring persons will listen more and be sensitive to another's reactions. It has even been suggested that the behaviour of caring persons is less rule-bound and displays greater variability and flexibility.[1] If this is true, we might be seeing the kind of sensitivity to the particular which we might expect in an Aristotelian moral agent, as opposed to the subservience to moral rules and principles which we might expect from a Kantian.

Let us consider *care* as a verb. We speak of caring for a person in the sense of taking care of that person. To take care of someone is to see to that person's needs and to provide comfort and assistance in light of those needs. Most often, the phrases "to take care of" or "to care for" are used with reference to some special need. People might take care of their aged relatives or their injured pets in this sense. There is also the more general phrase "taking care of business," which refers to an unspecified range of things that need to be attended to. Is caring, in the sense of taking care of, necessarily based on caring motivations? It might be assumed that the person who is taking care of business also cares about that business, and it is also likely that the person who is taking care of someone is motivated by a caring attitude towards that person. But I doubt that this is necessarily true. It seems quite possible that someone might take care of certain matters or certain persons without being motivated by a concern for those matters or persons. It might be that person's job to do so, and he or she might do so grudgingly. And even if this were so, he or she might still do the job adequately.

This point is of some relevance for the so-called "caring professions." Social workers, counsellors, nurses, and teachers are just some of the professionals who would describe themselves as engaged in caring. It is true that in the rhetoric of these professions, it is frequently said that these professionals care for their clients, and it is frequently suggested that some positive feeling towards the client is importantly involved in this.[2] In contrast, there will be others who argue that the basic requirement in these professions is that the job be done well and that the caring that is required in the practice of these professions consists solely in the fulfillment of this requirement.[3] In this latter professional ethos, taking care of someone in the sense of seeing to the needs of that person is the essential requirement of professionalism. Whatever the outcome of this debate, its very possibility demonstrates that there is no necessary or direct link between caring or taking care of, understood as an activity of seeing to the needs of clients or dependents, and caring as a motivational orientation. One might care for a client without doing so for that client's sake. Nevertheless, it does seem likely that the required professional behaviour would be more apt to occur in cases where the agent cares in a motivational sense.

We should turn now to an analysis of caring as a motivation. In this context, we will in most cases use *care* as a verb. We speak of persons as "caring about things" or "caring for things." Indeed, there seems to be a distinction inherent in the two most frequently noted locutions: *caring for* and *caring about*. Most frequently, *caring for* is used in relation to persons, as in "Mary cares for Peter," whereas *caring about* is more often used in relation to things such as precious items, ideals, or historical circumstances. Thus Sally might be described as caring about her antique vase, John described as caring about justice, and Lynne described as caring about the preservation of the rain forests.

However, I am not convinced that this distinction in usage marks a distinction of theoretical import. Indeed, even the distinction in usage seems less than firm. It does not sound wrong to describe Mary as caring about Peter or Lynne as caring for the rain forests. Perhaps, though, we can make at least this distinction between these two phrases: *caring for* is more ambiguous, as between a behavioural description and an attribution of a motivation, than *caring about*. Clearly, the latter phrase seems to attribute an interest and motivational orientation to an agent without making that attribution depend on the agent's typically behaving in certain ways. It may be true of Lynne that she cares about the rain forests, even if she never seems to do anything to aid in their preservation, but in that case, we might be less inclined to describe her as caring for those forests. Or Sally might be described either as caring about her vase or as caring for her vase, though in the latter case we might also be led to expect to see her dusting it or protecting it from harm.

Again, it seems possible to describe a nurse as caring for a patient while also saying that she does not care much about him. The important point is that both locutions allow us to attribute a motivational orientation to an agent which will allow us to interpret that agent's behaviour. We might say that Lynne subscribes to wilderness magazines and minimises her use of paper because she cares about the rain forests, and we might say that Mary talks to Peter on the phone a lot or sees to his needs when he is ill because she cares for him.

This last example demonstrates a further meaning that the phrase *care for* might have. When we say that Mary cares for Peter, we might mean that Mary is fond of Peter. Certainly her being fond of him will be motivationally effective in leading her to care for him in the sense of taking care of him when he is in need. And there will be many indications that she cares for him over and above her willingness to take care of him. The fact that she feels sympathy when he is hurt or disappointed or that she is vulnerable to being affected by his pain is an indication of her caring for him. Further, we would expect that she hopes for his advantage, seeks his benefit, and speaks well of him to others. We would also expect that she enjoys his company and shares his interests. Where the fondness borders on love, we may even expect that she desires him.

However, it is not my aim to fully explicate this meaning of *to care for*. I wish merely to point out that this set of motivational orientations is particular to this specific notion of caring for. The caring for others which is required in professional caring, for example, does not involve this set of motivational stances, though we have seen that taking care of someone is likely to be done more carefully when a caring attitude is brought to bear on it — when it is done more caringly.

What is this caring attitude if it is not a case of being fond of another? And what does this attitude contribute to acting caringly? Milton Mayeroff, in one of the few books written about caring,[4] places great stress upon the attitudinal aspect of caring. He defines caring as helping the other to grow. He sees this not only as encompassing a set of activities directed towards the other, but also as involving a number of characteristic virtues. These include patience, honesty, humility, hope, and courage. It is clear from this analysis that attitudes and an inner motivational orientation are essential to acting caringly. It also follows that, in this sense, caring can be subtly different from being fond of the other, and that it leads to behaviours that can include taking care of others, being careful in regard to them, and adopting a caring manner towards them.

But an important new point arises when Mayeroff says that the other for whom I care is a completion of my own personal identity.[5] In Mayeroff's view, caring for another involves some concern for the status of one's own being as well. This point is reinforced when we notice that if one describes caring for the other as involving a characteristic set of virtues in the way that Mayeroff does, then one's own ethical status is implicated in one's caring and becomes a matter of concern to the one who cares. It seems that caring for the other is an orientation which is not directed exclusively outwardly but involves a turning inwards towards oneself as well.

Nell Noddings[6] stresses this point even more. Her discussion of caring refers to both professional caring and parenting. Although she also places stress on the inner attitudinal and motivational aspects of caring, she offers a model of caring which is dyadic. It involves active contributions not only from the person who cares, but also from the person cared for. On the part of the one caring, there is an engrossment in the other. This engrossment involves a displacement of motivation away from the self towards the other, but one which is not elicited by a reasoned assessment of the situation or of the responsibilities which are inherent in it. Rather, it is the very dynamic of the dyadic relationship of which it is a part that elicits the motivation.

On the part of the one caring, the engrossment is motivated not only by a concern for the one cared for, but also by a concern for the agent's own ethical self. The person cared for contributes to the dyad by acknowledging the caring and by showing the one caring the growth or benefit to which the caring gives rise.

It is central to the dyadic relationship that there be a direct and intimate form of communication sustaining and constituting the relationship. The one caring is present to the one cared for in a direct way, and so is the one cared for present to the one caring. What the one caring communicates is the concern and willingness to care, whereas what the one cared for communicates is the acknowledgment and growth response which sustains the relationship. To achieve this, both partners in the relationship must be in an active, open, and receptive mode towards each other. This ultimately constitutes the basis for their mutual caring. It is clear from Noddings's model of caring that although it is the caring of one person for another which is central, a caring for self is integrally involved in this.

I want to return briefly to Mayeroff's analysis to pick up a point worth commenting on further. Mayeroff allows for the possibility that the object of the caring might include ideas and ideals as well as persons. Mayeroff does require that the person or thing cared for be capable of growth, so that the caring may be seen to be effective, but he does not require the same reciprocity to structure the caring relationship as does Noddings, and so the terms of that relationship may be different in kind.

Indeed, it may not be an accident after all that in the case where the object of our caring includes ideas and ideals, we more often use the phrase *caring about*. If it is true that this relationship does not involve the same degree of reciprocity, it may be that it does not depend on the same degree of behavioural instantiation either. Whereas caring *for* someone is validated by the response that the one cared for makes to the caring, and so requires action towards the one cared for in order, at a minimum, to make the one cared for aware of the care extended, caring *about* something cannot be responded to in this way. Outside of the romantic imaginings of some, a rain forest does not respond to or become aware of the care which environmentalists extend to it.

It appears, then, that the difference between the phrases *caring for* and *caring about* may point to a differing degree of reciprocity inherent in the caring, and this, in turn, may explain why there is a greater tendency to use the phrase *care for* in relation to persons and *care about* in relation to other things. And if that reciprocity requires behavioural validation, then we will also have explained why the phrase *care for* embraces both a motivational and a behavioural component, whereas *care about* seems more limited to the attitudinal. It seems that the intentional object of *caring for* is usually more specific than the intentional object of *caring about*.

That caring about things does not involve the same degree of reciprocity as caring for persons makes such caring more difficult to sustain. If Noddings is right, then caring for persons is in part sustained and encouraged by the response which the one cared for gives to the one caring. No such encouragement is available to the one who cares about justice or the environment. Only success in the struggle for these values will be encouraging, and in the absence of such success, this caring will have to be sustained by doggedness and courage.

In addition, such caring must be sustained by how we understand the thing cared about. With this we approach the cognitive element in caring.[7] Once again, I do not believe that a sharp distinction between caring about and caring for is being drawn. In the case where we care for someone, we are also encouraged to see the one cared for in certain ways. The professional caring of a social worker must be sustained by a positive view of the client, even in the case where the client is a criminal or deviant. But at least in this case, the client has the opportunity to support such a positive view by responding to the caring. And in the case where caring for a person consists of being fond of him or her, it usually follows that we see the one cared for in a positive light.

The more general way in which I will articulate this cognitive component of caring is to say that the subject who cares must see the object of that caring as important. Part of what we mean when we say that Mary cares for Peter or that Lynne cares about rain forests is that Peter is important to Mary and rain forests are important to Lynne. It is because this is an analytic relationship rather than a causal one that it is not viciously circular to also say that it is because Peter is important to Mary that she cares about him and because the rain forests are important to Lynne that she cares about them.[8] This link between caring and importance is common to both caring for and caring about.

We can also analyse caring in terms of its effect upon the one who cares. If Mary cares for Peter, then Mary is affected by Peter's states. She is vulnerable to grief and disappointment if Peter suffers harm. Similarly, if Lynne cares about the rain forests, she will be affected by what happens to them and is vulnerable to grief and disappointment if they are diminished or harmed. Many people feel depressed and disappointed on hearing about the burning off of the Amazon forests. This shows that they care about those forests.

Harry Frankfurt argues that the identity of the person who cares is bound up with the one cared for so that the fate of the latter becomes part of the fate of the former.[9] This shows, once again, that caring intimately implicates the self. If it were the sole indication of caring, however, this vulnerability to being affected by what happens to the object of one's caring would be rather passive. Though it is to be expected that people who care will be affected in this way, we might be disappointed in such people if the only indication of their caring was this set of affective responses. We might also hope that such people would act in pursuit of the well-being of those things which they cared about or those persons that they cared for.

This point becomes clearer when we return to the point that caring is linked to finding the object of our caring important. Bernard Williams[10] has suggested that *practical necessity*, the feeling that we "must" do something in a given situation, can be analysed in terms of the agent's finding the matter at hand to be important and giving the action which that situation presents a high deliberative priority. What this shows is that finding something important is not simply a cognitive judgment but a practical one. It is the cognitive, evaluative, and motivational context upon which practical necessity is founded. To find something important is to make it apt to be acted upon. If caring, in its turn, is linked to finding something important, then it follows that caring is inherently practical. If we care for someone or about something, then we are apt to act, as occasion demands, in pursuit of the benefit of that which is cared for. Merely being affected by the well-being of those objects is not sufficient. One must be inclined to act. This is the significance of my calling caring a motivation or a motivational orientation.

Let us explore the special character of caring as a motivational orientation. An intention is also motivational but in a more momentary way. An intention is formed at a specific time and is either put into effect immediately by way of an action or is changed into a plan or project if the fulfilling action is not directly available. We do speak of intentions as being held over a period of time, but this is distinct from the mental activity that leads us to act in any given situation. Intentions in this durational sense are more like projects or strategies in light of which specific actions might be engaged in and understood.

In contrast to an intention, caring is durational in its very nature.[11] When one cares, one envisages oneself and that which one cares about as having mutually intertwined futures. Caring for something is not simply a momentary want or impulse in regard to it. Desire and inclination are also longer-lasting motivational influences upon us, but they are less directly tied to action than caring. There is nothing anomalous in imagining persons as having desires or wants upon which they do not act. An agent may have a general policy or a specific reason on a given occasion to not pursue a desire. Caring, in contrast, is a motivational orientation which is strongly tied to realisation in action. It is anomalous to imagine an agent who cares about something but also has a policy to do nothing about it. To care about something or for someone is to want to act, as circumstance allows or demands, in pursuit of the good of what is cared about. This is merely another way of saying that the object of caring is taken to be important and that importance has a constitutive role in practical necessity.

It follows that caring and commitment are intertwined. If I am reflexively aware that I care, I will find myself with a commitment. As my discussion of Sartre's student in Chapter 1 demonstrated, commitment will flow directly from caring, except where there is a dilemma. Just as the test of commitment is action, so the test of caring is action. Merely being affected by harm suffered by the one that I care for, or merely being interested in what I care about, or merely wanting the good that is involved is not enough for caring. One must also be practically committed. Mary is committed to acting in pursuit of Peter's well-being if she cares for him and knows it, and Lynne is committed to doing whatever she can in pursuit of the preservation of the rain forests if she cares about them and knows it.

The central failure of caring is not caring. The person who says, "I don't care" is a person who refuses to be affected by the matter or the person at issue. Such a person is saying that the issue or person at hand is of no importance and that he or she has no commitment to do anything positive in regard to that issue or person. This stance is one of isolation. To not care about something is to cut oneself off from it. This is especially clear when we consider the various kinds of caring for another person. Let us consider a married couple. It is an expectation of our society that married people should care for one another in the sense of being fond of one another. For one person not to care for the other in this sense is regarded as an essential breakdown of the relationship. Whether or not the marriage is broken up in an institutional sense, the partners in such a relationship will draw apart from one another and will live lives which are in some degree isolated from one another.

Failing to care in the sense of not taking care of someone can also lead to isolation. If a professional caregiver were to be so careless and inattentive as to warrant the description of no longer caring for his or her clients, and if he or she failed even to do the things professionally required, no matter how summarily or mechanically, then we would have a serious case indeed. Such a person would require censure under the professional ethics which apply to that profession, censure which might involve professional isolation. But the more central point is that such a worker would establish no real contact with clients. And those clients, in their turn, would not feel themselves to have been dealt with in a caring way. There will have been no communicative contact in the professional relationship.

A more moderate and frequent case is that of the professional who performs his or her duties well enough in a behavioural sense but not in a very caring way. This person will not communicate as effectively to clients as others in the profession because his or her manner will not permit being present to clients in as full a way. And clients, sensing this, will not communicate as fully with this professional. In these ways the failure of caring can be seen to produce isolation, and by implication, caring can be seen to be a central element of deep communication.[12]

We sometimes describe a person who acts carelessly as one who does not care. We have already seen that acting carelessly or without due care involves a lack of attention. And this lack of attention can be motivated by the agent's not caring about what he or she is doing. If the agent does not find the matter to be of personal importance or is not committed to the matter at hand, then he or she will not give it the attention it may require. He or she will not care enough to do so. Once again, this involves a degree of personal isolation. It is a commonplace among psychologists that our personhood is expanded and deepened by the commitments and involvements which mark our lives. To not care about things, to have no commitment to them and to not find them important, is, therefore, a lessening of human possibilities and involves an isolating withdrawal of the self into itself.

It would be a confusion to equate this failure with failures in commitment. Persons can show themselves to be uncommitted when they fail to act on occasions when action is called for by what they took to be their commitment. Such failures may express a lack of courage, an ambivalent attitude towards the matter at hand, or a failure to understand the way in which the situation calls for action. But people who respond to such failures by feeling remorse or by resolving to act more purposefully next time show that they still have a commitment and that they still care. It is the person who shrugs his or her shoulders and says, "Oh well, it didn't matter anyway" whom we would disapprove of most vehemently. This person shows that he or she did not care in the first place and had no positive motivational orientation towards the matter at issue. In Aristotelian terms, this failure is not one of weakness of will, but of not feeling rightly about the matter.

Deep Caring

In Chapter 1, I identified a deep, inchoate level of commitment in our motivational sets which can be directed upon various objects to become the focused commitments of which we are reflexively aware. I suggested that this characterological level of commitment should be called *deep caring*. Deep caring is not yet intentional and gives rise to commitments and to more focused and intentional forms of caring. In the first section of this chapter, I explored these specific forms of caring and uncovered the interconnections between them and commitments. I should now explore the more primordial form of deep caring. I will do this with the help of certain remarks made by Richard Wollheim.[13]

In a far-ranging discussion of what is distinctive in our lives as human beings, Wollheim distinguishes between mental states, mental dispositions, and mental activities. Mental states are occurrences such as sensations, perceptions, thoughts, flushes of emotion, and so forth. They are episodic and occur at a specific time and for a specific, usually short, duration. Dispositions, in contrast, are ongoing. However, Wollheim does not understand dispositions in the way that a behaviourist might — as something whose function is solely to explain an occurrence in terms of a conditional description. Rather, a disposition is an ongoing background mental circumstance which is manifest in a variety of mental states or activities. Examples include desire, belief, skills, virtues, and vices. Mental activities, lastly, bring mental states about, enact mental dispositions, or inaugurate mental dispositions. They are exemplified by such activities as paying attention, volition, or thinking a thought.

Let us apply this taxonomy to the concepts of caring I have already described in this chapter. Examples of mental states seem to occur in our usage of *to care*. There might well be flushes of emotion involved in Mary's caring for Peter, and being a caring person might well involve experiences of sympathy or fellow-feeling from time to time. However, such occurrences do not seem as definitive of what it is to care as are the actions which express that caring. We would expect such actions to arise from settled dispositions rather than from occasional and unreliable feelings.

Those who are described either as caring for someone in the sense of being fond of that person or as caring about something might be described by Wollheim as having a mental disposition. Such persons have an ongoing mental orientation towards acting in ways that express their caring. On the other hand, caring in the behavioural sense of seeing to the needs of someone is not centrally a mental process at all and can be left aside for the moment like the other behavioural usages we have described, except insofar as they involve, as do all actions, volitions which are mental activities. Lastly, it would seem that caring in the sense of being careful involves a mental activity insofar as it involves paying attention.

As we try to capture the unique features of caring as a disposition, perhaps the closest analogy we can find among the heterogeneous list of mental dispositions that Wollheim offers is that of belief. Understood as a disposition, belief is intentionally determinable but not determined. We can be said to believe a vast range of propositions at any given time, but we do not have any particular set of those beliefs in mind as mental states at any given time. Although belief is mental, concerns something, and is therefore intentional, the set of our beliefs at any given time is not present to our minds as a belief about A, a belief about B, a belief about C, and so on. As I act intelligently in the world, these beliefs are operative, but often only as an effective matrix for my thoughts and actions rather than as their manifest content. It is only when some occasion arises that leads me to bring a belief to mind, rather than simply to act in accordance with it, that the object of that belief is specifiable.

As mental states, our beliefs would be determinately intentional, but as mental dispositions, they are only determinably so. To be determinately intentional is to be present to the subject for reflection, whereas to be determinably intentional is to be functionally operative, but not present to reflection. To explain an action, I could select and articulate a belief that I have, along with a relevant desire, and attribute causal efficacy to this belief and desire, whether or not that belief was present to mind as a mental state before or during the action.

It might seem that this distinction of Wollheim's between a determinable mental disposition and a determinate mental state is a distinction between vague intimations and articulate thoughts. But this is not quite accurate. Acting on a belief that I do not bring to mind as I do so does not imply that that belief is inarticulate, if by that we mean inadequately formed or not centred upon a specifiable object. If the action in question is successfully performed, then the belief was as formed and focused as it needed to be. It simply was not present in thought.

Wollheim's other example of a mental disposition, desire, might help clarify this point. There may be numerous things which we desire at any given time. But we might not, at that time, be acting in pursuit of any one of those desires, and we may not be fantasising about the fulfillment of that desire. I might desire to win a lottery, and this might be true of me at times when I am not thinking about lotteries or buying a lottery ticket. Nevertheless, this desire is quite definite, and it is one that I would acknowledge if asked, and might act upon by buying a ticket if occasion allowed. Indeed, even if I did not buy a ticket for some reason, I might still be described correctly as having that desire. But this quite specific desire was merely determinable so long as it was not in mind or acted upon. It becomes determinate when I consciously decide to enter the ticket agency.

So it is with caring. On specific occasions, I might experience feelings of solicitude or emotions of concern about some specific thing or person, or I might enact my caring for that thing or person. In this context I can speak of caring about X or caring for Y, and the notion is determinately intentional. It is clearly and specifically object-directed. But during the course of routine living, my caring is object-directed in a determinable rather than a determinate way. My caring is an effective matrix for a range of my activities. I do not at all times care about or for A, B, C, and so on in a determinate way. However, my caring is at any time determinable as to its object. Were I anxious to explain an action, I could select, from among the determinable mental dispositions of caring which I attribute to myself, a relevant determinate care which can be said to have led to my action.

Of course, as with belief, such an explanation must permit independent verification. There must be criteria other than noting my actions for saying whether I care about or for a given object. Otherwise the explanations would be circular. The same difficulty applies to belief. Are there ways of specifying one's beliefs other than by citing one's actions (including avowals)?

But caring is not only akin to belief and desire in admitting the distinction between determinable dispositions and determinate states, it is also like desire in that it is affective as well as cognitive. It is an affective as well as an effective matrix for my action. So we can speak of caring in three ways. We can speak of mental states, as when in the course of an action or event in which my caring for someone or something is a motivating or qualitative factor, that caring is present to my awareness along with the object of that caring. Secondly, we can speak of caring as a mental disposition, as when we characterise phases of our lives as being oriented by a determinable set of concerns which are enacted or brought to mind as occasion demands. The content or object of caring in this usage is specifiable but not usually present to thought in a determinate way. Reflection upon our thought and feeling or upon our actions would be required to identify the objects of our caring in this sense. Indeed, what we take to be the determinable objects of our caring may be part of a theory we hold about ourselves and may, as such, be debatable in public discourse. And thirdly, we can speak of caring as a mental activity, as when I try to be careful in what I am doing.

The various forms of caring which I have identified so far, including being careful, acting in a caring way, having cares, caring for someone, caring about something, making commitments, and so forth are determinate expressions of underlying determinable dispositions of caring.

Let me digress for a moment in order to further explore Wollheim's notion of a mental activity. Let us now speak of intentionality as that term is used in the theory of action. In discussing mental activities, Wollheim suggests that they are not intentional in the sense that normal actions are. Intentionality as applied to action is understood as a conjunction of desire and belief: an action can be explained and accepted as intentional in that a desire and a set of beliefs can be said to give sense to it. In contrast, mental activities do not require beliefs to explain them.

To explain mental activities, Wollheim conjoins instinct with desire in the place of belief. "Volition and attention, sometimes repression, come about solely through desire guided by instinct."[14] The observation Wollheim seeks to account for is that mental activities appear spontaneous. They are not preceded by volitions or intentions, whether explicit or merely specifiable. As his examples of mental activities include volitions, he must say this to avoid a regressive explanation of action. Just as remembering a partly forgotten name is a mental activity marked by surprise and spontaneity (even when I have been trying to remember), so paying attention, or beginning to act, or taking care are activities which enact intentions rather than being preceded by them. These activities seem to have no phenomenological volume. As Wittgenstein said while discussing agency, "doing itself is like an extensionless point."[15]

And there are further examples. Let me use Wollheim's terminology to further explicate what I mean by commitment. We can distinguish being committed from making a commitment. Making a commitment is a volition with a large temporal scope. Whereas volition is an act of will on a determinate occasion, a commitment is an act of will determinable by any occasion apt for the enactment of that commitment. As such, making a commitment counts as a mental activity in Wollheim's sense. It is a stance taken, but not one preceded by an intention. It is not to be explained by conjoining belief and desire. We can make commitments without first deciding to. Deciding to make a commitment *is* making the commitment. We can, as it were, find ourselves making one, or even find ourselves having made one which we only become aware of as we enact it. It has no phenomenological volume, but it is directed upon objects and projects in the world.

Just as Wollheim takes expression to be an instance of an activity which is not an action (his example is a smile which externalises pleasure), so making a commitment is an activity which is not an action. It expresses our caring without putting our care into effect deliberately and intentionally. In this respect, making a commitment is similar to adopting a policy.

Wollheim also argues that a mental activity can either express a mental disposition or bring it into effect. So, we might further say that once a commitment has been made, it continues as a mental disposition. To be a committed person is to have made a commitment and to characteristically enact one's commitments. To make a commitment is to inaugurate that disposition alluded to in describing a committed person.

Wollheim's notion of a mental activity also applies to other cases of caring. When a person behaves in a caring way, the quality of caring does not result from an intention separate from that which pertains to the goals of the action. Whenever we speak of behaviour which gives expression to a caring attitude or to caring in the sense of being fond of someone, whether it be a case of seeing to the needs of someone or of sensitive communication, the caring represents a mental activity which is not itself the intentional action. It is doing what is needful or speaking with kindness which is the intentional action, not the caring. One does not independently see to a patient's needs and care for the patient; one cares for the patient by seeing to that patient's needs in a caring way. Perhaps this explains why caring is so often described by way of an adverbial qualification of the action, as when we say that a person acted carefully.

The explanation for the intentional action will refer to the beliefs and desires of the agent, but the basis of the caring will be something other than a conjunction of belief and desire. Even if we identify this as a mental disposition called caring, we should again note Wollheim's proposal that mental activities are activities through which we bring mental dispositions into being. As we have seen, this allows us to identify the mental activity involved as making a commitment. We care and therefore commit ourselves. The result is that we care in the sense of acting caringly. A mental activity has given rise to a mental disposition. On those occasions when we act caringly or carefully and are aware of this quality of our action, we might even experience the mental state of caring. But this state originates in the mental activity of making a commitment.

The model I have been developing would suggest that this mental activity itself has a characterological basis, that is, the deep caring which I seek to theorise. In what way can Wollheim's concepts illuminate deep caring? We should not yield to the temptation of assimilating deep caring to that determinable mental disposition that comes to expression either in commitment or in acts of caring. Such dispositions are determinably intentional and are already expressions of deep caring. Deep caring is not yet intentional.

To help explicate this idea, we should note Wollheim's use of the notion of instinct to explain, along with the ever-present notion of desire, the occurrence of mental activities. What Wollheim is alluding to is a motivational substratum which is not determinable as a belief, even in reflection. But neither is it determinable as a cause in the way that a specific desire for something is. It would have to be identified independently of the resultant activity to be cited without circularity as a cause, and this is notoriously difficult. At best, instinct is an inchoate causal category which indicates an organism's basic orientation to certain goals.

Wollheim has a good theoretical reason for using the term *instinct*. In *The Thread of Life*, Wollheim tries to create links between an analytical philosophy of mind and Freudian theory. His use of the notion of instinct points to that biological, motivational, and meaning-generating substratum with which Freudian theory has enriched our understanding of ourselves. If we put the notion of deep caring into the place created for the notion of instinct in Wollheim's theoretical framework, it opens the possibility of relating caring as mental state, mental disposition, and mental activity to a wider horizon of deep caring. It allows us to make sense of the idea that our mental activities of caring — as when we pay attention to what we are doing or open ourselves communicatively to the person for whom we care — are expressions of or are grounded in deep care. To paraphrase Wollheim, we might now say that volition and attention come about solely through desire guided by deep caring.

I should explicate my use of *to make sense of.* I am not talking about causal explanations. Even Wollheim's notion of instinct fails to provide anything but a general explanatory schema. I use the phrase in a hermeneutical sense in which the basis for offering an interpretation of a phenomenon is the horizon of meaning present within that phenomenon or expressed in it rather than a causal explanation. In this way, I have suggested that we should understand manifestations of caring against a horizon of deep caring.

To understand caring in its determinate and intentional sense as a motivational orientation through which some things in my world will be important to me so that my attention will be drawn to them and my active engagement elicited by them, I need to uncover a basic orientation of concern regarding my self and my world through which the specific instances of my caring can be interpreted as such. But I will not uncover this orientation by reflection. In Wollheim's phrase, it has no phenomenology. Nor am I licensed to postulate it as a psychological or transcendental hypothesis, because to do so would be to beg the question of the meaning of my caring.

The suggestion that deep caring be understood as a determinable disposition borders on being a quasi-scientific hypothesis. Deep caring is present as a horizon rather than a content of consciousness or an a priori postulate. The function of this horizon will be to allow us to interpret commitment and specific manifestations of caring. The interpretation that it allows us to offer is that commitment and caring are expressive of deep caring. Part of the meaning of my commitments and of my focused caring will be that they give expression to deep caring.

But what further information or understanding will this give us? And if it does give us further information, how does deep caring provide this information if it has no phenomenological content other than what I can reflexively give it by reference to what I am committed to or explicitly care about? What is it that binds determinable and determinate instances of commitment and caring to this horizon of deep caring, other than a closed hermeneutic circle? Why should I postulate that it is deep caring which comes to expression in caring and commitment?

To answer this, we must remember that deep caring is not intentional, not even determinably; no object can be specified for it. Most importantly, we must not assume, as our talk of commitment and of specific caring might lead us to do, that deep caring is directed outwards from ourselves into the world. As we have seen in the analysis of caring offered by Nell Noddings, the self is an implicit object of caring, along with any determinate object. Caring is reflexive. The determinable disposition of caring is directed inwards even as it is typically directed outwards, although it is usually the outward orientation that becomes articulated. The same is true of deep caring, except that insofar as deep caring is not intentional, no distinction can be made within it between self and other-than-self.

In our own time, existentialist philosophers have stressed the centrality of the authentic self to our lives. This connects with the centrality of the notion of commitment to my notion of caring. For existentialist philosophers, commitment or resoluteness constitute the authenticity of the self. This would seem to suggest that our activities are authentic if they are expressive of a deep care for our own selfhood. But, as I will argue in Chapter 7, our actions in the world, especially those which are of ethical interest, are directed outwards. We care for things and for people. Our commitment is to help those people who are important to us, whether we are fond of them or whether we have accepted obligations with regard to them. And we are committed to work towards the good of those things which are important to us. It would be to reduce all this to selfishness to say that we ultimately pursue these cares for our own sakes, which we would be committed to saying if we understood deep care as a causal origin for our commitments and as primarily concerned with our own authenticity.

Rather, deep care, being not yet intentional, cannot be understood either as directed towards the self or towards the world. It is brute motivation, without object. In our existential makeup, it shares the same position but not the same ethical complexion as Nietzsche's concept of Will to Power. But although it is a motivation without an object, it is a motivation with a function, that of constituting the self. I will elaborate on this point in Chapter 3. For the moment, it is enough to note that this function provides the horizon against which caring can be interpreted as being genuinely concerned with what one cares about but as still being expressive of our self-concern or our self-project.

Such an interpretation is not arbitrary. The term *expressive* here means that commitment as resoluteness derives its strength from being the pursuit of authenticity. I am faithful to my commitment to something in order to be true to myself. I owe it to myself to be true to that which I care about. In this sense my faithfulness to what I care about, my commitment to it, is an expression of my deep care. Deep care is the horizon against which I can see the integrity amongst my commitments and the caring that issues from them. Even as I am anxious about my self for the sake of authenticity, I direct myself outwards and perform caring actions that constitute ethical community. And deep care provides the internal motivational strength so to act. When one acts caringly, one implicates oneself in what one does, and that is why it matters.

3

ON BEING HUMAN

Having argued that deep caring is not simply a contingent feature of human behaviour but that it is characteristic of human being, I will now explore the notion of *ontological being* which undergirds this thesis and develop a model of what it is to be a human being. This will allow us to understand caring in a fundamental form.

One methodological strategy I should stress again before proceeding is that of not thinking in terms of nouns but in terms of verbs. We are not asking what a human being is or what is described by the noun phrase *human being*. Instead, we should take *human being* as a verb phrase which means "being human," or "being in a human way." When existential phenomenologists use the notion of ontology, they refer to the various ways different things exist. A human being exists in a different way — has a different ontological being — from an ashtray. What we are curious about is what it is to exist as a human being. It is this existing or being (notice that these are verbs) that we are interested in, not the thing that is. I derive from Heidegger the hypothesis that our mode of being human is caring.[1]

A Model for Exploring Humanity

I propose a model through which we can see more clearly what is involved in being a human being. I propose that we understand our ontological being as functioning on at least four levels of formation and interaction which must be, in the mature person, integrated so as to constitute the wholeness of that person. These four levels are (1) the biological level,

(2) the perceptual and reactive level, (3) the evaluative and proactive level, and (4) the spiritual level.

Aristotle also posited a four-level model of human nature when he described four parts of the soul: a vegetative part, a desiring part, a calculative part, and a contemplative part.[2] However, Aristotle's model seems reified and static. It describes a synchronic unity of four levels of our being in terms of "parts" that make up our human nature. In contrast, if we understand human being as a verb, we will need a temporal model which describes levels of functioning rather than components of an entity.

At each level of my model, along with the observable relationships to the environment described by the various relevant sciences, there are dynamic and existential relationships which are expressions of deep caring appropriate to those levels of existence.[3] Such caring might also take determined or determinable forms in relation to objects. Further, the conceptual architecture that I propose posits deep caring as the dynamism which flows through these four levels of our being to combine them into the diachronic unity of our being. In this way I posit a model of human being which spreads across two axes: an axis described in terms of height or of depth in which the four levels are ranged one above another, and an axis of temporality in which deep caring, expressed, for example, as my self-project, flows through and combines those levels in a forward movement. This diachronic axis constitutes the narrative of my life as it moves from the past as I appropriate it, through my present with its concerns, towards a future which I envisage and hope for.

The Biological Level

The biological level of human being constitutes us as dynamic organisms with a definite genetic makeup and with metabolic and instinctual relationships to the environment. At this level are located all of those involuntary activities which we think of as instinctual or reflex; such pristine feelings as fear, pain, and pleasure; and a great many of our motivations. Our bodies cannot exist without the sustaining environments on which they depend. The very air we breathe is a prerequisite for our living and for all the other levels of existence we enjoy. In addition, our bodies contribute to those environments in a variety of ways and cause changes in it. At this level we also relate in a number of ways to other organisms, including some which are members of the human species. Some of these organisms we eat, some we avoid, and others we mate with. As a result, a preconscious form of caring might be said to operate at this level which, in its purest form, is the internal counterpart of need. It is the needs we have at this level which generate desires, anxieties, hungers, and fears.

However, the biological level of our existence has no phenomenology. Experientially speaking, it is completely absorbed into the higher levels. The relation of the biological level of our being to our experiences and actions is one of grounding. We are not present to ourselves as biological beings. Nor do we relate to others in a purely biological way. Whatever we do or care about has a meaning which cannot be reduced to a merely biological purposiveness.

Our sensory experiences and such activities as eating and mating clearly have a biological dimension. But they are meaningful to us, and their meanings are culturally formed. Virtually the only time in our lives when we exist in a purely biological way, when we realise only this first level of our existence, is when we are asleep and not dreaming. At such times our entire existence is fulfilled by our breathing, heartbeat, brain function, and other processes of the human body which constitute our being alive.

One may wonder why I refer to a biological level of our being at all if it disappears into the culturally formed levels of our being. One reason is that doing so permits us to relate Wollheim's notion of instinct to my model. Wollheim's appeal to a biological, preconscious explanation for motivations shows that a preconscious form of determinable caring can be located on the biological level of our being. Despite my use of Wollheim's notion in Chapter 2 to indicate the theoretical place occupied by my notion of deep caring, however, caring understood at the biological level of our being should not be equated with the notion of deep caring which I have suggested is central to our existential self-project, although it shares with it the quality of being hidden from consciousness. Deep caring is a preconscious dimension combining all four levels of our being, including the biological. Deep caring provides a deep motivational impetus to our intentional and purposeful lives as these are structured culturally and biologically. But for the moment I want to explore the hypothesis that a determinable form of caring already operates at the biological level of our being, a form often referred to as *instinctual drives*.

To argue this thesis, I will make use of that currently popular form of scientistic reductionism, sociobiology. Sociobiology is a body of thought which applies ethological studies of animals to human beings so as to explain the latter's characteristic behaviours. The idea is that many of our behaviour patterns, particularly those that might be universally present in human communities, are the result of our genetic makeup. A simple example might be the child-nurturing activities of mothers. Such behaviours would be explained as being instinctive or genetically imprinted by natural selection. As such, they would be immutable. Because of this inherently conservative consequence, and because the behaviours in question have included morally important ones, sociobiology has generated vigorous debate. The polarisation occasioned by the publication of E. O. Wilson's initial conservative statement on the subject[4] and typified by such vehement responses as that of the Sociobiology Study Group of Science for the People[5] has given way to a more moderate position on the part of Wilson (in conjunction with Lumsden)[6] as well as more moderate appraisals on the part of several philosophical commentators.[7]

I should note that there are some formidable methodologicaldifficulties relating to sociobiology. Too little is currently known about genes to support most of the claims that sociobiology makes. The correlation between genotype and phenotype (including the latter's behavioural manifestations) is much too complex and poorly understood to justify many of the detailed speculations in which the sociobiologists engage. Further, the assumption that descriptions of behaviour and its internal causes identify features of the phenotype rather than being theoretical or social constructs constituted by anthropological inquiry is made without justification.[8]

Yet the findings of the sociobiologists do seem to be relevant to my inquiries. If the basis for the sociobiologists' explanations is evolutionary biology and population genetics, then they must be speaking of the relation between the genotype and the phenotype. Insofar as behaviour is at issue, it can only be behaviour which is part of the phenotype. The technical term for this is *traits*, understood as biologically based behaviour invariant within the species.[9] The term *instinct* has also been used in this context to refer to the causal basis of such traits. Further, it may not be too great a departure from theoretical purity to also speak here of dispositions, as it can be observed that animals who are prevented by circumstances from behaving in the way that their biology dictates show displacement and frustration behaviours. Yet to confine ourselves to such purely biological categories as trait and instinct would be to deny what is clearly the case: namely, that it is appropriate to use intentional language in the description of animal behaviour.[10] This would seem to suggest that animals undergo such internal states as desire and frustration, raising the question whether such an imputation can be explained causally with reference to their genes.

But before we go on to ask whether our own internal states and motivations might be explained by our genes, we should note that there is a subtle shift in categories as we move from talk of instincts and traits to talk of dispositions, inclinations, motivations, and, finally, desires. This shift corresponds to an increase in the possibility of reflexivity and self-consciousness. Even if our genes cause our dispositions, it would not follow that they cause our desires. As we saw in Chapter 2 when we discussed the primordial level of our caring, dispositions need only be determinably intentional and come to expression in determinately intentional forms. Possible objects of desire which are culturally formed (such as consumer goods) have, therefore, a formative role in desires. And so does consciousness. Our desires cannot be formed by our genes, because our genes know nothing of the objects of our desires.

Perhaps we should grant that our genes might cause motivations. The advantage of the term *motivation* is that it does not necessarily entail full self-consciousness, so that it is not a vicious anthropomorphism to speak of animals as having motivations. Nor is it always the case that when human beings act in motivated ways, they are conscious of what their motives are, although they might be. This gives us a concept, therefore, which is causal in the sense required for sociobiological explanations yet also gives us an entrance into human self-consciousness. Given that a motivation may be necessary but not sufficient for an action to take place, we could speak of it as a force leading to action, one which, were it present to consciousness, could be felt as a desire or posited as a reason for action. Wollheim's "mental disposition," elaborated in Chapter 2, would then be applicable to motivations.

Given that needs can ground motivations, a great many of our motivations arise from the biological level of our being. This is enough to support my thesis that a determinable form of caring operates at the biological level of our being. I do not see the need to extend the sociobiologists' program to forms of cultural expression including ethics, however. To explain such behaviour in purely biological terms is to ignore the higher levels of human existence by which such behaviours are culturally shaped and transformed into lived projects. The explanatory program of sociobiology cannot succeed in telling us what such behaviour means and why it is important, because it has robbed itself of the essential dimensions of human significance which arise only at these cultural levels.

We cannot understand human caring as a purely biological phenomenon for the simple reason that we cannot understand anything that is of human significance at a purely biological level. This level of existence may be described and explained by biological science by way of theoretical constructs and entities such as instincts and genes, but it cannot be explored for its human significance for the simple reason that it is not available to human reflection. We do not think at the biological level of our existence. So, although we should grant sociobiology its due because we are basically biological beings, we should also recognise that sociobiology cannot account for all of what it is to be human without pain of reductionism.

One benefit of my four-level model is that it defines the applicability of sociobiological explanations. They do not reach up into the higher levels of our being. The biological and instinctual levels of our human being are absorbed into and hidden behind our conscious grasp of our own being as intentional and purposive. If there is a determinable form of caring at this level, it is one which takes the preconscious and causally efficacious form of need.

Deep caring, too, is expressed at the biological level of our being. Insofar as our own biological survival is basic to our caring as self-project, fear in the face of mortal danger is a direct expression not only of determinable, instinctual caring, but of deep caring as well. The meaning of such fear extends beyond a motivational pressure towards flight. It is a direct experience of what phenomenologists call our facticity. Through it we experience our biology as *our* biology. We appropriate our own instinctual being so as to combine it with and dissolve it into the higher levels of our being. The phenomenological evidence for this is that we experience ourselves as subject to inescapable biological determination and mortality. Through deep caring we experience our biology as that part of our temporality which we might call the ever-present past in the form of our genetic inheritance, and our inescapable future in the form of death.

The Perceptual and Reactive Level

When we turn to the perceptual and reactive level of our existence, my thesis becomes more complex. The way we apprehend the world sensorially is structured by the meanings our cultures make available to us. We do not simply see an item and only then make sense of it. We make sense of it in some way even as we see it.[11] As we walk down the street and see items moving along the road, we immediately recognise them as cars. We do not register shapes and colours in our perceptual experience as cameras do and then apply our separately learned knowledge of cars in order to recognise and identify what we have seen in some precognitive way. We recognise and understand what we see immediately.

That this understanding depends upon social and cultural formation is demonstrated by a thought experiment in which we imagine a New Guinea highlander with no experience of modern technology coming to our town and walking down the street with us. He would not recognise the cars for what they are. This would demonstrate that our recognition of cars depends on our cultural formation and education.

But neither is it the case that the highlander would experience the cars in a purely precognitive way, as if he could see the shapes and movements purely as what they are in themselves. He, too, uses some culturally mediated meaning to structure what his eyes take in. He might see the cars as magical monsters or as hard-skinned animals. Or he might simply take them to be highly puzzling items which he will inquire into when he has the time.

Whatever he takes them to be, the point is that he has to take them to be something. He does not simply have a brute, unprocessed perceptual experience. The thing is meaningful to him in some way. And the meanings which it can have for him depend on his culture. That he can see it as a magic monster or a hard-skinned animal, or even that he can see it as a puzzle as opposed to an object of fear, depends on his cultural formation. He must have knowledge of magic, or of animals, or of puzzles in order to form his experience in these ways. Part of what it is to be a whole, human being is to be able to experience the world in a definite, cognitive way, to have an understanding of one's world.

But all this relates only to perception. A second element at this level of existence is reaction. Not only do we immediately recognise and understand what we see in our environments, but we also immediately react. If I am walking down the street musing about this or that and a car suddenly bears down on me, then my perceptual equipment will directly cause a shift in my attention and I will jump out of the way. This will occur all at once, as if it were a reflex. What this indicates is that the perceptual level of existence is not only of purely cognitive significance; it is a part of my active orientation to the world. Although there is nothing in the way of deliberate decision making in such a case, my reaction is purposive and functional. Whether it is the result of learning or of instincts need not concern us, although if it were purely instinctual, it would be based in the biological level of our existence.

The point is that such reactions enter into our consciousness as expressive of our immediate practical understanding of the situation and are therefore to be assimilated into the perceptual and cognitive level of our existence. The intentional counterpart of this immediate practical understanding of our situation is that the world around us is discovered by us to be already meaningful. As Heidegger has put it, the world is always already there.[12]

What this shows is that behavioural or reflex reactions have an affective dimension. The world is not neutral to our gaze. As a result, emotional reactions can also be modelled at this second level of human existence. The word *emotion* covers a wide range of phenomena, and much of their origin lies in the preconscious sphere. Along with the affective turbulence and motivational pressures to action that one feels when one is angry, in love, or frightened, to name just three quite different examples, there is also a cognitive dimension.[13] When one is angry, one sees the offending situation differently. When one is in love, one sees the beloved differently. And in the example of the car bearing down upon us, we would not have noticed the make of the car, only its threatening presence.

But we should not think of this as a process comprising two stages, that of perception and that of reaction. As Maurice Merleau-Ponty has persuasively shown, the needs, practical orientations, and attitudes which guide our lives are expressed in a bodily comportment towards the world which structures our perception of it. We send out a "mute and permanent question" into our world,[14] to which both perception and action are the answer. This is clearly true when we are pursuing some specific purpose expressive of some determined or determinable care that we have. We more readily notice the things that relate to our concerns. It follows that reaction is not an aftereffect of perception but a schema through which what is perceptually given in the world is significant to us. Our determinable caring structures our world.

But a more fundamental a priori structure for the significance of the world to us is deep caring. The world and things in it are not only significant to us because of our contingent practical concerns, they are also significant in the sense that we always already find ourselves in a world that we acknowledge as our world. The world is neither a neutral field of brute facts nor a world whose meanings are merely a function of our needs. Rather, our world relates to and extends our self-project. We are ontologically related to this world just as we are to our past. It is the basis from which we project ourselves into our lives and into our future.

The Evaluative and Proactive Level

The third level of our existence as human beings is that of praxis, which I analyse as evaluation and proaction. The existence of this level in our being is indicated by the fact that human beings are agents acting in the light of values and purposes. This level is evaluative: we have attitudes and desires and act towards the world in ways expressive of these attitudes and desires. It is also proactive. It is at this level that we engage in that vast range of activities which constitute our everyday practical lives. Going about our daily business in relation to our jobs, families, and entertainments constitutes our common-sense practical orientation towards the world. This orientation, in turn, is the culturally shaped formation of an inchoate deeper level of needs and wants as motivators to action. These culturally formed attitudes, interests, and desires constitute determinable and determined instances of caring and provide us with our reasons for action.

It is the presence of what conventional philosophy of action calls *desire* at the third practical level of our existence that justifies my calling that level evaluative as well as proactive. The presence of reactive elements in the second level of our being and of evaluative elements at the third level serves to highlight the cohesiveness of those levels in the whole person. There is no sharp distinction that can be drawn between emotional reactions that express attitudes and practical evaluations that do so.

Insofar as I can sustain the distinction between levels two and three at all, I do so by saying that level two is completely preconscious, including as it does the cognitions and reactions with which I cannot but find myself, whereas level three is marked by a greater degree of reflexivity and presence to myself. Here I adopt projects, form intentions, and make plans with a greater degree of self-consciousness. Even in the many cases where I do not engage in fully self-conscious mental activities of deliberation, I do engage in mental activities of volition, and I can bring my reasons for action to consciousness by reflection.

Most philosophers seem to discuss human action in terms of the reasons that we have for action, where such reasons are analysed in terms of our beliefs and desires. Beliefs and desires, in their turn, are spoken of as causative realities, without regard to their being reflexively or prereflexively present. It is enough that they be determinable in reflection. In the vast majority of cases, we do not bring our reasons for action to mind explicitly, although we act in light of our beliefs and in a way motivated by our desires.

However, it would be inconsistent with my methodology if we thought of this as a purely causal process. These beliefs and desires are not only effective, they are also ontologically present in a prereflexive or determinable form. Further, the notion of desire is too limiting to give us an adequate interpretation of human agency. We do things based on our attitudes or what we care about, even when we neither desire to do them nor desire their objects.

Along with our beliefs (which are already affectively coloured, as I have argued), the motivational impetus for our actions can come from determined or determinable desires, needs, interests, attitudes, emotions, moods, habits, and compulsions. Some of these will be present to reflection and therefore able to be modelled at the third level of our being, and others not. Motivations that are not present to thought are not for that reason merely causes. They are prereflexive horizons for making our actions intelligible, horizons which display the caring nature of our being.

To actively and self-consciously assess and pursue what our motivations lead us towards is to act in a human way at the third level of our existence. This will involve a cognitive appraisal of our situation and the possibilities which it encapsulates, as well as an appraisal of our skills and abilities. It will also involve placing our desires, needs, interests, and so forth in an order of priority. Further, it will involve being able to adjust to frustration and disappointment when our interests are thwarted and our needs unmet. It may even involve major adjustments when our need for food, shelter, or security is radically unfulfilled, as when we suffer injury or illness. These are all things we care about in a determinable way and which give content to our practical lives.

Once again, we need to distinguish between determinable caring as it pertains to our conscious and preconscious motivational fields and the deep caring which I posit as the a priori structure for such determinable caring. What we do on a daily basis is important to us in varying degrees. It defines us as what we are at present, as that present directs itself towards our future. This importance is classically theorised by showing how our daily projects are part of a larger plan and how this larger plan is seen to be conducive to our overall well-being.

But these projects and tasks are not important to us simply because the specifiable goals that we contingently pursue through them are important to us in some ultimate way. Rather, they are important to us simply because it is *our* life that we are living. It is our self-project that we are engaged in, our future that we are directed towards, and we care about that in a deep and inchoate way. It may be that this is the true meaning of Aristotle's quest for *Eudaimonia* (happiness understood as fulfillment) as the fundamental objective of all our actions.

Before discussing the fourth level of our being, I want to digress for a moment to explicate one of the elements mentioned earlier as a constituent of our motivational fields: attitudes. Attitudes are a form of determinable caring. An attitude is a mental disposition in Wollheim's sense. It is a disposition not only to act in certain ways but also to react and feel in certain ways in response to given stimuli. I have noted that attitudes are present at the third level of our being. They are prereflexively present even at the second level of our being. Indeed, it will transpire as our analysis continues that attitudes arise at all four levels of our being. Attitudes are an expression of my individual being and self-project. The prerequisite for our having attitudes at all is deep caring itself. Accordingly, that attitudes can be seen to arise at all levels of our being will constitute an argument in favour of my model, in which the four ontological levels of our being constitute a unified diachronic structure by virtue of the deep caring that flows through all of them.

An attitude is not simply an affective reaction to a cognitive input. It expresses my stance or commitment. In the case where the exciting appearance of a fancy sports car gives a colourful dimension to our recognition of it and we also desire to have it, the full expression of that attitude will involve our trying to obtain it. Our attitude is one of approval of and wanting to own such luxury items. Yet such positive attitudes are not the same as desires. They differ from desires in that the latter are more determinately formed by the objects they are focused upon. Attitudes are the determinable stances which can generate desires in the presence of a suitable object. Of course, many attitudes, such as dislike or disapproval, bear no relation to desires at all. I might be displeased by the sight of the sports car because of my negative attitude towards conspicuous consumption.

The definitive feature of having an attitude is taking a stance (or finding ourselves with one when we first begin to reflect on such matters), by virtue of which something becomes important for us in a way that seems natural and self-evident. An attitude is either something we find ourselves with as a result of our upbringing, or something inaugurated by a mental activity such as making a commitment. One might speak of an attitude as a commitment that has become routine. Our interests can also influence our attitudes. Marx was right to suggest that our material interests form our attitudes. It is no accident that factory owners and factory workers often have differing political and economic attitudes. Our unreflected-upon opinions, our prejudices, and our predispositions to react in certain ways all constitute our attitudes and are largely formed in us by cultural forces of which we are only minimally aware.

And yet I also define attitudes as being stances which we take in a deliberate way. Is there a contradiction here? I would argue not. I understand "taking a stance" as being the voluntary but not necessarily self-conscious adoption of a position. It is often prereflexive. Even though we do not always consciously think about an issue so as to form a rational and sensitive attitude towards it, we can do so, and any attitude that we in fact have is therefore implicitly acceded to. In addition, there will be occasions in our lives when we are confronted with new situations, and we may form an attitude towards them via a creative and deliberate mental activity. We consider the matter, discern the implications of fact and of value, and adopt an attitude. This would seem a deliberate taking of a stance.

However, even here, the assessment that we make and the values we adopt will express attitudes that we already have. If I am a racist in one geographical context, then I will very likely be one when confronted by a different ethnic group in a new geographical context. If I have a sensitive attitude towards religion in one cultural context, I may well have that attitude towards different religions in another context. The problem now, however, is that in speaking of stances in this existentially foundational way, we are talking about the fourth level of our existence as human beings. We are talking about what we care about in an ultimate sense.

The Spiritual Level

To pursue only those things which constitute the pragmatic concerns of daily life would seem a limited way to live. After all, what are these concerns? Basic needs such as biological needs for food, shelter, and security seem to ground most of the cares of daily life. But "man does not live by bread alone," as the biblical saying goes. We know from Abraham Maslow[15] that our needs extend further. Self-authentication by way of the recognition accorded us by others and by the approval we accord ourselves is also an important need. But even then, if all we ever did was pursue these various needs, we would be limited to seeking food, shelter, security, and approval. Could we, on this basis, achieve fulfillment? Are there not activities and interests which we may freely adopt, other than in response to objective interests or needs?

Artists have needs and interests relating to the practicalities of life, but we admire artists precisely because they are able to dedicate themselves to goals that seem removed from such objective interests. The creation of a beautiful piece of sculpture seems to serve no useful purpose, if we measure usefulness in terms of the objective needs and interests of people or of the artist. A hat stand is more useful. Yet we admire the work, or, in those cases where we do not, we at least accept the idea that such work should go on. Moreover, we feel that artists should be interested in the work that they do for its own sake rather than for material gain and the fulfillment of objective needs. Although it may be inappropriate to espouse it, the traditional Romantic image of the artist starving in a garret expresses the important idea that we expect artists not to be concerned primarily with their own needs.

For us, too, there should be a level of caring which is independent of those objective interests of ours which arise at the first three levels of our being. To care in this new way is to have attitudes that accord importance to something other than our objective needs and interests. This constitutes our dignity and uniqueness as human beings. I will later explore the suggestion that this also constitutes our freedom. We are not limited to the biological or the pragmatic levels of living. The difference between level three and level four is that at level three, we do things because it appears to us that we need to in light of our real interests, whereas on level four we do those things which seem of intrinsic importance to us.

The fourth level of human being, that of the spiritual, constitutes the completion and fulfillment of human life. The words *completion* and *fulfillment* point to the further temporal dimension which deep caring constitutes: namely, our own future as hoped for and believed in by us. Once again, the distinction between the other levels of our being and this fourth level cannot be sharp. We envisage our future as we engage in the practical activities of level three. But at level four this future takes on a deeper resonance and becomes more definitive of our being, as we will see.

In speaking of a spiritual level in human existence, I do not want to suggest that a human being or a whole person has a component designated by the noun *spirit*. To avoid a metaphysical postulation of reified parts of human being, we should try to describe this fourth spiritual level of human existence with a verb, as we have done with the earlier levels. And the best choice would be *to integrate*. For human beings it is not enough to live, to recognise things for what they are, and to have proactive attitudes towards these things. The things we experience, and the attitudes that we have towards them, must be integrated into a whole. We want and need to have an integrated worldview, such that things in our world are experienced as belonging there and as belonging together over time, and we want and need personal integrity.

One dimension of this integrity is the synchronic dimension of the levels of our being which I have posited. Another dimension is the diachronic dimension of caring which I have proposed. It is this latter dimension which shows that the integration of our lives is an existential project, the most fundamental existential project that we can have: being ourselves. This project generates the spiritual level of our being and expresses the projection of our being through time. It is at the spiritual level of our being that we constitute our wholeness as persons, the wholeness of our lives, and the wholeness of our attitudes and worldview.

I can illustrate humanity's spiritual quest for wholeness by alluding to science. It is a tendency of science to want to explain everything, to seek to integrate the theories and hypotheses that explain different and various phenomena into a grand theory which explains them all. The attempt on the part of physics to describe the fundamental constituents of all matter is an example of this. So was Einstein's dream of a unified field theory which would explain all the forces that operate in nature. The attempt of sociobiologists to account for all human cultural and social events, ranging from social rituals to individual hopes and feelings, in terms of our genetic makeup is another example.

And such examples are found not only in science. The major task that philosophy has set itself through the ages is to develop an understanding of the diversity of the world we live in which would show this world to be the incarnation of metaphysically certain and unified realities. Whether it is Plato's Theory of Forms, Spinoza's Monads, Schopenhauer's World as Will and Idea, or Hegel's Spirit, philosophy has sought to postulate a unity lying behind the diversity of worldly reality.

There is a profound and important human project involved in these attempts to totalise our experiences of contingency. This project is nothing less than the attempt to make our lives meaningful as a whole. On the face of it, our existence is a sequence of apparently random events. We get up in the morning and go off to work or to other activities, and then we come home in the evening, eat, and go to bed. The next day is the same. And the day after. What is it all for? Is it simply a matter of filling time between birth and death?

Certainly there are joys as well as sorrows, pleasures as well as pains. But are these fleeting consolations all that there is to live for? Perhaps a life plan would tie it all together. But what if I die before my plans are fulfilled? Even if an overarching meaning based on a life plan could be established, it would ultimately be negated by death. Nothing of this meaning would seemingly remain after we die. How can any of our projects be significant for us if they might, in the very next moment, be completely annihilated?

We form short-term plans and purposes, certainly, but the achievement of any of these is dependent on the luck of circumstances and the cooperation of others. All too often our plans are frustrated and our hopes dashed. We desire what is difficult to obtain and then become disappointed almost as soon as we obtain it. What stereo buffs are long content with the expensive audio equipment they might just have purchased? How many of our relationships remain untainted by disappointments and resentments?

In the face of this, it is an important source of hope and courage to be able to see particular events and people as part of a greater whole. If this whole assigns a place to everything and perhaps even gives everything a purpose, then these ironies of existence may be seen to have a point. If the things that happen are precisely the things that should happen given the nature and scheme of things, then they may be accepted. At the fourth level of our existence, we seek assurance that the meaningfulness of our world arises from something less contingent than our own natures and wishes.

An example may be drawn from fiction. A story in a novel or in a film seems satisfactory to us only if there is a detectable plan to it.[16] Situations and events must contribute to the development of characters, and what happens to these characters at the end must make sense in terms of the story as it has unfolded. It would be a strange story where a person pursuing some ambition and relating to other characters in a way consistent with that ambition suddenly and accidentally died before any of that ambition was fulfilled or any of the subplots resolved. We want coherence and completion in our stories. We want them to have a point. Similarly, we want our lives to be coherent and to culminate at a point where we can look back and find it all to have been meaningful and without cause for regret.

Of course, real life is not always like that. It does indeed happen that we make wrong decisions that turn our lives into a collage of unconnected mishaps. Or it happens that a life, with all its aspirations, plans, and memories, is suddenly snuffed out. When this happens to a friend or loved one, we feel it to be a deep threat to the very possibility of making our lives meaningful. It is not simply that we grieve at the loss of a friend; we grieve at the lack of fulfillment and completion of a life as well. We are saddened that a life which was unfolding in a meaningful way is now frustrated.

As I have noted, death is the ultimate negator of meaning. Yet it is not always so. Elderly persons who die in their sleep after a life of achievement and spiritual fulfillment die in a way that puts the seal of meaningfulness upon their whole lives.[17] Alas, we cannot ensure that our own lives will end this way. The meaningfulness and completeness of our lives is always precarious. We do not have the sort of control over the story of our lives that novelists have over their narratives. Perhaps this is why Heidegger suggests that we should orient our whole lives towards our deaths.[18] If death is a horizon for our living, it cannot be a negation of the meaning of that life or a total frustration of its aspirations.

There is a further reason why we have need of this spiritual level of integration. In the modern world, people do not live only in one culture. We derive our existence and identity from culture, and we contribute creatively to it, but we may do this in relation to a number of cultures. Even though we live in one society or nation, this social entity comprises numerous subcultures. I might expect to derive multivalent identities from being of a certain gender, ethnicity, socioeconomic class, age, profession, and so forth. And these aspects of identity may conflict. My gender role may urge me to be competitive amongst my peers, whereas my role as a parent urges me to be caring and giving. My ethnic identity may demand of me that I behave demurely in the company of males, whereas my schooling has taught me to be boisterous and independent.

In the many conflicts that can arise from the ways in which human existence is socially formed, are not integration and coordination still possible? Psychologists might speak of this in terms of maturity and self-image, but for most people reflecting on their lives, what is needed is an order of meaning which will integrate all these conflicting attitudes and pressures. Every part of oneself must be seen to have a place. A concordance of roles must be established.

The spiritual effort that works towards the establishment of such integrity is part of what I have been calling our *self-project*. In using this term, I align myself with those existentialist thinkers[19] who propose that the self is a project rather than a metaphysical entity. To justify this will require a brief digression in which I will attack the traditional metaphysics of the self.

My self consists of nothing but the levels of existence I have described. These levels are all dialectically related to each other in a synchronic dimension and combine past, present, and future in a diachronic dimension. At every level of our existence, we are defined by what we do in relating to the world and by how we are transformed by what we relate to. We are what we are made to be. This might mean that in postmodern times we are made into confused and multifarious selves that have great difficulty ordering our lives.

Nevertheless, we do take a stance. However falteringly, we do order our values. We do adjudicate between conflicting desires and act as referees between opposing pressures. Most of us do make our lives coherent and meaningful. But who is the subject of all these verbs? The traditional answer is our true self. Does this mean that we "have" or "are" a true self? Is there a real self? Given my methodology, we do not need to ask whether there is a noun — self — which refers to a particular entity. Verbs are sufficient. We simply are. There is a taking of a stance. There is an ordering of values and an adoption of a life plan. There is pain and grief and love and hope. There is an integrating. Why do we also need an entity called a "self" standing behind these events so as to own them?

At the same time, we should not be tempted to think that we have no subjective reality. There is a product of the process of integration which is the self-image we have as a function of the relations we enter into at the four levels of our existence. There, too, is a hidden and prereflexive impetus to the process of integration which is our deep caring. This deep caring is the prereflexive basis of our self-projects which become focused as determinable caring and determinate projects and intentions as we engage our world. We are not something else besides this.

Although there was a tradition of Romantic thought which spoke at great length about crises of the self and of anguish in the soul arising from conflicts between social pressure and the true self and genius of each individual,[20] this was no more than a poetic and metaphorical way of speaking. What it described was real enough — the breakdown of the homogeneous traditional forms of society in which people had found a secure identity, and the consequent feelings of alienation and nihilism — but to have described these feelings in a manner suggesting there was a knowable and essential self whose destiny and promise were somehow being violated was to create hyperbole. What was happening was that a new socially formed self-image was emerging to replace the old secure and stable one. The anguished response was justified insofar as this new self-image was unstable and uncentred and left human beings with the unenviable task of ordering their own values from amongst the many conflicting values now on offer.

What, then, are we to make of the ancient nostrum "know thyself," of Shakespeare's "to thine own self be true," and of Nietzsche's "become who you are"? These sayings have emerged in contemporary cultures to such an extent as to seem like moral imperatives. Do they suggest that there is such a thing as a self to which we must be true? Is there a self to whom I am beholden, as when I say that I owe it to myself to fulfill an obligation? No, the explication is clear. What we are to come to know, what we are to be true to, that which we are fully to be, and that to which we owe a duty are the full four levels of our being, not some metaphysical entity apart from these.

To neglect our bodies through laziness, just as to ignore any of the ideals our cultures have taught us or to be disloyal to the commitments we have made, is to fail in these ways. It is ourselves as biological beings that we fail to understand and honour when we fail to look after our health, and it is ourselves as spiritual beings that we fail to understand and honour when we fail to adopt ideals or to be committed to them. To know ourselves is to recognise the various levels of our existence and what they hold out to us as possibilities and projects, and to be aware of the vertical integration which results from our self-conscious stances. To be true to ourselves is to acknowledge these many aspects of our existence and to be responsible for their fulfillment through such integrative stances. To be ourselves is to acknowledge what our cultural histories and biological destinies have made us and to align our hopes and aspirations with that. It is to accept and own our self-image.

There is no doubt that these sayings are often uttered in contexts where the commitments and plans of particular people are under threat from peer group pressures, social conformity, or other temptations. But to say that persons must be true to their commitments is not to suggest that they have inner entities called "selves" to which they owe a duty. It is to urge that people acknowledge their functional relationships with the world, and the integration of the levels of their being, as the basis for their self-projects and of the meaningfulness of their lives.

Though I will explicate these points more fully in later chapters, we need to be clear as to what I am and am not claiming at this point. What I deny is that there is some hidden metaphysical entity at the core of our being which we might call our "true self" and which is the ultimate subject of all the verbs ascribable to me, the ultimate referent of all the nouns and pronouns used to refer to me, and the ultimate owner of the four levels of my existence. What I do not deny is that I am a person with a definite historical and social situation who is grounded in a definite biological body, so that a large number of things can be truly said of me by others as a result of observation, and by myself as a result of reflection.

When I say that I want to go to the movies, I am referring to myself and describing what I want. My claim is that in doing this, I am giving expression to my existence by telling others or myself how I feel. I could equally give expression to my existence in this circumstance by simply going to the movies, but this would not convey the relevant information about me quite as explicitly to others. (Notice that although this is a description of me, it is not the same as when another describes me as wanting to go to the movies. In the case of third-person description, he or she is not giving expression to my existence. Only I can do that for myself.) First-person reports and avowals are primarily expressions of the speaker's existence. They are only secondarily descriptions of a self. And even then, the self in question is a socially constructed self. That we need to be able to refer to one another in various ways does not imply that there is an entity being referred to. There is only the self-project coming to expression.

The term *self-project*, then, aligns my thesis with that of those existentialists who would see the reality of the self as grounded not in a metaphysical entity, but in the project of becoming a self within the many formative influences that constitute our material and cultural world as we experience it. As I explained in Chapter 2, the primary expression of deep primordial care is our own being as self-project. This self-project can be an object of reflection. But one does not, in the course of such reflection, focus upon a formed reality with a fixed nature. One reflects on one's self-image.

This self-image is formed by one's hopes and expectations as much as by one's memories and past experiences. One holds before oneself an image which expresses what one wants to be as well as what one takes oneself to have become. Indeed, there might be many kinds of tension between these elements. What one hopes to be might be contradicted by what one has done or is currently doing, and what one hopes to achieve might not be enhanced by what one has been doing.

In this way, life becomes a struggle to realise what we hope for ourselves. It becomes a project of self-realisation or of self-becoming, where the word *self* refers to that hoped-for self or self-image which is the goal of my project. Modified by my realistic self-assessment, my hoped-for self is the object of my self-project.

Embodying as it does my memories, hopes, and aspirations, my self-project is more than simply a life plan. It contains my ideals and my most overarching goals. The spiritual level of my existence comes into being as I direct myself upon such ideals and goals to give my life coherence and meaning. The purpose of my life is to realise my self-project and the ideals it encapsulates. These ideals ought to resolve the confusions that flow from the breakdown of a traditional unified worldview, so that my life can be seen as part of a plan or even as reconcilable in an order of meaning that transcends the here and now. This would also establish a basis and justification for the particular meanings that things have for me in ordinary life.

To understand this more fully, we will need to explore what ideals are. We have seen how the first three levels of our existence ground the practical meaningfulness of things and incidents in our lived world. And we have seen how this is expressed in both cognition and attitudes. Cognitions are culturally and linguistically structured responses to whatever is the case in the world. The ground and justification of such cognitions would be that a cognition is true if it leads to our offering a description that fits the facts.

But what would be the basis of a justification of our attitudinal responses? Certainly, many of our attitudes will be learned as we are inducted into our culture, so that they could be justified simply by agreeing with prevailing norms. But what do we base the possibility of legitimating our responses and valuations on when we reflect deeply on our lives and scrutinise our accepted attitudes?

In the past, an overarching view of what is valuable and important in itself could have helped us achieve this. Then, there was a level of meaningfulness from which the meanings of particular things and events could be derived or against which they could be measured. But postmodernism would deny that any such overarching order of meaning is still tenable today. In response, I argue that all we can now appeal to is that inchoate, prereflexive basis of my being which is determinable as specific projects and plans — our deep caring.

As deep caring is hidden and nonintentional, it cannot be appealed to directly as a basis for our values. To ground our ultimate values, it will need to come to expression in a form which allows reflection. This form would be the self-image which integrates all our particular attitudes and cares and encapsulates our hoped-for self and our ideals. Rather than being objective realities, ideals are culturally formed intentional objects of our commitments. Such grand words as Truth, Beauty, and Goodness tend to fall on deaf ears in these cynical times, and there is no doubt that vague ideals can be dangerous if they replace caring for persons in their particularity. I will have more to say about this later.

Ideals, however, cannot be dispensed with simply because they seem jaded or empty. Character ideals such as integrity and honour, or sensitivity and warmth, are ideals which can give our lives meaning. Admittedly, ideals come into and go out of favour with the passage of time.[21] But whatever ideals are most forcefully conveyed in a culture and whatever are dispar-aged, they operate as frameworks of self-formation for individuals, whereby their lives become meaningful in an integrating way to the extent that they fulfill those ideals. All of the various tasks and agendas which preoccupy us on an everyday basis gain their meaning and importance to the extent that they bring our self-project and our ideals into being. To live in pursuit of ideals in this way is to live ethically.

The most prominent historical form of such a quest, however, is not eth-ics or morality but religion. Religious faith typically acknowledges a god or family of gods who rule earthly reality from a transcendental realm. Only in this realm can there be true knowledge, eternity, goodness, certainty, and meaning. There, everything is as it should be and everything that happens is what must happen.

Earthly reality, in contrast, is but an imperfect approximation of this. On earth, there is doubt, mortality, evil, contingency, and meaninglessness. The only way this absurd earthly realm can be made meaningful, and thus liv-able, is by relating it to the eternal. One might achieve this by calling the earthly realm a place of trial, such that our reward for meeting its challenges is entrance into the transcendent. Or one might attribute to the gods a prov-idential and guiding role over human affairs so that history becomes, despite any appearances to the contrary, the effecting of a holy will. The task of the individual within such worldviews is to fulfill the holy will of the gods and to bring one's personal projects in line with the fateful order of history or destiny. One way of living at the fourth, spiritual level of human existence, then, is to live with religious faith.

But faith does not need to be religious in nature. Determinable caring at the fourth level of our being can also be called faith. The core of such a non-transcendent form of faith is a positive stance towards one's life and a com-mitment to ideals even when no rational justification can be found for them. In this sense, faith is an expression of the fourth level of what it is to be a human being. It is the highest expression of deep caring. It involves an affirmative attitude towards life which is all-embracing and meaning-giving. Integrity involves seeing our whole lives — past, present, and future — as coherent and as an expression of our self-images and ideals. To live life positively, with faith, is to live as if our lives were indeed meaningful and coherent. It is to live as if our ideals were fundamentally important and attainable. It is to live as if we could indeed fulfill our aspirations and com-plete our plans. It is to live as if our loves and our friendships were indeed firm, as if trust and loyalty were indeed unquestionable. It is to live as if the disappointments, griefs, and pains did not negate the hopes, joys, and attainments which keep us going. There is no sound reason for adopting such a faith, yet we must do so if we are to live in an integral way. And we must live as if this were not an illusion.

Why must we adopt some form of faith? Because we reflect on our desires and fears, even if they arise from the merely biological level of our beings. We reflect on the meanings that things have for us even as we perceive them, and we reflect on the reactions that our environments elicit from us. We reflect on our attitudes and seek to justify them with argument and reconcile them with each other. Furthermore, we reflect on the things we willfully do, and we make conscious decisions to do them. All this reflection and thought seeks the meaning of it all, and in so doing combines the first three levels of our existence into the fourth. At this spiritual level, a coherence and meaning is posited by us for our lives.

Whether this positing is the product of explicit reflection as I suggest here, or whether it is the more implicit result of our upbringing and acculturation, it is this totalising commitment to life which constitutes faith. Yet this responding and positing is not the same as finding. We do not discover our lives to have meaning. We affirm that they have. This is an affirmation without rational justification and without external reassurance. It is an affirmation which remains a seeking and a questioning. It is a commitment grounded in deep caring.

Without faith we would not be enthusiastic about anything, for we would only be acting and reacting in accordance with our needs and interests. As human beings, living at once on all four levels of our existence, we do not simply go about our daily business because we have to. An animal in the field chews its cud or fossicks for food because it is driven to do so by its needs. It does not get excited about doing these things when it wakes in the morning.

Human beings, on the other hand, can pursue their goals with passion. To live life in a meaningful way means to be able to commit oneself to it. Were one to think that one was going about the daily round simply because one had to or because there was nothing better to do, then human life would become emotionally flat and absurd. Not only would there be no point to it, there would be no passion for it, either.

One of the consequences of having faith, of believing that living is worth the effort, is that one throws oneself into living with enthusiasm. Of course, such enthusiasm will wax and wane and be vulnerable to disappointment. The great spiritual illnesses of modern times are alienation and anomie.

These consist in the loss of this enthusiasm. It is an ideal of human character to suffer the "slings and arrows of outrageous fortune" with a reasonable
optimism, and it is a responsibility of society to allow everyone the circumstances that make this possible. What Plato called *thumos*[22] and what some of
his translators call "spiritedness" is this lust for life without which life would
not be fully human. Such spiritedness or passion is possible to the extent
that we have faith. We can be enthusiastic about life only if we take it to be
meaningful.

Faith is another term for determinable caring at the fourth level of our
being. But faith is not simply an open attitude of affirmation or a search for
meaning. Faith is commitment, and as such, it has intentional objects. These
objects are the ideals I have been speaking about. What ties my life together
into a coherent and meaningful whole might be service to others or the pursuit of my own pleasure. I might call it Love, King, Country, or Success.
Whatever it is, it is at once what I seek in my spiritual quest and that which
I think I have found as I affirm my life as meaningful. A medieval courtier
might attach his whole life in this way to a noble lady; a monk would dedicate himself unstintingly to his God. A modern executive might feel that he
or she belongs to the company; a member of an ethnic community might
identify with a national culture. Members of the environmental movement
might place the future of the rain forests at the acme of their priorities. All
of these are overarching attachments in which something or someone is
invested with the spiritual importance which allows a life to have meaning.
Whether one relates in this way to an ideal or to a person, the object of one's
commitment attains an ultimacy that elevates it to the spiritual level of
human living and makes it an object of faith.

But do we standardly live our lives with only one major ideal and one
major goal? Surely it is more common that people operate with a number of
major goals and objectives. There is nothing unusual or inappropriate about
loving one's family, pursuing business success, and also giving time and
energy to the conservationists' campaign to save the forests. Certainly, there
may be clashes and conflicts in such a life, but major aspirations can coexist.
However, I would suggest that our deep caring demands that there be a place
for an all-embracing ideal which ties these goals together. How would the
person we are describing resolve the conflicts that may arise from time to
time? Would he or she not have to decide which goal was primary? And even
if this person adopted a policy of giving each goal priority in turn, would
that not amount to a decision to adhere to an ideal of pluralism in values so
that this pluralism now becomes the overarching ideal?

Many of the particular goals and aspirations that people pursue belong on the third level of human existence. But at this level there is not yet any integration. There can only be conflict and confusion of priorities. If we were to live solely at this level, we would be steeped in anxiety about all the things we had yet to do and guilt for all the things we had, inevitably, left undone.

It is at the fourth level that integration occurs. Here, our faith orders our goals and combines them into a coherent program for life. We may or may not articulate this program by citing a single ideal which is the leitmotiv of our lives. But whether we identify our leading ideal or not, we have one to the extent that our lives are both meaningful and coherent.

The irony is that it may be only our determination to seek a single ideal, rather than any achievement of a single meaning, that constitutes the achievement of this ideal. Because it is not intentional, deep caring is not centred upon an identifiable metaphysical entity, spiritual object, or meaning-giving purpose. Rather, it is centred by determinable caring at the fourth level of our being — by the faith or commitment through which my pursuit of everyday goals becomes an expression of deep caring.

My self-project is both subject and object of this faith. If the logic of my argument requires an object for the striving which marks this faith, then it is the striving itself. Integrity as an ethical ideal means the affirmation of striving for wholeness as both the form and content of faith.

As explained in Chapter 1, I use the term *commitment* to designate practical and purposeful orientations towards ideals or persons. I can now add that they flow from my faith, or fourth-level caring. If I pursue meaningfulness in my life by pursuing business success, it would follow that I will be committed to giving priority to any action that is conducive to business success whenever a situation gives me that option. Given a situation in which I can either play golf with my friends or conclude a profitable deal, I will do the latter. That is the object of my commitment.

However, if I have decided or find myself with the conviction that the pursuit of close relationships is what makes my life meaningful, my commitment will be to pursue loving relationships whenever they arise. Given the choice between working at the office or going home to my family, I will do the latter. I am committed to loving relationships. In this way commitment expresses my faith, or what I care about as integral to my life.

Notice that commitments are just as rationally ungrounded as faith would be. I cannot rationally prove that love is more important than money, any more than my business acquaintances can prove to themselves, or rationally convince me, that business success is the most important thing in life. This is a matter of faith. The positive attitude to life that is the essence of faith is not justifiable by reason. Nor is the particular form of life that one person pursues justifiable as the best in and of itself.

I might not agree with my business acquaintances' priorities. I might feel uncomfortable with their venal attitudes. I might even disapprove of their unscrupulous methods. But I cannot prove, whether to them or to myself, that they are wrong. Their faith simply takes a different form from mine. Their commitments are different. If I were to force them to think differently by dint of logical argument or other forms of persuasion, their thinking differently would not then be a faith and a commitment of their own. It would be forced upon them, and they would not truly own that conviction. Mere acquiescence in logical persuasion does not produce the form of spiritual conversion which leads people to change their faiths and commitments.

When such changes do occur, it is usually in the context of some crisis in life rather than when detached rational argument is taking place. This is because faith and commitment arise from within us in a way that we cannot fully comprehend in reflection or reasoned argument. If I were able to say why I had this faith or enacted these commitments, it would be by alluding to a deeper faith and commitment which grounds those others, and this deeper faith would, in its turn, be without foundation. If my business acquaintances were sufficiently stung by my disapproval to say that they only pursued money to meet the needs of their families, and if this justification were honest and authentic, then we would have discovered that their deepest commitments were to their families rather than to business success, and that their most overarching faith was in love rather than in money. Any reason that I give for a commitment must itself be a deeper commitment. It is when this chain of justification stops that I have reached the commitments that are so ultimate as to express my all-embracing faith and the spiritual level of my life.

Through history, various schools of thought have held that there is one central concern that all people pursue as this ultimate fulfillment of their lives. Aristotle suggested that this was a special form of human happiness,[23] and many religious traditions suggest that it is salvation defined in various ways. But to suggest that there is only one goal that everyone pursues in life is as questionable as to suggest that there is only one faith that everyone shares, one commitment that everyone has, or one God that everyone believes in.

People make their lives meaningful in different ways. Different over-arching goals and different commitments are evident both across cultures and within them. If I had argued that deep caring demanded a single goal in a life, even if that goal was the striving towards such a goal itself, I would now have to stress that this referred to a particular individual's life. For any individual, there must be a single ideal, even if it is pluralism, which gives unity to his or her life. But it does not follow that there must be a single goal which all members of a given culture share. Still less is there a single goal which we all have by dint of our common participation in the human condition.

But the denial that there is one knowable goal that is universally sought does not entail that all people are free to seek whatever forms of faith and commitment they care to imagine. Postmodernism may be correct in challenging the universalist faiths whose times have passed, but it cannot undermine the human quest for faith. People learn to seek spiritual meaning as they are inducted into a culture. Cultures posit and teach historically specific ideals and ultimate values. The notion of what fulfills life in an ultimate way might differ from one culture to the next, but it will remain relatively constant within any given culture. The spiritual level of what it is to be a human being is formed by our culture and historical situation just as the perceptual/reactive and the evaluative/proactive levels are. Only our biology seems to enjoy a kind of human universality based solely on our species' characteristics.

However, despite these layers of cultural formation, the spiritual level of our being is the most intimate and individual level of our existence. Our sense of ourselves as unique identities and as individual projects in the lived world comes to articulation at this level. It is when I express the ideals I care about — my aspirations, commitments, and faiths — that I am most myself. My integrity as a person depends on the fulfillment and vertical integration of all four levels of my being. Moreover, my being in possession of myself as a person, my ability to own my life as mine so as to establish myself as an agent in the world, depends on my reflexive grasp of those four levels of being. It is in reflection upon my life as I live it at all four levels that I fully become what I am. At each level my intentional caring has differing objects and differing degrees of reflexivity, but all these levels are expressive of my deep caring as self-project. If this deep caring could come to expression at all, it would be at the fourth level of my being, in which my quest for meaning becomes its own object.

Nevertheless, although deep caring ultimately remains intimate and inchoate, it finds symbolic expression in culturally grounded public forms of communication which are historically available to me, whether they be the languages of religion, art, or philosophy. In this way my reflection on deep caring and the spiritual level of my being can be an expression which constitutes an authentic but virtual form of communication. Being human in the most complete and integral way involves authentic self-expression, and this self-expression remains a communicative gesture in its very nature, even if it is performed silently and privately in the context of a reflection upon one's own life.

This indicates an important fact about us as human beings. Despite the Romantics' imagery of the human ideal as soaring in solitary splendour towards the lofty heights of self-defined grandeur, the fullness of human existence, even at the spiritual level, is achieved in community. Equally primordial with our being as a self-project is our being as a caring-about-others. I will explain and substantiate this claim in Chapter 4.

4

CARING-ABOUT-OTHERS

In the preceding chapters, we have seen hints that we cannot exist in a human way by ourselves. In this chapter, I will propose that deep caring grounds a form of human solidarity which exists prior to cultural and linguistic differences. Solidarity with others is part of our being as caring and a form through which our deep caring comes to expression. In Chapter 3, I argued that our fundamental being as caring is expressed as the quest for our own integrity. My argument here is that there is also a comportment towards others implicated in this quest.

I have already described our deep caring as our self-project. But there is another equally primordial dimension to our being, apart from our self-project. Borrowing and adapting a term from Sartre, I might have called the comportment which persons have towards one another *being-for-others*, but following the argument that caring is central to the ontological structure of being human, I will call it *caring-about-others*. It is my further thesis that like my self-project, and equiprimordial with it, some form of caring-about-others will be a central preconscious motivational element in any analysis of our caring. Together, my being as self-project and my being as caring-about-others provide that preconscious dynamism which becomes the projects and commitments which constitute my ontological being as it is focused and determined by the intentional objects which form my world.

The simple meaning of the claim that our deep caring takes the form of caring-about-others is that at all levels of our being, others matter to us. And

I am not yet referring to other people: other things matter to us as well. Indeed, I think it would enhance our understanding of our relationship to such things as art and the natural environment to explore this idea further. However, as my present interest is ethics, I will focus on the way other people matter to us.

Self-project and caring-about-others must be equally primordial, because as pre-intentional structures of our being, they have no determinate content by which they can be delineated from each other. Others matter to us as much as we do to ourselves. There is a simple logical argument for this. Deep caring is not yet intentional. Accordingly, we cannot distinguish an aspect of it which is directed towards the subjective pole of our relationships with the world from an aspect which is directed towards the objective pole of those relationships. The mode of our being simply is relational. At this primordial level, our caring does not discriminate between the world and our own existence.

It also follows from this argument that our primordial caring-about-others should not be interpreted as a determinable regard for the welfare of others — others in general or in particular. All I am saying is that there is a deep caring at the core of our being which grounds our concern for our self and for the not-self which relates to us. My thesis is that our attitudes towards other persons and towards the world around us take their character from being the determinable formation of our own deep caring. It is too early to assign this thesis an ethical significance as if I were arguing for the existence of the kind of natural moral sentiments that Hume postulated. The point is simply that, to use a Heideggerian term, our deep caring is our "ownmost" being. I cannot disown the fact that others matter to me any more than I can disown my being as self-project. And this is a minimal prerequisite for ethics.

Sartre had argued that our being-for-others is a self-imposed form of vulnerability to the look of the other through which we gain our public identity.[1] It indicates our lack of self-sufficiency. We need the other to give us our identities, and therefore we must comport ourselves towards the other to make ourselves open to those interactions that create our knowable persona.

Far from viewing this being-for-others as a generous orientation towards others, however, Sartre regards it as a regrettable threat to the freedom inherent in our subjectivity. For him, our self-project is a more fundamental aspect of our being, and being-for-others is a development of it forced on us by the fact that we are not isolated individuals. For Sartre our self-project matters more than the not-self.

By contrast, in my thesis caring-about-others cannot be a threat to our self-project because it is equiprimordial with it. The caring that is most fundamental to our being — and most concerned with it — already looks outwards. It does not follow that such caring is inherently altruistic any more than that it is inherently selfish or competitive. These more determinable forms of caring are grounded in deep caring, and it will be my task in this chapter to indicate how our determinable attitudes towards others constitute expressions of this primordial level of our being.

In keeping with my strategy of using a four-level model of what it is to be as a human being, I will analyse our caring-about-others as it might be expressed in determinable forms of caring at those four levels. These determinable forms of caring will include forms of dependence upon others, of sociability, of solidarity, of affection, and of responsibility. It is inescapable that they will also include forms of fear and loathing.

The Biological Level

At the biological level of existence, I can think of only a few examples where our caring-about-others appears in a pure form. Take, for example, the caring-about-others of the human infant. In its earliest weeks, the barely self-conscious human infant enjoys a mode of being not yet structured by the acculturation to which it will become subject. It has no awareness of itself as a person, no awareness of its parents as separate persons, and no awareness of the world as a field of objects separate from itself. It can hardly be said to direct itself upon another in any way. And yet we do feel inclined to say that the infant turns towards others with some form of selectivity and expectancy even before it first acknowledges others with a smile of recognition. Even its earliest reflexes, by virtue of which its lips close upon the mother's nipple and its fingers grasp its caregiver's finger, show that its very biological being is directed outwards and towards others.

It may not be obvious that these others must be persons (those infant chimpanzees who cuddle up to furry puppet surrogate mothers demonstrate that this biological drive for contact can be deceived as to its object), yet the drive is there. Evolutionary theory has no trouble accounting for this. Infants who do not direct themselves towards their caregivers in this way would not survive as readily as those who do. Minimal and self-motivated as it is, we may identify this primary comportment towards others as a first-level caring-about-others which already establishes relationships.

A second form of biological caring-about-others is much more difficult to extricate from the higher levels of human existence which envelop it. I refer to the sexual attraction between two adults which leads to physical love. It is obvious that many layers of cultural meaning and learned expectation separate physical love from the purely biological level. Yet when all is said and done, reflection does discover a purely physical feeling of desire for and self-offering to the other. Parts of the culturally formed rituals and practices surrounding sex, whether at the stage of selecting a partner or of giving physical expression to the liaison, have as their purpose precisely the production of this feeling of abandonment to the other. The word *abandonment* is revealing in this context. What it seems to convey is the stripping away of all self-possession as a fully formed person with the cultural and social identities and self-images this involves. In moments of sexual abandon, we seem to return to a primeval level of existence which is purely biological.

I say *seem* because this point is not uncontentious. There are many[2] who would want to say that no matter how abandoned the lovemaking becomes, we never do, or never should, revert to an animal level of existence. The dimensions of meaning which arise from the higher levels of our existence as human beings are never absent, and our lovemaking will always have a human meaning. There will be communication and fellow-feeling of some sort in any loving exchange where two lovers are human beings who exist at all of the four levels we have described. Of course, the biological level of human existence is not the same thing as being "merely" animal (I will not comment on the implied denigration of the animal kingdom). To suggest that it were would be to suggest an almost automatic or driven form of coupling which was totally devoid of significance for the participants.

A counterargument might be that the human biological level is from the very first communicative. Certainly, I suggested as much in regard to the human infant. If I am right, then when all self-consciousness is stripped away and we abandon ourselves to sex, we may be becoming communicative and expressive through the most direct physical form of fellow-feeling available to us. Our caring-about-others is then purely bodily. We are not conscious of ourselves as persons. It is as if we direct our entire selves as whole persons into our bodies and towards the body of the other. Although the completeness of our embodiment at such a time may lead us to suppose that we cut ourselves off from others by reverting to a preconscious self, in fact, the quality of that embodiment is communicative and expressive in that it arises from a sexual caring-about-others. At such moments, my closeness to the other is complete because it is unencumbered by a consciousnes of self.

Kant grapples with these notions in his all-too-brief remarks on sexuality. He speaks of persons' giving themselves to one another in such a way that each receives himself or herself back from the other.[3] Though he uses an excessively legalistic language, with its notions of property and rights, it seems clear that he is trying to express the mutuality which sexual relations establishes.

In my model, this mutuality consists of a prereflexive physical rapport established sexually, whether in inclination or in action, such that reflexive consciousness becomes aware of a focused desire and affection of each for the other. The idea of receiving oneself back from the other refers to the experience of feeling that the loving consciousness which each partner has of the other has arisen from that pre-existing physical rapport. Insofar as this rapport is prereflexive, it is a nonindividuated but determinable sexual orientation.

At the first level of our being, sexual rapport establishes a bond. When we reflect on this bond, we discover that we are not as we were before. The relationship of love exists prior to our experience of it. What we experience is a culturally shaped emotion in which we identify ourselves as "in love" or sexually enraptured. But as we emerge into this ontological individuation, we sense that the bond we had with our partner and in which we were prereflexively implicated is the source of this new joyful self which our relationship has created. In this way we "receive ourselves back" from our partner, renewed and enlivened out of a first-level rapport which is a bodily caring-about-others.

The Perceptual and Reactive Level

The reader will recall that at the second level of human existence — that of information processing and reaction — the organism organises its perceptual grasp of its world and responds behaviourally to that world in more or less appropriate and intelligent ways. Is there at this level of human existence a mode of caring-about-others which is prior to any self-consciousness but more than a directly physical comportment towards the other?

We might turn first to some possible analogues in the animal kingdom. Take animals which hunt in packs. We find that lions, for example, instinctively fall into a cooperative pattern of behaviour in which one member of the pride stalks the prey while others form a semicircle to trap the prey when it flees. There seems to be an instinctual rapport amongst pack members as they move with one eye on the prey and the other on their companions, coordinating their movements. When the time to strike is at hand, the pack moves as one. We might say on the basis of such an example that the lion comports itself both to its prey as the object of its quest and to its fellows as cohunters. It is this orientation towards its fellows that I want to highlight to illustrate a basic form of caring-about-others which seems to antecede any explicit formation of intentions.

On a number of occasions in the lives of human beings, fundamental kinds of fellowship similar to those illustrated in the animal kingdom may exist. Merely travelling on the same train with others can set up such a basic comradeship.[4] Even if one does not in any conscious sense acknowledge the other passengers, one may occasionally become aware of a commonality of purpose. This would become clear if the train were to break down. On such an occasion, everyone in it would share the frustration of the ensuing delay. At this point one might be inclined to pass some comment to the others, even though they are strangers, in order to acknowledge more openly the shared circumstance.

And what if the train were to have hit and killed a pedestrian? Would there not then be a spontaneous rush of concern for the deceased and many expressions of pity or sympathy, along with immediate patterns of cooperation? Even before we notice an attempt by someone to render assistance, do we not notice how everyone in the train is united in their thoughts and feelings towards the unfortunate deceased? Although it is the victim who is the object of their concern, they are also united in their sharing of this concern and oriented in some way towards one another by it.

This spontaneous preconscious solidarity is more obvious where human beings are engaged in a common enterprise. Even travelling on that train was such a common enterprise, but not one which would normally be reflected on. Were the enterprise more deliberate and self-conscious, as when a number of people gather together to build a house, form a football club, or go on a picnic, the sense of solidarity and comradeship is more apparent to reflection. But then we would be on the third level of our existence. A common enterprise is a consciously adopted practical project which we share with others in a deliberate way. Is there a common enterprise which is preconscious in a way that permits us to say that it belongs to the second level of our being and which sets up feelings of sociability with which we find ourselves, irrespective of our conscious intentions?

Although it may seem sanguine to say so in a period of history rife with struggle and turmoil, I would suggest that the maintenance of society is such an enterprise. Without wanting to claim that society is a completely homogeneous community with a commonality of interests, I nevertheless want to suggest that most of us do find ourselves with a positive and basically cooperative attitude towards fellow members of our society. We are willing to help others in need, and we identify with the social whole in a variety of ways. An earthquake within our own society elicits a greater caring response than does such a disaster in a more exotic locality. Perhaps my point would be more plausible if I attempted to differentiate various strata of society in which my claim might be variously true. An attempt at such a description will of necessity fall short of the sort of rigour one would have the right to expect in a treatise on sociology, but it may serve.

We could create a model for our feelings of sociability by drawing a small circle.[5] Let this be the most intimate circle of our relationships, which, for most of us, is our family. If it is true that our caring for others is equally primordial with our self-project, then there are only relationships, and we should not put a dot in the middle of the circle and call it our self. There is no true self. Perhaps we could draw an even smaller circle in grey at the centre and call this the trace left by our relationship with our parents when we were infants. This will be as close to a self as our model will let us get.

Outside the initial circle, we could draw any number of further concentric circles: the first might be the group of our wider family; the next circle our close friends; then less close friends; then our workmates; then our acquaintances, such as friendly shopkeepers and tradespeople; then those we do not know personally but still relate to in specifiable ways, such as our political leaders; then groups with which we identify, such as our local community, cricket club, ethnic group, gender, age group, and so on. Many people feel a solidarity with their coreligionists, irrespective of nationality, and the human family as such is also often alluded to as an object of responsibility which would be represented by a wider circle still.

My notion of human society covers these last few circles. In addition, in these days of greater awareness of animals and of the natural environment, we may want to include these, too, in a still-wider circle. It should be stressed that there is nothing precise or fixed about this model. Some people may feel closer to their pet cat than to any other human being, and others find their spontaneous allegiances constantly shifting from one of these circles to another.

However large our diagram becomes, it is a picture of what we are in terms of our preconsciously formed determinable caring relationships and a map of the varying ways people matter to us. Meet a specific family member and he or she immediately fills a place on the inner circle. Meet a workmate and he or she determines a less central position on the map of our social being. In this way my own identity is constantly formed by the relationships I enter into from moment to moment. I am a potential for relationship, determinable in my relational being by having innumerable places to fill on the map of sociability that represents my being.

Moreover, these circles of my being are dynamic in a further way. If there were arrows in the diagram linking the concentric rings and indicating formative influences, these arrows would point in both directions. My life contributes to what my group is and becomes, just as my group contributes to what I am and become. The relative positions of the circles in this model represent gradations of care and responsibility for others, as well as varying potentialities for the fulfillment of my relational being as a caring-about-others. The graded structure of my being as a caring-about-others which is represented by this model is something which I will have internalised as part of my acculturation and is therefore preconsciously adopted. Accordingly, this model constitutes a large and admittedly vague map of my caring-about-others at the second level of my being.

Of course, this map does not only include such positive feelings as solidarity and care. There are also barriers that develop between people at this preconscious level of existence. Just as there are bonds that seem to arise naturally in that they precede any deliberation or intention, so there are divisions which seem to arise spontaneously. I speak of racism, sexism, and various other forms of sectarian prejudice which arise in people's lives. I may feel a solidarity with all the people on the train except one: one who is Black, or elderly, or handicapped, or Jewish, or a member of any of the other groups who have been the object of prejudice, hatred, or embarrassment in human history. It need not concern us whether the aetiology of these reactions is natural or based on cultural formations. Whether these reactions to those who are perceived as different from ourselves are innate because they are instinctual or because they are internalised as part of our acculturation is probably undecidable. I am inclined to say that they are learned, but I cannot deny that they run very deep. Xenophobia is an almost universal human phenomenon.

If we confine ourselves to the second level of our being, it would follow that the spontaneous positive feelings of solidarity with others that we become aware of in ourselves are ethically on a par with such negative feelings as prejudice. Insofar as we are dealing with second-level preconscious reactions, we are not yet at a level where it is appropriate to pass moral judgment. Morality is traditionally thought to apply only to the deliberate.

Although it behooves us as human beings who exist at levels higher than the second to consciously appropriate these feelings or not, the fact that we have, at the second level of our being, reactions to others which can be positive or negative is not yet of moral significance. These feelings arise preconsciously in our awareness, and they constitute modes of basic orientation towards the not-self. They are a modality of our deep caring as caring-about-others. Each of the circles of our model sets up a sphere of exclusion and rejection as a counterpart to the sphere of inclusion and acceptance.

On the other hand, because the four levels of existence that I have been describing do not exist by themselves — because the level of preconscious orientation becomes the basis for attitudes and stances which we adopt or acknowledge as conscious subjects —moral significance may come to be attached to this second-level caring-about-others. The notion of character is often used in moral discourse to express the idea that our preconscious motivational set can be of moral significance despite the fact that deliberation or decision does not constitute this level. I will return to this matter later.

The Evaluative and Proactive Level

The third level of what it is to be a human being is praxis marked by intentions and attitudes formed by the agent in a given cultural context. I place the more or less self-conscious orientation of human beings towards their world through desires, interests, plans, intentions, and practical projects at this level. Most of our conscious life is focused at this level as we go about our daily affairs. And this conscious and intentional life is the determination of a preconscious determinable comportment arising from our being as deep caring effected by suitable objects.

The question that now arises is whether and in what way the daily world of work and practicality is marked by an individual's engagement, describable in ontological terms as an instance of our being as a caring-about-others. By virtue of the simple and obvious fact that people in our complex society cannot obtain what they need and want by themselves, there is need for interpersonal cooperation. Even those who sacrifice a great many of the comforts of life and seek to establish a self-sufficient lifestyle on a country property cut off from the rest of society find that many of their needs and provisions must be purchased or borrowed from others. We seldom notice these forms of interpersonal cooperation because they are institutionalised in a variety of ways. When we go to the local shop to buy a carton of milk, we do not allude to the fact that we are participating in a network of cooperation. My expectation that the shopkeeper will stock milk and will give it to me in exchange for money, along with his expectation that I will offer him money for the milk, constitute part of a large pattern of interactions and expectations that are taken for granted in our daily lives.

It would be a major exercise in sociology to detail all of the ways in which such practical cooperations interact and combine to form a society operating more or less effectively to meet the reasonable needs of its members. There will be tensions and conflicts which it is the business of politics to resolve, and there will be dissatisfactions and struggles as the interests of various groups and individuals clash with those of others. But a society will remain more or less stable for as long as most people most of the time recognise that it is in their interest for it to do so. Even if we consider our taxes too high or a particular bureaucratic decision harmful to our interests, we do not regard things as bad enough to require civil disobedience. We recognise that, on balance, the maintenance of civil order is worth the few disappointments and injustices which it might bring with it, and we choose to cooperate with this order. To the extent that we give thought to this matter, this form of cooperation with our fellow citizens becomes a mode of our caring-about-others which functions at the third level of our existence as human beings.

Upon this stance towards others, which is one of the grounding structures of our existence as social beings and which has already begun to arise at the second level of our existence, is built the edifice of political and social discourse through which our practical relations with others are structured and changed. What I propose here is a form of that venerable social contract theory, whose proponents include Plato and Rousseau, which would suggest that the acceptance of the duties of citizenship is based on a more or less implicit recognition that the benefits of citizenship may not be fairly enjoyed without a commitment to those duties. The solidarity of our being with others is partially constituted by a commitment in that our identity as citizens depends upon an implicit commitment to that citizenship. And this commitment expresses our being as a caring-about-others.

There are also more focused examples of caring-about-others that arise on the third level of our existence as human beings. Positive instances include parenting, professional caring, and engagement in a wide variety of cooperative ventures and tasks with others at work and at play. One feature which should be present in all these forms of determinable caring is trust.

Trust is another interpersonal stance or commitment which establishes solidarity at the third level of our being. There are many variations of this phenomenon, involving varying degrees of intimacy. One example is the trust implicit in bureaucratic structures that involve delegation of authority. When managers assign tasks to more junior employees, they display a trust in their co-workers as effective persons. This is more than a prediction that they will perform the task. It is also more than an imperative or command that they had better perform it. It is an expression of confidence in the junior which may bolster the latter's self-esteem. As such, it sets up a relationship between the manager and the operative which sustains the latter. The manager, in an implicit way, cares for the operative in giving him or her the task. The delegation also involves a degree of vulnerability for the manager, because if the underling fails to perform the task adequately, it is the manager who carries the responsibility. Although this example involves the public sphere, it is interesting to notice the nature of personal involvements which it embodies.

I can use the phenomenon of trust to illustrate how the ontological being of agents emerges from the relationships in which those agents exercise their being as a caring-about-others and as a self-project. It is because of relationships such as trust that a large measure of our fulfillment as human beings can be achieved at level three. Although the majority of our projects at this level are of a worldly and practical nature, we also seek, and sometimes achieve, a form of self-authentication at this level. Because others place their trust in me, even routinely, I find a form of recognition and validation of my being which I could not achieve were I closed in upon myself. Abraham Maslow's hierarchy of needs, referred to in Chapter 3, includes the need for personal fulfillment in this sense. I find the mutual trust and reliance which sustains me in the various forms of practical association which constitute my caring-about-others at level three.

There are many forms of caring-about-others at the third level of human existence which are not exclusively present in the world of work (though they may be present there) but which are not yet so profound as to belong to the fourth level of our being. They both express and consolidate our being as a caring-about-others. They demonstrate the fact that we cannot live life in an isolated and independent form. They form part of the way we comport ourselves towards others to define our own being.

One such form is shared interests and attitudes. To the extent that people belong to the same culture or subculture, they will have similar interests in, and attitudes towards, a wide range of matters. People living in one suburb may support the same football team. People belonging to the same ethnic group may share an interest in the music and other arts of their home country. People in the same occupation may be interested in similar issues relating to their careers. Perhaps it is fair to say that most people in societies such as ours share an interest in consumer goods, although this shared interest might generate envy and competition, rather than trust, as the modality of our social caring-about-others. Not all shared interests lead to harmonious forms of sociability.

Many attitudes are shared. The extensive range of shared attitudes that one might discover in a given society constitute a common ground upon which people can meet in genuine communication and rapport. Attitudes are part of the shared outlook of a community to which people belong, and form the horizon for the individuality in outlook which community members do have. In this way, shared attitudes constitute the ethos of a society.

Indeed, part of the basis for the sociability and cooperation which allows civil societies to exist is shared attitudes. Individuals learn to accept shared attitudes as part of their acculturation. Such attitudes come to individual and determinate expression in the way we perceive the world and in the way we act and relate to others in the practical, public, and interpersonal spheres. Shared attitudes constitute a preconscious interpersonal horizon for the third level of our being. They demonstrate that our being grounds solidarity even before we form explicit practical projects and commitments. Shared attitudes are a deeper mode of our being as a caring-about-others than are shared practical projects. Shared attitudes are determinations of our preconscious caring-about-others.

Of course, caring-about-others as realised in shared attitudes can be the basis for conflict as well as solidarity. Conflict can be generated not only when interests clash, as when employers and unionists clash over the distribution of economic wealth (in which both have a mutually understandable interest), but also when attitudes differ, as when conservationists clash with developers. In the latter case, even dialogue and mutual understanding seem impossible because attitudes are so different. People are able to enter into genuine dialogue with one another when they care about the same things, as in the case of employers and employees who both have an interest in money. But there is no more effective way of closing off communication and rapport than to respond by saying, "I don't care about the things you care about." It is because the conservationist does not predominantly care about profits and the developer does not predominantly care about unspoilt nature that their disputes are so often intractable. They have differing attitudes. They live by different values.

The Spiritual Level

When I use a phrase like "live by different values," however, I allude to the types of commitments that constitute the practical expression of our determinable caring at the fourth level of our ontological being. Acting at level four of our existence involves acting with enthusiasm about what we do. It involves fulfilling commitments which involve the pursuit of our highest ideals. The fourth level of our existence is the level on which we live our faith, understood as a positive acknowledgment of the challenge of living life so as to give it a unified meaning. These meanings may be articulated by high ideals towards which we dedicate ourselves, or people whom we love and to whom we commit ourselves, or an image of ourselves as ethical agents which we feel called upon to preserve, or a religious faith.

Now, how might we be a caring-about-others at this fourth level? In what way do others matter to me with a depth that confirms my faith? We may suggest that just as shared outlooks, interests, and attitudes constitute the expression of our caring-about-others at the earlier levels, so shared faith expresses our caring-about-others at the fourth level. Two or more people may discover a community of spirit based on a shared outlook on life, a shared set of attitudes towards a number of things which both find important, and a shared faith. Whereas at the third level of existence, there may be associations and friendships based on shared interests, mutual benefits, and the mutual pleasure that the company of one gives to the other, at the spiritual level there can be a community of faith.

An individual's spiritual caring will colour his or her experience of things relevant to that caring. Thus, a person committed to art will find deep interest in artworks from many places and eras. Such a person will read about art, go to the galleries, meet artists, and, perhaps, practise the arts. The point is that confronted by a work of art and a fancy car, he or she will evince a greater interest in the artwork. Similarly, confronted by an artist and a businessman, he or she will, all other things being equal, evince a greater interest in the artist. There will be a rapport with the artist based on shared commitments which will be absent in his or her relationship to the businessman.

Such a rapport with another person expands upon the dedication or commitment to a particular life project, with all the reorientation of attitudes and priorities which that implies. By itself, such a commitment pertains to the agent in a solitary context. It requires a social context and a social formation, but it nevertheless constitutes part of the individuating self-definition of the agent. Rapport with another based on shared faith or commitment expands this self.

Perhaps such a rapport can even ground a love for the other. Of course, I am not using the term *love* in the sense of romantic love. It would be absurd to suggest that two people who share the same deep commitments have in that circumstance alone the basis for romantic love. Such love also requires sexual attraction. The interpersonal love I speak of is a form of intimate rapport based on the most profound feelings and commitments that each party has. Aristotle described such relationships as friendship based on the mutual recognition of goodness of character.[6] However, the English word *friendship* is not sufficiently deep to capture the idea I am after. In addition, the notion of goodness of character is too moralistic for my purpose. Therefore, I will use the word *love* and hope that the ambience of popular cultural conceptions can be abstracted from it. By love, I understand the fulfillment of the fourth level of our ontological being as caring-about-others.

It would be vain to expect that I could offer an explication of interpersonal love on so slim a basis as shared faith. Nevertheless, it might be a hint worthy of further exploration to suggest that love between people involves, among other things, a spiritual rapport understood on this model. Our commitments draw to our attention those things which are pertinent to our commitments just as the artist is drawn towards works of art; therefore, we will be selectively drawn to people who share our commitments.

It is important to notice that I am not talking simply of shared interests here. Friends and acquaintances are people with whom we share a range of interests and, indeed, attitudes. Love between persons is both deeper and more mysterious. People may love one another who do not share many interests and whose outlooks on life may differ. Yet they are drawn together in a way that they hardly understand themselves. This mystery can be explained by the hiddenness of our deepest attitudes. We do not understand our loves by understanding our own commitments and faith. Rather, knowing whom we love is one of the several ways we have of discovering who we are and what our faith is.

Just as we live our lives with enthusiasm and passion to the extent that we have faith, so we relate to others with enthusiasm and passion when we discover a consonance of spirit. Or perhaps we discover that we have a spiritual rapport by noticing that we are drawn passionately to these others. By *passionate,* I do not mean sensual or romantic. I use the notion of passion to capture the depth and commitment involved in our caring-about-others when we love someone. The passion I speak of is not the turbulence of the heart which is the stuff of popular romance, but the sense of commitment, excitement, and also peace which comes from meeting someone who shares our ultimate concerns.

We can illustrate this more fully if we do, after all, discuss sexual love. I said earlier in this chapter that two people might be attracted to one another physically and thereby establish a bodily rapport which exists purely on the first and second levels of their existence. Such a sexual attraction is not yet a case of love, though it is often an element of it. There are many social liaisons between people which are lived solely on these levels. Whether it be a visit to a prostitute, or a "one-night stand," or even a relationship of longer standing involving friendship between the partners, there can be many forms of sexual rapport which do not involve full love. There is nothing wrong with this. These would be cases where, provided no one's integrity or freedom is compromised, human exchanges take place with full mutual recognition of what is involved.

However, what is involved here is the sensuous rather than the passionate.[7] These exchanges are based on a mutual interest in physical pleasure (or, in the case of the prostitute, an interest in pleasure on one side and in money on the other). As one loses oneself in such sexual activity, one is expressing a purely sensual dimension of one's being. One is enjoying and being enjoyed for the sensuous physicality of one's being. As the more self-conscious and practical level of existence is recovered, we may find ourselves enjoying a friendship with the other based on this mutual pursuit of pleasure. We are now on level three of our existence, where we share an interest.

But should we discover in the other person a consonance of spiritual commitment, a shared attitude towards things which we regard as profoundly important, a shared faith in the sense of a similar stance towards life, then the passion we bring to living out these commitments may turn into a passion for that other person. The enjoyment of one another in sex becomes a passionate commitment to one another in spirit. The physical dimension of level one comes into contact with the spiritual dimension of level four, and the wholeness of our being is completed. This is why the experience of romantic love is so often accompanied by the feeling that this person is our exact and unique counterpart. The rapport that we establish with this person involves all four levels of being. This love becomes more than a sensual fulfillment mutually sought and mutually satisfied. It becomes a passion for each other in which longing, fulfillment, and profound commitments are never absent. As expressed through our caring-about-others, our faith becomes love.

It is one of the miracles of human existence that the sheer animal magnetism that exists between people can be the vehicle for expressing this highest spiritual passion. Indeed, it is when we discuss such cases that descriptors such as "higher" and "lower" levels of existence or "animal" dimensions to our lives lose all meaning. Whatever the level to which an aspect of our lives belongs, it is human through and through. The four levels of our existence infuse one another fully. Love is at once the most intimate and the most intense form of caring-about-others which we can express. It is the most intimate because it involves our most deeply held attitudes and commitments, and the most intense because it combines the variety of our involvements into one focused passion. This passion is directed upon the object of our love so that the latter embodies all that is most important for us.

But how is this rapport grounded in deep caring? Our deep caring is our being as a self-project and as a caring-about-others. It is expressed at the four levels of our being as caring which is determinable by objects or persons which, as intentional objects, would then be experienced as important. But our ontological being as deep caring does not individuate us as persons. It is only when it is expressed in commitments, actions, or reactions in relation to the world or to other people that it contributes to our emergent identity.

Faith is the part of this identity which is grounded in our being as self-project. It becomes love as we also express our being as caring-about-others in a rapport with someone of a similar faith. To this extent the faiths and the beings they individuate must already be defined. But the rapport logically precedes the completion of those individuals as defined by their love. Our faith does not make us complete. Like the severed beings of Aristophanes's myth in Plato's *Symposium,* we are looking for our other half.

This is explained by the fact that our caring-about-others is equiprimordial with our self-project. The completion of our self-project by itself does not fulfill us. We need to love another. We do not enter into relationships with others from the basis of our formed individuality. Rather our individuality is formed by the relationships with others that we enter into. Our deep caring as self-project and as caring-about-others moves us towards love, where such love includes sexual love, love between close friends, and familial love.

When our being is considered in its aspect as a self-project, the faith and deep commitments that we have constitute our existential identity and individuality, but when it is considered in its aspect as caring-about-others, our loves enlarge that identity. What one is as an individual is not finally achieved by oneself as an individual. Though there may be some who follow their own private genius into the realm of spiritual solipsism, for most of us the completion of our being and the formation of our individual identity requires the fulfillment of our commitments and faith through love for another.

Our caring-about-others is a foundational structure of our being as human beings. Love establishes the most intimate circles of our concentric circle model. Whereas the outer circles represent the most general and least individual involvements constituted by our caring-about-others, those circles which are closer to the centre represent our most unique, intimate, and specific involvements. The wider scope of our caring is readily recognised as socially formed and establishes our shared social and cultural identity. But the particularity and individuality of our stance towards life comes to expression in our innermost circles of intimates. Our loves establish who we are.

But it would be too limiting to suggest that the completion of our being as a caring-about-others at the fourth level is achieved only in the particularised form of love or friendship. To say this would be to suggest that the orientation we have to others who are outside of the more intimate circles of our affection could only be understood to exist at the first three levels of our being, and this would imply that such relationships could only be functional in nature. Although there is no doubt that our relationship with the vast majority of others whom we meet and have dealings with on a day-to-day basis is largely functional, there is no doubt either that there is a deeper interpersonal exchange involved in these relationships. This needs to be true so as to provide the horizon of intelligibility for such phenomena as sympathy extended to strangers and feelings of concern and acts of charity extended to those who belong to more distant circles of my model. If our being comprises all four levels of my model, then we might expect that even our daily relationships and our everyday orientations to others with whom we have functional dealings should be expressive of the fourth level of our being and include acknowledgment of this level in the other.

This proposal has been explored by Emmanuel Levinas.[8] He develops the point in the context of the rather startling claim that both the other and the self are "infinities." This term *infinity* is not meant as a quasi-mathematical or scientific description of the being of a human being. It is an interpretative and poetic characterisation of our ontological being. Applied to my model, it would mean that caring, in the twin forms of self-project and caring-about-others, as it unfolds at all four levels of our being, is without limit. It is a projection that admits of no final satisfaction. Neither is Levinas using the notion of infinity in a theological or metaphysical sense, in which it might be said that God is infinite. This idea, if it can be made clear at all, claims an objective, real, and limitless greatness for God, as well as ascribing to the Godhead a real transcendental relationship to finite creation. Levinas's notion of infinity is a phenomenological one akin to that of mystery, depth, and aesthetic power.

Moreover, in saying that persons are infinite, Levinas does not deny the equally important thesis that persons are finite in a number of senses. It is clear that if we were to confine our discussion of human being to the first two levels of that being, then it would be as finite as any physical and biological object is and as finite as any information-processing system is. Moreover, at the third level of human being, persons are subject to error, bad luck, and the defeat of their powers by a myriad of forces and agencies. As Paul Ricoeur has argued most eloquently, human beings are fallible in numerous ways at all levels of their ontological being.[9] And yet we experience the other as infinite, and we experience ourselves as infinite. We cannot contain our own being, and we do not place limits on our aspirations or ideals or on the scope of our caring. In short, I am interpreting Levinas's term to refer to the fourth level of our being.

Levinas bases the idea that the other is an infinity on an observation common to us all: the other's face, when it gazes upon us and is perceived by us, is experienced by us not as an object among other objects, but as an opening into the mysterious reality of that other person. The face of the other is an opening onto a radical otherness which I cannot encompass. The most obvious examples occur in the context of love. Our experience of the way our lover looks at us allows us to discern the endless depth and limitless meaning which resides in the other's eyes, and our looking at them produces no objectification of their being for us.

In contrast, we might think that many of our everyday exchanges with others look to the face of the other merely to discern responses and reactions so that we, in turn, can adjust our communications for practical purposes. If this were all that there was to these functional exchanges of looks and glances, then they would exist on that pragmatic third level of our being which seems to acknowledge others only at the third level of their being. Only deeper and more significant exchanges would disclose others to us at the fourth level of their being. However, Levinas argues that all interpersonal exchanges, no matter how cursory, partake of the mutual acknowledgment of infinity.

Others appear to me as unlimited by the categories and classifications through which we understand them. The words *mother, lover,* or *child* might be categories and classifications which have functional uses in a number of social contexts, but when they are used to address someone, they bespeak a relationship of such depth and scope as to burst out of those categorisations. Similarly, I do not relate to postal workers or shop assistants as I would to a functional object — as if their function summarises their total being for me. At the very least, I bid them good day, something I would never do to a vending machine. In Kant's terminology, the other must always be related to as an end rather than as a means.[10]

An important difference between Kant's position and that of Levinas, however, is that whereas membership in Kant's Kingdom of Ends is gained simply by having the universal characteristics of a rational being, Levinas argues that the nonobjectifiable otherness of the other is a particular mystery, a localised and specific epiphany of infinity. We encounter the other in his or her particularity. Of course, Levinas does not mean that other persons do not belong to the order of reality that everyday things also belong to. The other has weight in the way that a chair does, has appetites in the way that an animal does, and pursues needs in the way that any pragmatic and self-conscious being does. But others also transcend all this to be unencompassable by us. We cannot cognitively grasp them and insert them into our world without remainder. Although I can experience this most directly in the case of those others who are significant to me, it is true of all others. In this, they are infinite. My own model of what it is to be a human being allows us to understand this by saying that the other is potentially an object of faith and love at the fourth level of our being rather than an object of use at the third.

This is not to say that the infinity of others makes me finite, which, translated into his own terms, would be Sartre's thesis.[11] For Sartre, the ontological nature of the being of a human being is that of a nothingness or freedom seeking to realise itself by appropriating its world unto itself. It follows that every nothingness seeks to appropriate every other nothingness. It also follows that the being of others is always a threat to my being as a nothingness or freedom, because their nothingness or freedom seeks to incorporate me into their world as a thing, just as I seek to incorporate their being into mine.

As I have already noted, this thesis might be true if our deep caring took only the form of self-project. But I am also a caring-about-others. My being is bound up with and dependent upon that of others. Yet if others are infinite, they must be radically other. It is not the case that my infinity and theirs mutually constitute each other. I do not constitute the infinity of the other, because if I did so, he or she would not be radically other. The other would then be dependent upon me and would enter into that web of mutual dependencies which Sartre sees as a threat. It is my deep caring as a caring-about-others which allows others to be infinite even as I depend upon and need them. This is why my being as a caring-about-others cannot be reduced to, or subsumed under, my being as a self-project. My caring-about-others permits me to acknowledge the infinity of others without appropriating them; in this way, I realise my self-project. Levinas expresses this by saying that insofar as I acknowledge the infinity of others, I am myself infinite. I reach out without reservation to others so as to allow them to be. And their limitlessness is what elicits that reaching from me. The infinity of the other, discovered in the face-to-face encounter, draws me into that infinity so as to make me aware of my own.

Levinas goes on to argue that the meeting of infinities in the face-to-face encounter is the foundation of ethics. For Levinas, ethics is an interpersonal, dialectical, and limitless set of relationships marked by mutual acknowledgment and responsibility between people. It grounds the possibility of any form of solidarity and mutual caring. Its fundamental tenet is to let the other be in his or her otherness. According to Levinas, the other calls me to acknowledge his or her infinity: "The being that imposes itself does not limit but promotes my freedom, by arousing my goodness."[12] It is by acknowledging others, by entering into encounter with them, that I accord them the recognition that gives their infinity an infinite openness to expand into.

But the other also calls me to my infinity. It is because there is limitless depth in this call, in this appeal of the other to my being as a caring-about-others, that I realise the limitless dimension of my being as deep caring. Nor is this mutual calling into being to be understood in the purely ontological terms of infinity and transcendence. The other has real needs, and so do I. My four-level schema makes it plain that my fundamental aims include my biological and pragmatic needs. The dialectic that I set up with the other is not only a realisation of the fourth level of our mutual being. The other calls to me in his or her need, and I am present to the other in mine.

I can illustrate this in practical — if extreme — terms, using the call to action which a trapped person directs to me from a burning building. That call is a challenge to help another survive and to exercise courage and self-sacrifice of a magnitude that both embraces and goes beyond the practical solidarity of the third level of our being. The need and infinity of the other calls to my need and to my infinity. My willingness to sacrifice my life for the other is a willingness to move from the first three levels of my being to the fourth, where commitment without limit can be called for.

Though I will examine the ethical implications of Levinas's views more fully later, I will not follow Levinas's suggestions as I demonstrate in subsequent chapters how our being as deep caring is the foundation for ethics. For the moment, I want to delineate those implications about solidarity which I mentioned at the beginning of this chapter. At the third level of my being, solidarity implies that I am a social unit whose identity is defined by social context and which contributes to that context in a variety of practical ways. I am a functioning cog in the machine of history. At the fourth level, in contrast, solidarity involves the mutual acknowledging of infinities or faiths which establishes what I will later call our ethical community.

This fourth level of my caring is not only realised in such circumstances as being in intimate love, when I uncover the infinite depth of the person I love, it is also present as a dimension of all my authentic relationships with others. The infinity of the other can be revealed in any and all particular relationships. And this infinity calls upon, and calls into being, my own infinity. My being as a caring-about-others grounds not only my developmental and functional relationships but also relationships of depth and openness, such as trust, courtesy, and love.

5

COMMUNICATION

I established in Chapter 4 that equiprimordial with our deep caring as self-project, our ontological being takes the form of deep caring as caring-about-others. The central thrust of my argument was that at all four levels of our being, we need others in various ways and that, therefore, they are important to us. This fundamentally alters our mode of being. I now want to add that our deep caring as caring-about-others is expressed as a will to communicate. We are communicative at all levels of our being. Maintaining communicative relationships with others is one of the things we deeply care about because we are a caring-about-others. If we were simply or more fundamentally a self-project, we might envisage living as single and separate individuals in the world, but as a caring-about-others, we need to overcome the isolation that such a radical individualism would imply.

So far I have only explicated our being as caring-about-others as a comportment towards others, as a prereflexive orientation. I need to further explicate the dynamic nature of this comportment. In its dynamic form, our being as caring-about-others expresses itself as communication. Communication is much more than the mere imparting of information from one person to another. It should be understood broadly as the overcoming of human isolation. *To communicate* is the verb we use to describe the dynamic processes through which we express our being in relation to others.

Communication is a relation we engage in, rather than one we simply find ourselves with. At the higher levels of our being, we engage in it intentionally, whereas at the lower levels, our relations with others are communicative in a prereflexive manner. But at all levels of our being, to exist communicatively is to exist differently from those things existing in isolation or in passive relationships as recipients or propagators of causal influence. Insofar as they constitute our mode of being, communicative relations are an expression of what we are as a self-project as well as a caring-about-others. That is why such relations matter to us and why they are an object of our deep caring. Once again, I will explicate this at each of the four levels of our being.

The Biological Level

As applied to the biological level of our existence, we must understand communication as being more than an exchange of information with the environment in the sense of negative entropy developed by information theory. Even at this prereflexive level of our existence, we project ourselves towards others communicatively. This can be illustrated when we think of involuntary expressions such as cries, gestures, or expletives which I utter when I am in pain, in fear, or in other states of distress. Shedding tears is a further example, as would be, in a more positive context, a smile or a burst of laughter.

Yet insofar as such events are involuntary, it seems at best inappropriate to regard them as an immediate and direct means of communication. Communicative intention appears to be lacking, and therefore these examples do not appear to show that my being as a caring-about-others seeks to communicate itself through them. Normally, I do not seek to communicate with anyone when I cry out in such ways; I cry out whether there is someone within earshot or not. Of course, given that I am a self-conscious and purposive being, I might allow such cries to escape me in an attempt to manipulate the emotions of another, but in such a case, it can no longer be said that the event is involuntary. In this case we are no longer analysing an event that occurs at the purely biological level.

The claim that direct groans and cries might not be genuine cases of communication is further supported when we note an important difference between direct expressions of pain, for example, and the reports and descriptions of my pain which I might offer a medical worker in the course of therapy. I do not directly express my pain when I tell a nurse about it in the way that I do when I groan because of it. The groan is caused by the pain, whereas the report is offered intentionally.

To explain this difference, we might say that I do not own such groans as a conscious agent, but they are events causally linked to my body. My body seems to be operative in these spontaneous cries without reference to my intentions. Indeed, there might be cases where the intensity of the pain or distress (or pleasure, for that matter) are such that the cry is wrung from my body despite my attempts to suppress it. This would seem to indicate that it is my body rather than my conscious self which is the origin of these events.

However, this is a misleadingly dualistic way of putting the matter. It is not true that I do not own groans and spontaneous gestures. If it were, it would have to follow that I do not own my body. Rather, what we have here are events which are mine at the purely biological level of my being. They are instances where I am pressed back to the most fundamental level of my existence. These cries are extensions of my bodily being and are therefore as bound to my own being as is the rest of my body. If we remember that the word *being* here is a verb, then we will see that this conclusion implies that the mode of my being is, through my body, expressive. I express myself pre-reflexively and involuntarily through my body.

Are involuntary expressive gestures and cries then cases of communication? I suggest that they are, because even though there is usually no communicative intention, I must own these gestures as an expression of my being. But the word *own* can have two levels of meaning in this context. It can mean both "acknowledge" and "allow to come to expression." In the second meaning, the term has the largely negative connotation of "doing nothing to prevent." It is like relaxing. When we relax, we do not engage in any specific activity called "relaxing." We simply do what we do (it could even be quite intense work) in a way that is free of pressure, hurry, or anxiety.

In the same way, to own an action is not to engage in a mental activity described as owning, acknowledging, or accepting what we have done. It is simply to respond to the action without anxiety or embarrassment. In the case where an action or gesture is socially acceptable, it is easy to own it in this sense. However, when the action or gesture is not acceptable, the first meaning of *own* must come into play.

Cultures dictate which expressions and involuntary gestures are acceptable and which not, by whom and under what circumstances. As a result, there is embarrassment involved in allowing proscribed involuntary expressions to become public. But to be embarrassed when I offend against cultural norms in such ways requires that I acknowledge the expression as mine and see it as an expression of my being. I need not be embarrassed about something that happens to me purely causally.

To own offending gestures, which is a prerequisite for embarrassment, is not simply to let them flow without internal hindrance, however. My acculturation has taught me to suppress such expressions, and therefore I would prevent them if I could. Rather, to own such a gesture is to acknowledge that despite my embarrassment, the gesture is an expression of my being. But an expression of my being can only give rise to embarrassment if my being were preintentionally in communication with others. It is only because I presuppose that my gestures, however involuntary, are going out into the world as communications that I can be embarrassed about them if they offend cultural standards. I can only take my gestures to be potentially offensive if I take them to be communications from me. In this way I not only own the gesture but also the offensiveness of it. I acknowledge that it is not simply a matter of someone's taking offence, but of my giving it; I acknowledge that it stems from me. I can only take myself to have given offence with my involuntary bodily reactions if such gestures or cries were an expression of my caring-about-others at a biological level.

Despite their involuntariness, there may be, in the complexity of an actual lived situation, various ways in which I can allow spontaneous gestures to emerge so as to communicate my feelings to others. I can be more or less inclined to suppress these expressions, depending upon my intentions towards others. I may be happy to allow others to know how I feel and thus put less of a curb on these apparently involuntary gestures. As I have noted, the likelihood of such expressive events occurring may depend on the degree to which such expressions are socially acceptable. Wailing at funerals is acceptable in some cultures but not in others. Yet when it occurs, it seems to do so involuntarily. Although not all intentional acts need be conscious acts, the freedom that comes from an awareness of one's own caused expressive states is the freedom to make use of those states to communicate, even though, at the purely biological level, such states are not intentionally communicative.

As it enters into the complexity of human life, the biological level of human being is absorbed and transformed by the human meanings and intentions which cover it. But, then, the biological level must be communicative in some sense in order for this to be possible. I cannot manipulate your emotions with an admittedly inauthentic cry if cries were not expressive as such. It must be the case, then, that however private and purely bodily they are, such cries and groans have a biological communicative meaning. Like our bodies, they are expressive in and of themselves.

If we wanted to explain this, we might suggest that the processes of natural selection will have favoured those species of animals which accompanied their experience of pain or fear with cries and yelps, because other members of the group would thereby be warned of danger. If this were correct, then species of animals with an instinctual tendency towards externalising their intense feelings would have greater chances of survival. Even in the absence of any deliberate communicative intentions, their gestures would still have communicative significance and be of help to others.

However, this significance is entirely general in form. At the fundamental biological level of spontaneous bodily gesture, such events lack any direction towards a specifiable audience. There is no intended recipient for the communication. They are wrung from the body in the intensity of experience and thrown into the world without direction. They are not yet formative of relationships. At the biological level of our being, our bodies and the gestures and sounds that they generate in response to a variety of stimuli are not yet formative of specific relationships, even if they do express the essentially relational nature of our being.

Through our bodies, we are determinably communicative. As biological entities, our bodies are expressive and meaningful in and of themselves. This expressiveness arises from the movements and sounds that they generate. Indeed, even the stillness of a body can be expressive. By virtue of their every comportment, bodies externalise their inner states. At the higher levels of our being, our intentions can shape the determinable communicativeness of our bodies. As human beings we can be expressive and communicative because we are bodily.

Our bodies are the embodiment of our being. They are the expressive means of all four levels of human being. But my thesis presses even further: I argue not only that our bodies are meaningful, but also that we are determinably communicative through our bodies. The gestures and cries which issue from our bodies are not simply expressive means of communication; they are expressions of our very being as communicative, of our dynamic caring-about-others at the biological level.

Prereflexively, we project ourselves towards others with a will to communicate; indeed, this grounds the meaningfulness of our bodies. This is the famous thesis of Maurice Merleau-Ponty,[1] and it explains the fact that we can have body language, expressive gesture, and bodily adornment — that we can communicate through physical love, through eating meals in a context of sociability, and through the myriad of meaningful movements that constitute ritual and social forms of communication and celebration. In addition, it grounds the communicative significance of health and illness, pain and pleasure, and birth and death as events of a biological nature which are given a profound meaning in the context of human existence and culture.

For human beings, there is no separately identifiable purely biological level of existence which we can choose to make communicative or not. Rather, the bodies that constitute our biological being are expressions of our existence and communication with others from the very first. As absorbed into the wholeness of human existence, the biological level is communicative in the sense that our full human being is present in our bodies, with their gestures and cries, so as to make them expressive of our whole being.

The Perceptual-Reactive and Evaluative-Proactive Levels

At the second and third levels of our being, our caring-about-others, lived as a will to communicate, requires language for its expression. Language has been a central issue in philosophy for much of this century, but I do not intend to embark here on a full discussion of this topic.[2] My thesis is simply that the meaningfulness of language, both in receiving and expressing it, depends upon our ontological being as deep caring in the twin forms of self-project and caring-about-others. My argument is that in its everyday use, language extends beyond functional communication so as to express our attitudes and thereby our caring. Moreover, this expression of our attitudes is grounded in a prereflexive purpose of establishing community with others. As such, language expresses our caring-about-others in the form of a will to communicate.

If we could isolate it from the wholeness of our being, the second level of our existence would involve a level of communication consisting of an exchange of signals which operate as behavioural triggers. At this level of existence, I live in a world of behavioural triggers only, even if some of those triggers are words uttered by others. At this level I can only react. Yet these reactions are based on, and expressive of, a comportment that I have. Foreign workers on a building site do not need to know what *slab* means in order to respond to that word as a signal.[3] All that those workers need to be able to do is associate the sound of that word with the reaction that is expected: namely, bringing the slab. This reaction can be learned by demonstrating the required reaction rather than by conveying the meaning of the word. However, the workers must want to learn what is required of them.

They can respond appropriately to the command "Slab!" because they know they are there to work. There is a practical orientation of their being which allows words and other gestures to be triggers so that the reactions that take place issue from that orientation towards the world and towards others. Even at the second level of our being, a purely behaviourist account of the meaningfulness of words, which sees them as mere triggers for behaviour, would be inadequate for our ontological being.

Confined to the second level of human being, I would exist in a world that is purely prereflexive. I would not yet engage in intentional action, and I would not yet recognise things in a self-conscious way. In short, I would not yet have language in a full sense. To recognise things for what they are requires that we be able to name them. If our foreign construction workers come to see that "Slab!" is a command pertaining to some things on the building site and not to others, they will eventually see that the word in some way refers to the slabs themselves. The workers may even come to see that the word is a name. And when they do, they will be able to refer to other slabs at the site, talk about them, and even refer to slabs that are not immediately present. They will be able to recognise slabs for what they are by applying that name to them. Moreover, they will be able to engage in intentional actions which involve slabs because they will be able to plan and deliberate in relation to them. Insofar as the workers' prereflexive determinable practical orientations can be focused as determined intentions and thoughts, those workers will be able to be reflexive. Not only does our linguistic grasp of things at the third level of our being combine with our practical interests to give us a fully articulated world, but it also establishes our identity as reflexive agents. It follows that our deep caring as self-project requires language.

A further essential function of language is one taken as primary by most commentators: namely, that language is essential to us as communicators if we are to speak to each other about this world. The ability to name things is an ability to embrace them into the lived world of a language community. Anything that cannot be named is so foreign as to be absent from the world of speakers. Nameless fears cannot be dealt with because they are outside of our linguistic grasp. It is only when they are identified that they can be embraced, rejected, or placated. It is one of the intractable problems of caring for those in pain that pain is so hard to describe, to name. This confines it to the private and ineffable experience of the sufferer. Without some way of naming that pain, there is no way of bringing it into the shared world of linguistic expression, in which sympathy can effect its comforting influence.

Nameless things have no place in a culture and are nonentities so far as that linguistic community is concerned. It is the language we share, with all its concepts and meanings, which allows us to share a world which is communally ours, to communicate about it with each other, and to act within it. This is why so many philosophical discussions of language place such stress on the referring function of language. Unless words are known to refer to the same things for everyone in a language community, they are meaningless. A common lexicon gives us a common world to refer to and thus establishes a linguistic community. It is because we wish to communicate our new experiences that we are pressed to create new words and expressions. The lexical richness of language provides evidence for this primordial drive to communicate, which I interpret as an expression of our being as caring-about-others.

But at the third level of human existence, there is not only a shared world of things that can be referred to, but also a shared context within which each person can communicate with others. Such a communicative context comprises shared attitudes, evaluations, and practical projects. Linguistic communication depends not only on the referring function of words, but also on the common values held by the relevant communicative community. Language is not merely a set of behavioural triggers in word form, as it would have to be if it operated only on the second level of our existence.

If we take language to be a way of referring to the world so that a shared recognised world is a prerequisite for communication, then we have moved to the third level of our existence. But at this level our active, affective, and purposive engagement with the world sets the agenda for communication. We communicate purposively. It is because the world is now seen in the light of our needs and attitudes that it becomes *our* world. It is understood in the light of our practical orientation towards it.

The slab on the building site is not simply an item without meaning or significance in the way that a clump of grass on that same building site would be. Insofar as the people on the site are there for a common purpose, they understand the slab as an item conducive to that purpose. In referring to the slab and giving one another instructions regarding it, they share an outlook on it. Boldly, I generalise from the microcosm of the building site to the macrocosm of the shared world of a given culture. At the third level of our existence, the common and everyday shared understanding of the world is established and maintained by the commonality of attitudes and purposes of a given language community.

Further support for the claim that our understanding of, and ability to communicate about, things not only depends on the shared and learned concepts by which that understanding is expressed but also involves our attitudes to them will arise from thinking about what it means to say that we appropriate the world through language. At the very least, this means that our world, even as we merely name things, becomes familiar to us. We feel ourselves at home in it. Adam was able to feel at home in Eden when he had named the things in it. But this feeling is an attitude. Our linguistic grasp of these things, the way we speak about them, and the connotations of the words we use, encapsulates our attitudes towards them, as well as our knowledge of them. The words we use to refer to them embody the culturally established place which they have in the world as it is lived in our culture.

Even though a New Guinea highlander may be able to refer to a car by saying, "There is a car" when he sees one, he does not mean the same thing by that utterance as I, who am familiar with cars, do. For him, the word is not at home in his language and in his worldview, and he is not at home using the word. In the same way, the non-English-speaking worker does not feel at home with the word *slab* even though he or she uses it successfully to make a reference. In such cases, the word might involve a connotation of puzzlement and fear, whereas for me, its meaning is perfectly ordinary. Were I to talk to the highlander about cars, it is possible that we might misunderstand each other because of this difference in attitude and cultural understanding.

This expressive function of language becomes part of the lexical meaning of words in particular cultures. Insofar as members of a given society share an attitude, the words they use to express it will acquire a certain connotation (as opposed to a denotation). Take the word *death*. It is not possible to utter that word in a purely neutral way. Even in contexts in which no actual grief or loss is being experienced, as when we note the death of a plant —such as a dandelion — in which we have no interest and for which we do not care, this connotation will be present as part of the affective content of the word. We do not refer simply to an altered biological condition when we refer to the dead dandelion. We express a negativity or a loss. I do not mean that we feel such a loss and then express it; I mean that the word we use brings that sense of loss into being by conveying it as part of its meaning. Of course, apathy, routine, or relative unimportance may prevent us from noticing or responding to this connotation. The point is that the meanings of words comprise affective elements as well as referential ones.

Further, these affective elements are not injected into words by the expressive intentions of speakers. Rather, the expressive intentions of speakers can be fulfilled in speech through the affective connotations that words actually have in a given language community. One can fail to communicate or be caught up in confusion if one fails to recognise the affective tone of an utterance or chooses words that have connotations inappropriate to one's expressive intention.

It follows from this that the infinite number of successful communications that occur in everyday situations are evidence that human beings in a given culture share a large set of attitudes simply by virtue of being users of a given language. These attitudes are so basic to a given culture that they are seldom alluded to or made explicit. It is only when someone fails to evince the appropriate attitude and so becomes thought of as strange or even insane that these attitudes become apparent. If one characteristically uses the word *dead* and its cognates in a happy tone and with a smile on one's face, then one will be thought to be unusual at the very least. A sad attitudinal connotation is inherent in this word as shared and is the basis of forms of communication such as sympathy and rapport. The word cannot be used simply for referring to objective events without carrying this connotation. This is also demonstrated by the experience of those whose profession it is to care. If all communication requires language, and if those for whom we care belong to a different culture or language community, we often have severe communication problems. And this is so even when we successfully refer to the same things.

What all this shows, then, is that at the first three levels of our existence, communication and the use of language are already matters of great complexity and depth. It is not acceptable to try to reduce this complexity and depth by explaining the functioning of language as being reducible to the function of referring. We do refer with language; indeed, we might suggest that language is at its most efficient and unambiguous when it is used to refer. However, this impression of ease of linguistic functioning presupposes unquestioned and shared points of view on the part of the speakers and listeners. Given that the third level of our existence includes the practical orientation that each of us develops to a world of recognised material or theoretical realities, an analysis of language at these levels must include the affective, evaluative, and attitudinal dimensions which our shared culture encapsulates. There would be no literature without this dimension of depth in language.

There is another point worth noting. We have been speaking thus far of language used in practical, everyday contexts, such as the many communications that take place on building sites, in offices, on committees of management, or between nurses and patients in hospital wards. Most of these words will be uttered to convey information and trigger behaviours. But it is probably fair to say that even more words are uttered or written for quite a different purpose. When we say, "Good day, how are you?" — or when we answer such greetings — and when we tell our loved ones in the evening about the day we spent at work, we are not engaging in practical activities. Why do we want to tell others about the enjoyable things we have done, the new things we have bought, or the new plans we have just formed? Will this information be of use to anyone, or would telling it be of any use to me? I would think not. Yet I venture to guess that most use of language is actually of this kind.

Language is a medium of sociability and self-expression: two functions which are closely connected. That self-definition and self-expression are among the functions of language explains the existence of language arts. Literature and literary style exist to bring to a standard of excellence the self-definition and self-expression of human persons. That whole communities seek to retain their distinctive language despite pressure from neighbouring countries — or from a dominant group within national boundaries —even when it would be more useful and practical to speak the language of the surrounding culture is another indication of the importance of language for self-definition and self-expression.[4] This example also shows that retaining a distinctive language is not merely a matter of individual self-expression. For whole cultural groups, language forms part of the communal identity which is lived and expressed in everyday speech.

Linguistic communication requires and establishes shared attitudes. It presupposes and establishes community. As such, it is an expression of our being as caring-about-others. Even at the functional and worldly third level of our being, where linguistic communication is grounded in shared contexts that embrace our concerns, aspirations, and desires as well as objective reality, the basis of these shared contexts is not simply the communal projects and hopes which unite us in any given historical and cultural period. These projects and hopes are themselves an expression of our being as a self-project and a caring-about-others.

In purely functional concerns, the bottom line is survival, but our earliest experiences have taught us to reach towards others as we pursue this goal. The will to communicate which this reaching has engendered in us makes deep, successful communication a matter of importance beyond the functional levels of our being.Communication is something we care deeply about because it establishes community with others. Communication is not only a fulfillment of our being as self-project, but also an expression of our being as caring-about-others. Successful and deep communication is an expression of our deepest being, and even our worldly practical communications share in this deeper significance. At the third level of our being, our caring-about-others uses modes of communication to establish practical communities and fellowships of purpose. But there is more to these communities than shared interests or projects. Our deep caring comes to expression in functional communication, but it is not satisfied by it.

The Spiritual Level

This lack of satisfaction points to the fourth level of our existence, at which we transcend the practical exigencies of life and seek to ground our faiths. That we pursue ideals and excellences which are not reducible to practical needs and gratifications is what constitutes the fourth level of our existence as whole human beings. It is this level which I have called, without any metaphysical implications, a spiritual level of existence.

I have argued that the first three levels are transformed in meaning by the diffusion through them of the fourth level. The way we affirm our lives in our faith, the way we unify the meanings of our various daily activities, and the way we give our lives one or more goals is the way we realise this fourth ontological level of existence. The meanings, aspirations, and faiths which we realise or articulate at this level constitute a framework in which both the routine and extraordinary activities and experiences of our lives are given their deeper meaning. Even such clearly biological activities as sleeping, along with the daily activities of our practical lives, are inserted into a life the unified meaning and purpose of which I constitute at the fourth level of my existence.

And so it is with our communicative relationships with others. The expressive and pragmatic forms of our being as caring-about-others which are evinced at the first three levels constitute our everyday relationships with others. But if we confine our attention artificially to the first three levels of our being, then we not only constitute ourselves as a reduced being-who-cares — a being who does not seek to integrate life and give it an overarching meaning — but we also constitute the other as a reduced object for caring. If my model comprised only these three levels, then I could relate to you only as a source of need satisfaction, as a cognitive object, or as a functional entity in my world. For example, I would relate to a police officer signalling me to stop in much the same way that I relate to a stop sign. I would relate only to those aspects of the police officer which pertain to directing traffic.

Moreover, the scope of my communicativeness would be confined solely to my proximate practical and linguistic community. If we were completely formed as identities and as purposive and thinking agents by the practical, social, and linguistic reality into which our birth had placed us — if we existed at only the first three levels of our being — then we would have no reason to seek communication with any being outside of that operational sphere. In such a case, we would be convinced, as tribal peoples were of old, that the people over the mountain were either ghosts or barbarians. Because they did not share our language, and the worldview which it encapsulates, they were perceived as not sufficiently like us to be open to communicative approaches. It would have been only when early peoples recognised something shared with others that the will to communicate with them would have been born.

We may call this "shared something" their common humanity, or the human condition.[5] Given my preference for verbs, I would call it sharing the project of being human. And in my model, this project is focused by the fourth level of our being as self-project and caring-about-others. If our communicativeness or our being as caring-about-others is to extend to all humankind, then it must transcend the first three levels and embrace our pursuit of faith and ultimate meaning, and it can do this to the extent that we recognise others as engaged in the same four-level self-project as we ourselves are.

Although we all have in common the project of being human, it is not a project that would take the same essential form for all of us. There need to be culturally defined ways of engaging in it. I may unquestioningly adopt the meaning-giving worldview of my society through an implicit commitment, or I may seek and formulate a faith of my own. But even if I do the latter, it will be in reaction to the cultural formation and upbringing to which I have been subject and will therefore have various dialectical internal relations to the dominant cultural forms of my society.

But behind the culturally formed self-projects which I could readily recognise in others of my culture, there is an inchoate project which is open and determinable as to its specific form and content and which expresses deep caring. We are infinity. All that we can generally say about the fourth level of our self-projects is that it will involve creating a unified and meaningful orientation towards living. But if our being as self-project might take differing forms in differing cultures, how can it be the basis of a universal extension of our caring-about-others? If the practicalities of life only ground an extension of our caring-about-others towards those with whom we enjoy a pragmatic solidarity — and then only in relation to the pragmatic aspects of their being — how can an indeterminate quest for meaning ground a more universal communicativeness towards others in their full humanity?

Perhaps Levinas can help answer this question. In Chapter 4, I reported Levinas's view that our experience of the face of the other discloses the phenomenological infinity of human being. The face of the other person is not an object for me in the sense of a cognitive item appropriated into my functional and pragmatic world. Encountering the face of the other always involves the fourth level of our being.

The experience Levinas alludes to is that of perceiving in the face, and particularly in the eyes, of the other person a mystery and a depth which seems fathomless and transcendent. Even in the case where I know a person very well or even love that person, there is a sense of otherness which seems unbridgeable. Indeed, it is almost as if the more I know that person, the more I feel I still need to know. It is this mystery of the other which constitutes the full humanity which I am in contact with as I reach out to someone at the fourth level of my being.

But this only answers part of the question I have posed. Levinas indicates how our day-to-day communication with others tends to transcend everyday practicalities and meaning structures in order to disclose the infinity of the other. My question also asks how our communication with others takes on a universal dimension. How does my ontological being as caring-about-others become extended to all others beyond the circle of those who are of immediate concern to me or with whom I have some pragmatic solidarity?

For Levinas, the face-to-face encounter is but a specific form of a wider phenomenon. The infinite distance between us which this encounter reveals calls us to communicate with each other, calls us to speech. Rather than switching to Levinas's term *speech*, however, I will continue to speak of communication and expression. As it happens, the latter term is appropriately ambiguous for our purposes, because expression is attributed to faces, as well as being the term used to describe both the external and internal activity of speech. Expression is that form of communication which embraces and transcends the biological and practical spheres; it is a form of which the other's meaningful gaze is a nonlinguistic example.

For myself and the other, in my model, Levinas's call to speech or expression is the fourth-level communicative form of our being a caring-about-others. The face of the other discloses infinity in the sense that it discloses the spiritual level of the being of the other. This fourth level of the other's being calls out to the fourth level of my being as self-project and so constitutes me at this fourth level as a caring-about-others. This drawing towards the other transcends the exigencies of ordinary life because it is the infinity of the other — the phenomenology of the fourth level of the other's being — which calls out to me. Whereas my being as caring-about-others was always implicated with my being as self-project at the first three levels of my being, in that my will to communicate with others was always linked to my own needs and purposes, at the fourth level of my being there is a pure fascination with the humanity of the other.

In this way my being as caring-about-others takes on not only an infinite depth in relation to the individual other but also a universality of scope. Levinas argues that the call to expression is itself infinite to the extent that the difference between us, as infinities, is infinite. Expression is understood as encounter between infinities arising out of the infinite caring-about-others of the parties to that encounter. The call to communicate elicited by the face of the other awakens us to what we are in common as human beings.

For Levinas, expression is an activity. Expression, or speaking, gives rise to, and also depends on, language.[6] Language has, therefore, an inescapable fourth-level dimension. However useful it might be for making a success of our lives at the third level of our being, it also embodies the mutual seeking and acknowledging of our infinite mysteries as persons. In this way, language is necessary for our self-project and our caring-about-others at all four levels of our being. I have already argued that language is central to our self-project as individuals in that it gives us a reflexive grasp of the world. Further, insofar as language includes amongst its functions the self-definition of a people, it also grounds our collective being as a self-project.

It now transpires that language is central to our communicative being as caring-about-others because it is needed to establish solidarity and community with others at all levels of our being. And for Levinas, this means that the act of expression and communication through language has an inescapably ethical dimension. Levinas's thesis that ethics is founded on the dialectic of the face-to-face encounter and of speech appeals both to the experience of the other's face and to the nature of dialogue. The expressiveness of the face and the expressiveness of speech are of a piece for Levinas.

On this basis, I interpret him as offering us a communicative ethics not unlike that developed by Jürgen Habermas.[7] The central idea behind Habermas's ethics is that communication between two people requires a mutual recognition of one another as speakers. One is allowed to be a person, a speaker, a communicative partner by the necessary conditions of the speech situation. When Levinas speaks of the needs of the interlocutor calling me to my responsibility,[8] he speaks not only of the needs which that interlocutor might have on the first three levels of being, but especially of his or her need to be heard and recognised as a speaker in the communicative context. We hold the power to satisfy this need, and we are called upon to do so whenever persons speak to us or express themselves to us. This is our responsibility arising out of a communicative situation. And it is the responsibility of our interlocutor in relation to our speech and expression.

Levinas argues that it is the call to the other inherent in expression, either through the face or through speech, which is the foundation of ethics. In this context, ethics simply means letting the other be, as opposed to appropriating the other into my own life. It is a matter of respecting the humanity of the other. In my terms it would be an expression of my being as a caring-about-others.

An illustration of this point arises in ordinary life. When I engage in even so mundane and functional a communicative exchange as buying a railway ticket from a ticket seller, I generally say, "please" and "thank you." This is so routine a requirement of etiquette and is so seldom informed by an explicit communicative intention that we are apt to think of it as an empty formula. Yet we can give offence by neglecting it, and there would be a cultural loss if the practice ceased to be observed. But what does it mean?

I suggest that even in everyday situations, these locutions express our acknowledgment of the other as infinity and as freedom, as not being merely a functioning unit in a practical matrix. Moreover, they express our own infinity and infinite longing for communication with the other, or, to put it in my own terms, my fourth-level caring-about-others. Further, the phenomenon of social chitchat can be taken as evidence for this yearning we all have to reach across barriers and express ourselves to others. Far from being the "chatter" which Heidegger has suggested threatens to overwhelm us and defeat our quest for authenticity,[9] idle social communications are expressions of our deep caring as caring-about-others. It is only when speaking transcends practicality and functionality that it becomes expressive of and acknowledges all four levels of the being of the speakers. This does not mean that expression should renounce communicative action in the practical sphere, but only that communicative action should not renounce expression. It must remain ethical.

Though I find it suggestive, I do not espouse Levinas's thesis that ethics is founded upon expression or speech. To accept this view would be to found ethics upon our being as caring-about-others only. This might even suggest the Humean thesis that ethics is founded on some sort of natural sympathy that we have towards one another as human beings. In my view, ethics must be founded on our being as self-project as well as our being as caring-about-others if it is to be integral to our lives and a product of deep caring. That our being as self-project is as fundamentally involved in ethics as our being as caring-about-others is shown by the fact that we frequently disagree with each other about ethics. If caring-about-others were all that was involved, then we would do everything to reach agreement with one another. Let me elaborate.

The willingness to communicate beyond the sphere of practicalities and even beyond the discourses of our own cultures is an expression of all four levels of our existence as human beings. Of course, this point is most likely to impress itself upon us if we concentrate on discourse that pertains to matters of moment. Communication at the fourth level of our being frequently requires a shared awareness of the depth and importance of the matters at hand in such communication.

Two cultural discourses that exemplify this are religion and morality. It is striking testimony of their relevance to the spiritual level of our being that these are spheres of communication in which division and disharmony are at their most intense. Insofar as these discourses deal with the very project of what it is to be a human being, they deal with an area in which our interest is profound and foundational. The cultural and linguistic formation that we give this interest will be a matter of great seriousness in our lives. These will be matters towards which we cannot be noncommittal. They are matters about which we inevitably care. As a result, disagreements about the basic projects and meanings of our lives involve breakdowns of communication which are usually quite intractable. If one person says that helping the poor and destitute is important and ethically good while another says that doing so is worthless and merely distracts one from pursuing one's own interests, there would be real difficulty in resolving the disagreement.

Such difficulties have given rise to such disciplines as ethics understood as a theory of morality. One of the most frequent projects of such moral theory is to seek to ground the objectivity of moral norms. Though I will discuss moral theory at length in the following chapters, I will at least indicate my own line of argument while my brief discussion of language is still fresh in our minds.

There are some moral theorists who insist on a referential view of language, allowing them to argue that such words as *important* and *ethically good* refer to objective moral facts which we can appeal to in resolving disputes. They would say simply that there is a moral requirement to help those in need which we must recognise and follow. Parties to our dispute should be able to refer to this requirement as to a reality, just as parties to a dispute about the height of a horse should be able to refer to the animal, measure it, and so resolve their dispute. The view that there are moral facts of this kind is called *moral realism.*

One classical formulation of such a realist approach is the Ten Commandments. Here we have a view of morality which is so objective and real as to be represented in the Bible as tablets of stone handed down directly from God. Within the context of religious faith, the reality of these norms cannot be disputed, given the power of the mythic formulation in which they are presented. Similarly, the moral requirements set out by that greatest of modern philosophers, Kant, have an objective reality which they derive from our natures as rational beings. This is less easy to refer to than tablets of stone, but it still admits of objective disputation, description, and agreement. Once again, the power of the presentation, based now on the brilliance of the argumentation, seems to underwrite the reality of the norms.

In this age of postmodernism, by contrast, the quest for moral autonomy has challenged these apparent objectivities. The simplest explanation for moral realism now is that such norms of behaviour are externally imposed upon agents by others. The model for this would be criminal law. I refute moral realism by arguing that moral discourse belongs at the fourth level of our being and that at this level language does not refer so much as articulate and express the being of the speaker. It would follow directly that moral discourse does not refer to or describe any reality but expresses and articulates the speaker's ethical commitments.

The problem with this argument is that the reality of moral norms seems to have been displaced by the mere preferences of human subjects. If this were so, ethical disagreements would be both endemic and irresolvable. Although I will wait until the next two chapters to discuss this matter at length, I hold that our ethical lives need not dissolve into a rootless subjective relativism. Insofar as our identities are social constructs, our feelings of what we ought to do, what it is important to do, and what it is good to do will be taught to us within the contexts of our families and larger cultural formative groupings and will thereby acquire an objectivity or necessity for us.[10]

Admittedly, in a heterogeneous society such as ours, these influences will not be uniform and will be localised in various ways. People from different ethnic groups will have different attitudes to such matters. In some communities female circumcision is a practice encouraged by moral and religious norms, whereas in other communities this practice is regarded as abominable. Is there an objective norm that both communities can refer to? The civil law might provide such a norm in that the law forbids the practice in some places. But in these places the communities who favour the practice will argue that their cultural rights are not sufficiently acknowledged by the law.

Given this variation, it would seem that the moral realists' demand that an objective moral standard apply to everyone, irrespective of background or social circumstance, and exist in some realist sense beyond our own intentions cannot be met. It is possible for moral norms to be an operative reality in the practical lives of real people with a form of objectivity but without their being real or universal. People do operate with standards and ethical norms which they regard as imperative or important to adhere to, and these are not simply their own personal and individual creations. Social contexts of varying scope provide the only kind of objectivity that ethical norms can have. Individuals learn as part of their social formation to take a specifiable range of action-guiding norms as important and relevant to them. Most of the time most people seek to actualise what they take to be independently existing moral requirements.

But these points have an air of sociological observation. They articulate an aspect of the cultural contexts in which we exist. They do not show how we come to commit ourselves to those moral standards. We are passive in relation to the processes of acculturation. To show that morality is an issue of importance which arises at the fourth level of our being requires that we understand morality as an expression of our being as self-project and as caring-about-others, an expression which extends beyond the pragmatic realms of life and is relevant to our pursuit of meaning and faith.

Social scientists are content to say that ethical norms are, firstly, socially learned but internalised standards of behaviour and, secondly, gradations of importance in values. But I would insist that as internalised standards and values, they form part of people's prereflexive being as self-projects and caring-about-others. They become matters that people care about in a primordial and determinable sense. The theory that I need to develop to underwrite this view and to build on Levinas's must explain how these standards are internalised so as to seem objective and compelling to us, because the impression of objectivity and stringency which ethical norms have is what leads people to think that these standards exist as realities or as effects of cultural causalities.

My view is that we prereflexively seize upon some social formation or other for such standards and values because, as human beings with a spiritual level to our existence, we have inchoate determinable hopes and ideals, the fulfillment of which requires a determined historical form. Because these ideals and aspirations will be expressions of our being as a self-project, they will ground our commitments. Moreover, because we are a caring-about-others with a yearning for communicative relationships with others, these ethical ideals will have a social dimension and an other-directedness. They will be means whereby we not only realise ourselves but also forge solidarity with others.

What follows from this is that the importance, objectivity, and stringency attached to ethical standards and ideals results from their being the determinable form given to our deep caring, understood as an internal will towards self-fulfillment and communication with others and the affirmation of living as a human being.[11] The two forms of primordial caring – caring as the pursuit of self-fulfillment and caring-about-others – ground our ethical commitments and the concrete forms of caring which these commitments lead to.

But there is a problem. I can explain the apparent objectivity of our ideals in terms of our deep caring, but can I also explain what the motivator for ethical action is if it is not an external imposition of rules and requirements? It is one thing to regard ideals and norms as objectively important; it is another to be moved to adhere to them or to give them deliberative priority. In my view, one motivator is our being as self-project. Once I recognise ideals and norms, I can only fulfill myself by adhering to them. A second motivator is that adherence to socially established ethical norms is a communicative act in the sense that I establish and maintain solidarity with others through adhering to the standards which they observe. In this way, ethical action becomes an expression of my being as caring-about-others in the form of a will to communicate and establish solidarity. I find the moral standards of my culture important and give them priority because I wish to maintain community with those who also find those standards important. But insofar as my self-project is also involved, I will not compromise those standards simply to achieve social harmony.

Let me spell out the two stages of my argument in more detail. Let us first take the notion of ethics as grounded in our being as self-project. Our image of ourselves as fulfilled, social, and excellent human beings, though it is a function of external social formation and acculturation, will be committed to by us as an internal standard of behaviour and virtue. Psychologists speak of an ego ideal or of ethical ideals in this context. These are aspects of the operative understanding we have of ourselves and of what we hope to become. They are an expression of our being. Although many of our everyday aspirations will centre on career ambitions, the acquisition of worldly goods, proper regard for others, the enjoyment of companionship and physical love, and so forth, these will be matters which largely belong to the first three levels of our existence. But some of our projects take on an importance and depth which make them seem ultimate and unconditional. This is because our aspirations will also include such spiritual quests as deep loving relationships with others; moral excellence and virtue; meaning and significance in all that we do; communion with beauty; and, for those with religious faith, salvation, immortality, and God. The first three of these, and possibly all of them, will involve an understanding of ourselves as ethical projects.

By using the phrase *ethical projects,* I make use of the existentialist understanding of what it is to be as a human being in terms of projects, and I add to it the notion of goals of behaviour and of standards of character which are central to ethical thinking. When I mentioned the psychological category of an ego ideal, I was referring to a self-image which is a product both of how others see me and of how I would like to see myself. It is a prereflexive set of beliefs that I have about myself and of aspirations that I have for myself. It is based upon my being as a self-project and a caring-about-others in that it involves the way I am defined by others and the way I come to define myself as a person with a characteristic set of virtues. As it comes to determinate expression in reflection or action, it is largely a social construct and may include some elements of projection and fantasy. In that way, my ego ideal may involve a degree of bad faith and self-deception.[12] It follows that I may choose to own this self-image or not. If I wish to be the person my cultural formation has made me, I can commit myself to it simply by relaxing into it. If not, I need to devise an alternative and throw myself into this new persona. To own this new ideal, I need to commit myself to it rather more forcefully.

It is in identifying the impetus to such commitments that one approaches the notion of a self as an ethical project. This project is the most inner and the most primordial level of my being. It is my deep caring as it issues in faith. It is the project which lies behind my comportment towards the world and others and my beliefs about myself as an ethical agent.

My deep caring, or ethical project, this deepest and infinite ground of my being, will be inchoate and unavailable to explicit reflection. I will be able to think about my objectified self-image, but I will not be able to think about the origin of that thinking in my innermost caring and ethical project. The phenomenological reason for this difficulty is that it is not possible for reflection to ever capture the subject of that reflection. If I try to reflect upon the one who is reflecting at any given moment, I will constitute a new object for that reflection in the form of a self-image. The one who is reflecting will always be implicit and hidden.

How, then, can I know what my most fundamental orientation and commitment to living is? The biblical saying "By their deeds you shall know them" gives us a clue. Given what I am as ethical project, there will be actions which I feel that I must perform when suitable occasions arise. Such feelings of practical necessity disclose me as what I am at the level of ethical project. If I fail to perform such actions as situations demand of me, I will feel the sort of disappointment with myself, or the sort of disharmony with what I am and what I aspire to, which is called guilt. Guilt, too, is a disclosure of self. Guilt is not a feeling induced by failure to respond to something objective, something our moral language could refer to as to a reality. It is the feeling induced when we acknowledge our failure to live up to our own ideals and aspirations.

What traditional ethical discourse calls moral obligation illustrates this point. To act out of moral obligation is to act in response to our feeling that an action placed before us is important and at hand. That the action is at hand means that it is available and possible for us to perform. This is certainly a factual matter which can be referred to and explained. But that the action is present to me as being important, such that I feel that I would have failed to live up to myself as an ethical project if I did not perform it, requires a different explication: the importance of an action derives from my taking it as an opportunity to actualise my faith or realise my deepest aspirations as a self-project. This gives such actions a centrality to my identity and sense of self, and I will apprehend them as supremely important and feel compelled to perform them.

So much for the grounding of ethics in our being as self-project. But what of the grounding of ethics in our being as caring-about-others? My thesis is that our primordial caring is directed towards communication and solidarity with others. At the fourth level of our being, this caring is expressed through our quest for faith and meaning, and it directs itself upon the spiritual level of the being of the other. It is as infinity to infinity, or humanity to humanity, that I wish to be related to the other at this level of my being. Such relations will be central to my achieving that sense of meaning and faith which I need to make my life whole. Ethics is one of those grand spiritual enterprises of humankind, along with art, religion, and pure science, through which our quest for significance and spiritual solidarity with others is exercised. The implications of this view for our understanding of ethics will be explored in the following chapters.

6

PREREFLEXIVE ETHICS

Deep caring is a primordial orientation towards living a life expressive of our being as a self-project and a caring-about-others. It is a mental disposition towards commitment in all spheres of life. This notion of deep caring is not that determined or determinable notion which we use when we describe someone as caring about a particular issue, or as caring for a particular person, or as being characteristically a caring person. Such behaviours and motivational sets as these are a consequence of the commitments which we might make or find ourselves with.

Though *caring about* and *caring for* are determinably intentional mental dispositions focused upon particular objects or persons and express this more fundamental caring, deep caring is the caring which constitutes the most fundamental horizon of intelligibility for these commitments and cares. Deep caring is a prereflexive mental disposition. It is a pre-intentional motivational structure through which what we are committed to, what we care about, and what we care for acquire their importance for us. It is because they are implicated in our self-project and caring-about-others that the things we care about, or the persons we care for, have a practical importance for us which standardly leads to our giving them deliberative priority in instances of choice. The motivational impetus for according this importance is our pre-intentional deep caring.

Just as Aristotle identified a fundamental goal for action which requires no further reasons to justify it, so I have identified a fundamental motivational comportment which requires no further motivational force to enliven it. Unlike Aristotle, however, I do not claim to have identified its goal. Whereas Aristotle has identified our *ergon*, or basic drive, as the pursuit of *Eudaimonia*, understood as happiness in the sense of active self-fulfillment, I do not claim to be able to identify a goal or object for deep caring. That is why I call it pre-intentional. It is not even determinably intentional in the way that caring about and caring for can be. Nor do I identify this caring with our biological instincts or reduce all expressions of it to such drives, as if being a fundamental and inchoate disposition meant that it must belong exclusively to the first level of our being.

Rather, I suggest that this primordial caring can provide the horizon against which we interpret the functioning of all four ontological levels of our existence as human and social beings. Biological instincts are the expression of deep caring at the first level of our being, whereas our pursuit of a cognitive grasp of the world expresses our deep caring at the second level. At the third ontological level of our being, deep caring is expressed in our practical concerns, whereas our ethical self-project and pursuit of ultimate meaning give form to it at the fourth level.

Throughout, these levels of existence are marked by a combination of cognition and evaluation in the form of attitudes which are culturally formed, constitutively expressive of self, and practically oriented towards our meaningful world. But these levels are also expressions of deep caring as self-project and caring-about-others. Because deep caring is not focused upon any particular object or class of objects, these two orientations are equally primordial and together constitute the motivational substratum of our lives.

It is my theory that deep caring grounds ethics, and in this chapter and the chapters that follow, I will explicate and justify this theory and posit mechanisms whereby deep caring is determined and focused to become ethical motivation. As a preliminary definition — which I will have reason to modify — I understand ethics as comprising action-guiding norms which tend to align people's actions with social and interpersonal requirements. My theory will require that ethics be manifest at the four levels of our being. It follows that a viable description of how ethics emerges at those levels will support the theory. In this chapter I will focus on the first two levels of our being.

The Biological Level

Many would argue that it is not possible to discern the emergence of ethics at a purely biological level. This is because ethics involves reasons and norms which are the object of reflection and choice, and these are mental activities which do not occur at the first level of our being. This level, together with the perceptual-reactive level, is essentially prereflexive. Those who hold this view claim that ethics and morality by definition involve reasoning about our actions, and any exercise of this function of reasoning elevates us above the instinctual level at which the biological elements within us operate. But this view implies that our reasoning arises from a faculty which is a distinct, and perhaps biologically later, development and which is free from any constraints which might arise from the biological level of our being. This assumption is often linked with further assumptions to the effect that our desires are more basic than reason in that they arise from levels of our being closer to the biological, and that it is the function of reasoning in general and ethics in particular to control these desires.

I will begin my discussion by challenging these assumptions. One way of doing this is to recall my strategy of using verbs instead of nouns when speaking of human being. Reason and desire are not entities or faculties to be ordered in a classificatory hierarchy. They are ways of human functioning distinguished from one another by virtue of the varying roles they play in our active lives. If we bear this in mind, we will find it easier to accept the suggestion that reason is operative at even the most basic level of our being, albeit in a prereflexive form.

We can approach this matter from yet another angle. In Chapter 2, I reported on the view of Richard Wollheim, inspired by Freud, that our spontaneous mental activities (which I take to include making ethical commitments) are explainable by alluding to desire conjoined with instincts, just as our intentional actions are explainable by alluding to desire conjoined with beliefs. The mention of instincts in this context is intended to point to a prereflexive level of our being which, in accordance with Wollheim's Freudian inspiration, is taken to be the biological level. It is also meant to point to a functionality or purposiveness in relation to our biological goals which renders such spontaneous mental activities rational in some sense.

A book by Mary Midgley has much to contribute on these themes.[1] Midgley has little patience with the reductionism inherent in sociobiology,[2] yet she agrees broadly with the explanatory program which it implies. For example, she argues that our natural desires and inclinations are not only sometimes good; they are also naturally ordered. As opposed to the traditional notion of the passions as unruly forces which need to be controlled by reason, where reason is understood as a "higher" faculty whose function it is to control the lower ones, Midgley would suggest that in animals at least, there is some sort of ordering mechanism whereby the various desires, drives, and instincts are maintained in an ordered balance.[3] A hungry animal that sees food in a clearing but also senses the presence of a predator nearby will not proceed into the clearing. The instinct for safety overrules the instinct for food. This example would be described by Midgley as a form of rationality. It is reasonable for the animal to stay out of the clearing. There is no suggestion of ratiocination, of course, but there is behaviour which can be described as rational. Moreover (and this is the burden of Midgley's argument at this point), this is precisely the same form of rationality displayed by human beings.

To provide the theoretical basis for this acute observation of Midgley's, we need to distinguish between theoretical reasoning and practical reasoning. Theoretical reasoning involves thinking about abstract and purely cognitive matters, whereas practical reasoning involves making practical decisions. However, as any reader of Habermas knows, this distinction is not sustainable, because even theoretical reasoning in this sense is infused with cognitive interests that ultimately have a practical import.[4] It might be better, therefore, to map this distinction using a range of cases distinguished in terms of immediacy to action and degrees of reflexivity.

Ratiocination and deliberation, even when concerned with practical matters, involve a distancing from the immediacy of action which allows us to describe them as tending towards theoretical reasoning. They often involve a form of counterfactual reasoning requiring imaginative projection of possibilities and a degree of experience and knowledge of the world. Practical reasoning, in contrast, can be exercised implicitly in the actual courses of action we engage in. Although practical reason is traditionally discussed in terms of such explicit deliberative reasoning procedures as the practical syllogism so as to suggest that it is disengaged ratiocination which leads to decisions to act, it can also be understood as the kind of judgment which is implicitly exercised when we act in situations with options, whether we explicitly deliberate or not. It is the kind of judgment that sees what is required in a given situation, apprehends the means to effect it, and leads to appropriate and therefore rational action. Aristotle called this *phronesis*.

There seems little doubt, as the preceding animal example illustrates, that practical wisdom or prudence in the sense of *phronesis* could be selected for if it were a biological trait. There also seems little doubt that human action is often marked by a form of implicit practical reasoning of this kind, although a better way of describing this would be to attribute the quality of rationality to such actions rather than the activity of reasoning to the agent. Although Aristotle argued explicitly that virtue (*phronesis* is an example of an intellectual virtue) is an acquired skill or habit rather than a biologically caused trait,[5] I am inclined to agree with Midgley and with sociobiologists that a basic and innate ability to order our inclinations and desires is present within us at the first two levels of our being.

Midgley does not, however, conclude that there is no role for conscious thought (or even moral philosophy) in harmonising our various desires and inclinations in an explicit way.[6] We can, perhaps, use one of her own distinctions to suggest that if *phronesis* can be instinctual, then it is an open instinct rather than a closed one. The distinction between an open and a closed instinct corresponds to the distinction between a behaviour pattern which arises from an ability to respond to input from the environment in a variety of ways, and a behaviour pattern which is so fully ingrained as to be closed to any variation which might be occasioned by learning.[7] Perhaps the animal in my earlier example cannot but stay out of the clearing, but another species of animal (and a human being) could run the risk of going for the food, albeit in a quick and furtive manner. In one case practical reason is fixed fully in the genes, whereas in the second, it is only partly so and is reinforced by learning, habit, or thought. In this case it can be overruled by other instinctive inclinations such as hunger. If it is true that practical reason in the sense of *phronesis* is an instinct in human beings, then it is clearly an open one.

The relationship between open instincts and the freedom which they seem to imply is very complex. As Midgley puts it, "With closed instincts, desire and technique go together"[8] so that the animal has no opportunity to doubt or reason about what it should or should not do. In contrast, an animal that can assess its situation and decide what to do needs to have not only a well-ordered system of priorities if it is to do the appropriate thing, but also strong desires to do it. Whereas closed instincts require no motivating force over and above the programmed response itself, when the acting organism has options, it needs to want to perform the appropriate one. Such an animal must not only be able to discern what it needs to do but must also want to do this thing most. Its desires are a central component of its practical rationality. Therefore, the ordering of its priorities must arise as an object of innate desire rather than of open choice. Rationality does not take over at the point where desire leaves off but is exercised in the prereflexive assignment of priority to some desires over others.

Are there, at the apex of such an inherently ordered set of values or desires, inclinations based in our genes to which practical reason would apply the moral notion of good and which we would, therefore, rightfully choose? Midgley supports this suggestion when she says that "our structure of instincts, as a whole, indicates the good and bad for us."[9] But these notions of good and bad introduce moral notions which will need to be developed more gradually. Perhaps it would be better to say that our structure of instincts indicates what is important for us. Indeed, Midgley does say something like this: "Calling something important means that it *concerns* us deeply, that it *means* or *imports* something essential to us, is linked with a central part of our nature."[10] Clearly, our biology is a central part of our being and is the basis for some of our most intimate needs. To speak of such matters as important is to say that they can be operative as reasons and as motivations in our lives. This notion of importance will have further significance for us later when I discuss Bernard Williams's recent account of the feeling of obligation.

It will help clarify the causal nature of the processes which generate *phronesis* if we stay at the biological level and look briefly at a text which discusses these processes in relation to the ideas of Charles Darwin. Jeffrie G. Murphy[11] discusses Darwin's contributions to the questions we are discussing as set out in *The Descent of Man*. Darwin does not seek to derive moral principles from evolution in the way that J. S. Huxley and C. H. Waddington later tried to do,[12] but he does argue that our accepted moral principles must be consistent with the human biology which that evolution has produced. The sort of genetic explanation Darwin offers is that moral feeling and conscience (for reasons that will become clear later, I will not use the phrase *moral feelings;* rather, I will speak of *ethical feelings* or *caring feelings*) are not derived from reasoning, but neither are they simply to be identified with the instincts of sociability.

The way Darwin explains this is helpfully theorised by Murphy: "According to Darwin (as expounded in my language), the moral sense or conscience is the secondary desire to act out of certain primary desires, particularly those of sociability and sympathy that have the well-being of others as their object."[13] I take it that it is the causal origins of these primary desires which the sociobiologists have subsequently worked out in detail. I take it also that these primary desires express what I have described in Chapter 4 as the biological level of our caring-about-others. The instincts of sociability are the product of natural selection acting at the level of genes. The crucial problem for sociobiology becomes explaining the origin of the secondary desires which Darwin suggests constitute conscience without postulating a faculty of reason which has other than biological origins.

Darwin understands conscience as an internal monitor and control which obviates the need for ethical reasoning at every point of decision. Its role is to make ethical living habitual. It does so by reinforcing the social instincts and by delivering an internal punishment in the form of shame or remorse when we fail to act in accordance with these instincts. If there is to be an aetiology for it, it must arise either from the prereflexive realm of instincts, just as the first-order desires do, or from that apparently independent source called reason. According to Murphy, Darwin opts for the prereflexive aetiology and appeals to sympathy as the relevant instinct. Somewhat unusually, Darwin defines sympathy as "the innate desire for approval of others."[14] It is this instinct which grounds shame, which then acts as the negative reinforcer of antisocial behaviour.

It is perhaps a moot point whether shame is an instinctual response or a learned one. Perhaps the aetiology of ethical or caring feelings is entirely biological; or there may be room for a Freudian account of the superego as formed by the Oedipus complex; or it may be that a sociological account of the internalisation of norms through social pressure based on the sanction of shame will provide an adequate explanation.[15] Whatever the best account turns out to be, we will be dealing with a prereflexive, causally produced feeling which will constitute the desire to act in accordance with the first-order desires of sociability. It follows that Wollheim's notion of instinct is still to some degree appropriate to it and that my own concept of primordial caring designates a complex mental disposition which is causally produced. The complexity of caring is reflected in Darwin's distinction between orders of desire and in my distinction between primordial, determinable caring and focused, intentional caring which is expressive of my being as a self-project and a caring-about-others.

Of course, one may object that this account does not deny that when it comes to matters of conscience, reasoning can intervene. After all, I can assess whether the social approval of my peers is worthy and whether I should concern myself about it. If my peers are all rogues, their approval may not be important to me at all. The moral loneliness which this would occasion may be unwelcome, but reasoning could certainly play a part in making my conscience independent of social approval in this circumstance. On the other hand, this deliberate moral independence may be possible only for a mature individual, and this maturity would have to be based on, or consist in, an already strong moral conscience. This, in turn, would need to have been developed on the basis of the internalisation of shame, if Darwin is right. And this would still give the biologically based feelings of sociability the primary position in our ethical lives.

It seems, then, that Darwin is at odds with the traditional separation of desire and reason, where only the latter is a source of moral worth, because he locates the moral sense or conscience with instinct and desire, where those primary desires which are the energising wellspring of our motivations are also located. Darwin improves our account of moral psychology by attributing both primary desires and conscience to prereflexive causal influences which are at their root biological. He sees moral conflict not in terms of desire contending with reason, but of desire contending with desire, although there is a distinction between orders of desire.

Yet Murphy also reports Darwin as proposing the more traditional view that reason, having once evolved, takes over from the instincts so that natural selection ceases to have explanatory value. Murphy sums up Darwin's position as follows:

> Darwin's basic points about the moral role of reason, then, are these: (1) Reason is a crucial part of the moral life of all civilized human beings; (2) Reason is an instrumental faculty that allows human beings to compare present experiences with past experiences and to anticipate future experiences; it thus allows the introduction of deliberate planning, through trial and error, into the moral world of civilized human beings; (3) Though the faculty or instrument of reason was improved and developed through natural selection, the *actual use* of that faculty in particular circumstances is not biologically determined.[16]

Now, it is striking that the main exercise of reason that has been mentioned here is that of practical reason exercised instrumentally as deliberation. And this is precisely what one would expect in a doctrine which requires that anything which survives natural selection must be functional. Reason must serve our goals. Darwin assumes the Aristotelian point that we do not deliberate about ends. Our ends and ultimate purposes are simply given. However, it should not be assumed that these ends are predetermined by our biology. Even if reasoning were purely instrumental, it is not determined in its objectives by its evolutionary origin. The fact that reason has evolved does not imply that it is predetermined to pursue evolutionary ends whatever they might be.[17] Human *phronesis* is not preprogrammed as to its goals.

This raises the question whether there are any overarching values in service of which we engage in reasoning, and if so, what would be their nature and origin. They either would be prereflexively given or would have to be conjured up in some other way. That they might be derived from pure reason in some Kantian manner seems a possibility denied by Darwin when he sees reason as purely instrumental. Yet neither does Darwin take the Aristotelian course of asserting that our most pressing concerns are given us by our telos.

Murphy accuses Darwin of being less than clear and consistent on the role of reason[18] and argues that the exercise of distinctively mental functions emancipates moral thinking from its biological basis. Reflection, reasoning, and resolve are what differentiate human ethics from instinctual patterns of sociability, even if the latter are reinforced by an instinctively based conscience. Murphy agrees with Darwin in drawing the boundaries between reason and feeling at a different point from that of the traditional conception. The moral feeling of conscience belongs to the same sphere as the rest of our desires and feelings. Nevertheless, Murphy, in expounding Darwin, is still tied to the traditional notion of reasoning as transcending the influence of biology.

When he turns to the sociobiologists, and to E. O. Wilson in particular, Murphy is more generous in his reading than most. This is because he sees Wilson as part of a long tradition of moral scepticism or relativism, of which the most noted exemplar is Nietzsche. This tradition seeks to undermine moral convictions by showing them to be the unwitting expression of amoral or even immoral drives or motivations. Murphy calls this *moral relativism* because he understands it in Wilson's case as involving the view that our moral norms are relative to our innate tendencies and instincts. However, we should not suppose that there is some sort of reductionism in the offing here, as if our norms were "nothing but" the expression of our instincts. Moral reasoning does take place and it does make a difference to the practical decisions we make, but it is based on a "set of pretheoretical convictions that cannot themselves be rationally defended because they are definitive for rationality in this particular domain."[19]

This set of convictions, in its turn, is to be accounted for biologically. Murphy describes Wilson's position as being a hierarchical one, with moral discourse at various levels supported on a biological base of instincts. Murphy describes this as a Humean position in which "reason is the slave of the passions" and the passions in question include those many and conflicting inclinations and dispositions which occur in us through natural selection. "At the most ultimate level, support (for moral judgments) becomes causal rather than rational."[20] This allows us to understand the basis for moral motivation — why the good appeals to us — at the price of that form of moral realism which asserts that the good is independent of our desires. Moreover, sociobiology provides us with the answer to the question Darwin left unanswered: namely, are there overarching values which are to be served by reason, and what is their nature and origin? Propagation of one's genes is that value, selfishness its nature, and natural selection its origin.

However, one might object that to say that biology provides the pretheoretical convictions of ethical living begs the question of the moral relevance of this grounding. Even if sociobiology could causally explain our pretheoretical convictions or our prereflexive motivations, would it follow that they are thereby justified? Surely our intuitions or inclinations in favour of violent aggression and our intuitions or inclinations in favour of parental care are not morally equivalent simply because they are equally present at the basic level of our being. These dispositions need to be evaluated in light of moral thinking and only those that pass muster accepted into our moral lives. And this evaluation will involve the exercise of reason. To answer this objection by saying that such reasoning will be based at its most fundamental level on biologically grounded instincts and dispositions is to accept a circularity which many thinkers seeking a grounded objectivism in ethical thought would reject.

However, this circularity takes on a vicious appearance only if we maintain a dualism between reason and desire. If reason and desire really are separate and distinct, and if reason is being asked to provide the ground for moral thought, then we would indeed be either standing on thin air or caught in a vicious circularity. But reason cannot provide the ground for moral thought because it is not distinct from desire.

The debate about sociobiology arises from an ambivalence in the word *ground*. It might mean "ultimate justification" or it might mean "deepest level of our being." The first meaning appeals to reason exercised reflexively, whereas the second refers to those prereflexive levels of our lives which the biological level exemplifies. Sociobiologists have raised the ire of traditional moralists because they would seek to reduce ultimate justifications to the operations of our biology. This is wrong only because it is an attempt to reduce the reflexive to the prereflexive, as if the prereflexive were all that mattered. But it is no defence against this to reinstate autonomous reason as a reflexive ground for moral thought.

I would argue that the prereflexive biological level of our being is rational and motivational but that the prereflexive levels of our being should be seen as levels of our total being. My schematic postulation of a biological level allows us to conceptualise a prereflexive level of caring which partakes of the qualities of both reason and desire. This overcomes the dualism of reason and desire and allows us to recognise that even if reasons can no longer be offered and a basic preference is simply caused at a fundamental point, we still have a fundamental juncture of reasons and desires. A reason is only a reason because it appeals to us in some way; some attractive element in it draws our attention to it and urges us to take note of it. The difference between reason and motivation is merely one of more or less reflexivity.

The strength of Murphy's commentary lies in noticing that the sociobiologists are not tied to the traditional notion of pure reason as separate from, and adjudicating over, our desires, instincts, and motives. But it does not follow that our lives are unruly and amoral. *Phronesis* is an inherent function of our being by virtue of which certain things come to reflexive consciousness as being important to us or required of us. The primordial caring which constitutes the deepest motivator of our being is marked, at the biological level, by an inherent rationality of appetite. It follows that I can only answer the objection about the apparent amorality of *phronesis* by saying that if socially acceptable behaviour does not flow from it, the body politic will simply have to defend itself against it. This conclusion is not as pessimistic as it sounds. A further reason that our lives are typically not unruly and amoral is that the biological level does not exhaust our being.

The Perceptual and Reactive Level

The second level of our being still involves prereflexive influences upon our actions. Can learned patterns of cognition, behaviour, and affective response which are of ethical significance be established at this level? Processes of behavioural learning and habituation lead to characteristic overt reactions to stimuli, whereas attitude formations which are part of the causal processes of socialisation for human beings, and perhaps for other species of animals as well, lead to characteristic modes of affective reaction and thus to culturally shared ways of understanding the world. Not only behaviour patterns but also many action-guiding norms develop or are inculcated prereflexively in the form of habits at the second level of our being.

Our ability to train animals seems to confirm the possibility of inculcating action-guiding norms at the reactive level. Training animals consists of producing conditioned responses to a variety of stimuli so that an animal will behave in particular ways on command. The required behaviour becomes a conditioned reflex. That it is a reflex on the model of a purely bodily reaction is indicated by the classic Pavlovian experiment, in which a dog was conditioned to salivate at the sound of a bell. But because it is not a reaction that could have been under the dog's direct control, salivation is not a case of behaviour at all.

In contrast, the jumping and prancing of circus animals at least exemplify behaviours that the animals can initiate in other situations, should they want to. A thorough behaviourist program would seek to make such behaviours as reflex as salivation. There is no doubt that this would constitute a thorough inculcation of behaviour patterns, though it is not as clear that we could appropriately describe this as an inculcation of norms of behaviour or of action-guiding principles. Whether such behaviourist techniques used in a human context constitute a stage in imparting ethics turns on this distinction between patterns and norms.

Yet the inculcation of habits was recognised even by such a venerable teacher as Aristotle as being a necessary basis for the ethical education of human beings. In his view, the instilling of habits, which allows a person to conform to social requirements, is not yet the development of ethics in any full sense, but it does provide the necessary basis for a more reflexive development of policies for living. A human being is a project for living that is historically and culturally formed, and this formation will include the inculcation of habits.

But at the second level of our being, the behaviourist inculcation of habits is, for human beings, augmented by the formation of affective bonds amenable to causal description. Given his stress on feelings, Aristotle probably had in mind not only the overt behaviours of his young Athenians, but also their habitual affective reactions. The habits of which he spoke included those patterns of feeling which we describe as attitudes, concerns, affiliations, bonds of affection, and senses of responsibility. As they mature, people find themselves with feelings of obligation, along with many other patterns of feeling. They feel that they "must" act in certain ways in certain circumstances, that they are bound or beholden to act in this way. Darwin's concepts of moral sense and conscience also seem appropriate here, because we are talking about reinforced prereflexive patterns of reaction and attitudes through which the material and social world is understood and responded to. I argue that this pattern includes bonds of affection and responsibility through which specifiable persons and things in the world assume an importance for us. They are aspects of the world that we care about.

Much of the traditional discussion of ethical and moral issues assumes that agents are autonomous and rational individuals existing only at levels three and four of my model and initially beholden to no one. As a result, such discourses have had to invent moral theories which provide reasons to underwrite the obligations agents felt themselves subject to. But the error here is thinking that persons have no developmental history and exist as solitary agents so that all their obligations and responsibilities must be either willfully adopted or externally imposed.

The fact is that at all levels of our being, we are a self-project and a caring-about-others. We come into the world with relations to our family environment that blossom on their own into bonds of affection and responsibility. When we are born, although we exist on a primarily biological level in a symbiotic relationship with our mothers, we are already undergoing events in that relationship which will underwrite the meaningfulness of later experiences. As we noted in Chapter 4, it is central to the ideas of psychoanalysis that the relationships of our earliest youth, even if they seem functional on a purely biological level, continue to colour and influence our subsequent experiences throughout life. Meaning is being created even at the mother's breast. This bond with our mothers is so fundamental that it provides the groundwork for all the other relations of affection which we form with others throughout our lives. It is striking that even at this pristine point in our lives, while the focus seems to be upon the purely biological level of our being, the foundation is already being laid for the fourth level of our existence, in which love is a central experience.

Psychology teaches us that the most fundamental distinction we make in recognising the world for what it is is that between ourselves and the rest of the world. It is the relationship with our mothers that teaches us to make this distinction. Insofar as I have needs that I cannot fulfill for myself, I have need of another. And so the distinction between myself and that which is not myself is born. Not only my cognitive abilities but also my attitudes to things and other people will be affected by these early experiences.

What psychologists call my personality will be affected by the amount of confidence I have been able to build up in the context of my family.[21] The basic pattern of my affective responses to life's myriad situations will have been set in the earliest years of my childhood. The social and cultural formation that results from the development of habits, the training of skills, the inculcation of values, and the imposition of norms — whether these occur in the family, at school, through the media, at places of work, or in churches and community groups — is but the further development and transformation of these earliest patterns.

What psychoanalysis adds to this picture is the deep structure of the bonds that are set up in the family context. If an infant relates to its mother solely to the extent that it has needs, then one would expect such a relationship to dissolve to the degree that the child became able to fend for itself. However, families are knit together by bonds of responsibility and affection that never disappear, even when they transform themselves throughout the lives of family members.

Readers of psychoanalytical literature may be surprised at my use of such a positive-sounding word as *affection* to designate the bonds of mutual responsibility which tie family members together. *Fear* and *loathing* would seem more apt words to apply to the relationships within the family as described by Freud.[22] The formation of the superego, with which we are mainly concerned, would seem to depend upon an Oedipal situation involving fear of castration or mutilation on the part of the child and envy and hatred on the part of the father. The infant introjects an all-powerful figure which it fantasises as its father, with whom it is in competition for access to the mother. This father figure is all-seeing and all-punishing. The infant's total dependence on its parents and its desires for sexual gratification turn into total terror and an all-consuming but ever-frustrated desire to please.

With such an aetiology for the exigencies of the moral imperative, it is little wonder that morality has been conceived of as such a pitiless taskmaster. As long as we focus on unconscious or prereflexive processes, as we must when we remain at level two of human being, we cannot but see family ties as wrought by such relationships. That these bonds might be transformed into affection requires that subjects develop a degree of self-consciousness that allows them to convert introjected figures into conscious role models.[23]

This is a process to which we will return later. For the moment, we can draw the conclusion that insofar as the formation of the superego, which is taken by Freudians to be the basis of conscience and the internalised norms of morality, depends upon family relationships and takes place prereflexively at the first two levels of our being, we can legitimately regard ethics as having a prereflexive basis in what happens to us in early life.

Of course, we do not need to conclude that childhood is destiny. It is not the case that the patterns of our early upbringing are so rigid as to leave us no freedom to create the narrative of our own lives. The multifarious developmental influences that act upon me are such as to gradually accord me greater rights and responsibilities in a moral order. I draw this idea from the writings of Rom Harré,[24] who speaks of a process of psychological symbiosis as a prerequisite for our ethical formation.

Taking his starting point from what he calls a "moral order," Harré explains the moral formation of an individual in terms of a transition from one such order to another. Harré defines a moral order as "a collectively maintained system of public criteria for holding persons in respect or contempt and the rituals for ratification of judgments in accordance with these criteria. The moral value of persons and their actions is publicly displayed by such a system."[25] A moral order is a discourse and a set of practices in which people find themselves, by which they are valued and categorised, and through which they can value and categorise others.

Moral development is not based on the development of a capacity for moral judgment or action but on the distribution of rights and permissions to act with more or less autonomy and to accord respect or blame to others in a given moral order. As a child grows older, it acquires not only more abilities but also more rights as a participant in a moral order. There is no stage at which a child is premoral in the sense of not having the capacity to be part of a moral order or of not being inserted in a moral order by others. The kindergarten playground is just as much a moral order (and its denizens moral agents) as the world of adults is.

The smallest social context in which this can be displayed is the symbiotic dyad between mother and child. When the child is very young, its mother supplements its identity and being by externalising its inner states on its behalf. In this way the child learns who it is and what to value. Already, therefore, the child is being given a role in a moral order. Harré notices social groups in which the father-child dyad, as structured through their talk, is different and accords the child greater autonomy than the mother-child dyad. Similarly, as the child grows older, its relationships with others and with its parents, as defined by social discourse, typically lead to its having more right to display its own practical wisdom. It seems that changes in its psychological symbiosis, rather than changes in its moral decision-making capacities, are central to what psychologists have called its moral development.

These points are significant for Harré because he is engaged in a polemic against Lawrence Kohlberg, for whom moral development is dependent on growth in reasoning capacity, but they are significant for me for two different reasons. Firstly, they display the essentially relational nature of ethical development and ethical maturity and, secondly, they show that ethical development occurs even at the prereflexive levels of our ontological being as a self-project and as a caring-about-others. Moral growth is not a growth into ever more autonomous agency. Rather, it is a change in our patterns of symbiosis. Harré's account gives us a second-level diachronic developmental model which prepares us for Levinas's fourth-level model of personal interaction, a model in which I acknowledge your infinity and you acknowledge my infinity in the context of a communicative exchange.

Psychological symbiosis is an apt model for the dialectical nature of my being as a caring-about-others. My ethical formation and development require such symbiosis and therefore require me to be a caring-about-others. It is not only my being as a self-project but also as a caring-about-others that is essential to the process of maturation, through which I attain a degree of autonomy and discernment.

Autonomy is something I am given as my parents display confidence in me and permit me to pursue my own goals and make my own mistakes. Autonomy does not mean that my motivations can transcend that field of concerns, desires, hopes, and projects which has been formed in me by my biology and my upbringing. Rather, it means that I can reflexively own what I do and acknowledge it, with all its motives and consequences, as something for which I am responsible. Indeed, it is this feeling of autonomy that the traditional ethical discourse has taken as paradigmatic of what it is to be a human being. But this also explains why most modern philosophers begin their discussions of moral problems by assuming an isolated, autonomous agent motivated either by some form of self-interest or by an impartial altruism.

Autonomy is the product of our socialisation and upbringing rather than something we strive for despite these. Even as self-conscious, deliberative, and autonomous agents, we are relational in our being. I call this relational mode of ontological being *caring-about-others*. It is not simply that relations with others have formed us into what we now are, as if the relations in question were all in the past. In the present we remain essentially relational. This is true even at the cognitive and reactive level of our being.

As we apprehend our world and recognise things in it for what they are, we are reaching out with our knowledge to apprehend and appropriate the world as our own. Even as we walk down the street, we are related to that street as part of a world which is meaningful to us. As we act, we make use of things such as tools and thereby throw ourselves into the world through objects in it. Through his cane, the blind man extends himself into the world. It is a part of his sensory and active system.

We are related to our worlds in ways that make it hard to draw boundaries. Are our clothes part of us or part of our world? Is the chair we sit in part of us or part of our world? Of course, if we think of ourselves purely in terms of our biological bodies, the answers are clear. But if we think of ourselves as our existence, as our stance and presence in the world, and as our self-projection into the world, then our clothes certainly, and our chair probably, should be seen as part of our being.

It is even more obvious that we are relational in our very being when we recall my discussion of our being as a caring-about-others in Chapter 4. If our most pristine selves are symbiotically related to our mothers, then our natures are from the first relational in respect to persons. The centrality of our families during the years of our upbringing highlights this further. We will seek to reproduce the intimacy and sensuality of our first relationships in our rapport with our spouses. But our subsequent relationships contain more than the qualities of the mother-child relationship upon which psychoanalysis tells us they are based. There is also the intimate communication, the sensuous touch, and the passionate loyalty of lovers. And what of the love of parents for children? Is this not love of another kind again, a kind in which the balance between giving and receiving has been tipped towards the former? And what of our friends? How are we related to them — because we admire their qualities and can then recognise ourselves as having them also, as Aristotle suggests? How are we related to our colleagues at work? Do we feel solidarity with our fellow workers at large? Do we identify with our ethnic group or our church? And what is the nature of our relationships to our compatriots? It may be that some of these relationships and feelings of solidarity are spurious and would evaporate if placed under critical scrutiny, but there is no denying the prereflexive processes that go into their formation. To some degree or other and in a variety of ways, my being is tied up with that of others. My identity is found in others as if they were mirrors. And my autonomy arises from them.

But I am not simply related to others by bonds of affection of various kinds and degrees. I am also bound by bonds of responsibility. And these bonds of responsibility do not apply only to people. They might link us to institutions or ideals. And they might link us to various things. I might have a fondness for my car and be concerned not only with keeping it running efficiently, but also with keeping it clean and sparkling.

For most of us, our deepest bonds with things tie us to nature.[26] However, to suggest that this is a direct consequence of our biological level of existence, of the fact that we are of nature ourselves, is simplistic. Certainly, our first natural relationships are purely metabolic. But for this fact to be given an imperative charge requires that it be assimilated into the pattern of feeling formation which takes place in our earliest childhood.

It is not without significance that many of humankind's earliest myths speak of the earth as a mother, as if that first symbiotic relationship had become the model for the relationship that we have with our whole natural environment. We do indeed come from the earth, from material, and from flesh. Not only do we come from these, but we are embodied still, and our destinies point to a return to earth which none of us can escape. Perhaps the peace that can be felt when we go into the wilderness is a reminder of these things, of the womb, and of our organic links with the earth we inhabit.

Whatever the truth of these matters, one thing is clear. These relationships, whether with nature, with institutions or ideals, or with persons, all carry with them a dimension of responsibility. We are not a clean slate upon which fate, the narrative of our life, or our inner self writes a set of responsibilities. We are born with responsibilities, and we grow into more as we achieve maturity.

I do not refer here to that determinate set of responsibilities which I have by virtue of the social position into which I am born or into which I introduce myself in the course of my life. A prince is born with such responsibilities, and we all acquire responsibilities of this kind as we enter into employment, into marriage, or into any one of the myriad roles that social life offers us. These responsibilities belong to the third level of our being.

I am speaking here of a sense of responsibility which we find ourselves feeling towards certain people and things as we achieve our autonomy. We do not simply feel a sense of responsibility for our children because we occupy the social role of parent. We feel that sense by virtue of the inner bond which exists between us and our children. Whatever the deep psychological dynamic of this feeling, it is most often felt as affection and as a feeling that these children are importantly in my charge in a way that other children are not. My being as a caring-about-others is more immediately called upon by these children than by others.

Our being is defined as much by our responsibilities as by our projects, our upbringing, and our present experiences. Living life meaningfully involves acknowledging these responsibilities along with our ideals and aspirations. But lest it be thought that our imbeddedness in a world of persons and things leaves us with a field of responsibilities that is limitless and unmanageable, we should remember that it can be prioritised. Although we must not expect to be able to map the intricate pattern of our obligations and their relative stringencies in generally applicable ways, we can once again make use of the concentric circles model of relationships. This model, as used in Chapter 4, shows that there is a pattern of varying bonds of affection and responsibility such that we respond differently to the demands of others, depending on their location in that pattern of relationships.

Although I use Peter Singer's model of concentric circles to map the bonds of feeling which constitute the structure of the biologically and developmentally based elements of my caring-about-others, I do not agree with his use of it. For me this map shows the differential degrees to which certain people and things are important to me, so that the circles that are closest to the centre represent the spheres of affection and responsibility that are of greatest importance to me. For his part, Singer uses the model to show the scope to which our responsibilities should, and in time will, extend. He argues that no affection of mine should interfere with a rational assessment of worth or merit in making moral discriminations. But if this is so, then we will see a growth of conflict between the demands of a universalist morality as historically evolved and the prereflexive motivations of our actions.

Singer himself recognises this when he discusses the celebrated case of Fenelon and his valet.[27] If a person passes a burning building containing Archbishop Fenelon, who is a great man making significant contributions to the betterment of humankind, and his valet, who happens to be this passerby's father, then a universal rational ethics would demand that the passerby seek to save the archbishop from the building rather than his father. Singer admits that such a morality transcending our natural sympathies is hard to subscribe to, because he argues for the necessity of ethical codes which will soften these harsh demands and make a compromise with our natural tendencies.[28] I reject Singer's reading of the Fenelon example because I take my feeling of affection and responsibility for my father to be a valid aspect of my being as a caring-about-others and thus a valid component of my ethical stance. Ethical stances are expressions of caring rather than the products of abstract rationality.

Another way in which we could highlight the difference between my position and that of the traditional moral discourse is by focusing on the way my father in the burning building would feel, were he to see me. The archbishop might see me and say, "Thank God, there is someone who can save me." But my father, on seeing me, will say, "There is my son; surely he will save me." My father acknowledges our relationship as relevant to the situation just as I do. Because of this relationship, he has the first call upon my efforts. Figuratively speaking, his presence in the building calls out to me for my help more loudly than does the presence of the archbishop. And the archbishop typically calls out to me more loudly than would a trapped dog in the building. And the trapped dog typically calls out to me more loudly than a beautiful artwork in the building. (Is there room for argument on this point?) The artwork typically calls out to me more loudly than the furniture, and so on. If I had the time and the ability, I would save them all. But if I do not, then my priorities are set by my affections and sense of responsibility. My caring-about-others is structured.

Let us examine the phrase *calling out* in this example. In suggesting that even the furniture and the painting on the wall have some call on my responsibility, I assume that I have some respect or concern for such things, that I care about them. I might recognise the furniture as the precious possession of its owners, or I might consider it to be beautiful furniture in itself. Either way, it will have some importance for me. Similarly, the painting may be important because I know its owners love it, or because it is a picture of my mother, or because it is a great piece of art. Either way, I am not indifferent to it. If I were indifferent to it, it would not call out to me in the situation of danger.

As for the two persons in the building, my father elicits my response by virtue of being my father, and the archbishop calls out to me firstly by virtue of being a fellow human being and then, perhaps more importantly, by virtue of being recognised by me as a person of worth and value who can do much good in the world. This is why the example makes him an archbishop: in this case, the appropriateness of my according priority to saving my own father is not as obvious as it might otherwise be.

However, my central point is that the fact that, figuratively speaking, people or things call out to me indicates that I feel a responsibility to them, that my being as a caring-about-others and as a self-project is completed in them. Both the responsibility and the calling out are grounded in the relationship that exists between us. I might express this relationship as an explicit ideal or an ethical norm, or I might simply find myself feeling concerned. There will be situations in my life which will present a phenomenological dimension which I interpret as a call to action because of their nature and because of what my upbringing has made me.

One last point needs to be made before we move to the next chapter. The concern, sense of responsibility, and affection which I discover at the second level of my being and which motivate my actions are prereflexive or implicit expressions of my caring-about-others. Were I to make them explicit to myself in reflection, they would typically take the form of commitments; commitments, therefore, are explicit expressions of my caring. Moreover, they standardly express intentions and projects for the future and are in this way future-oriented. Whereas my behavioural reactions are the making public of my caring-about-others in the present and at the second level of my being, my commitments are an expression of that caring marked by a degree of latency and an orientation to the future. They are one way in which my caring-about-others and my self-project enters into self-consciousness. With this entry into the sphere of the reflexive, we enter level three of our being. And here, we need to refine our understanding of what ethics is.

7

ETHICS AND
PRUDENCE

The Evaluative and Proactive Level

As we move to the third level of our being, we enter that sphere of living where we are conscious of ourselves as agents and of the world as the arena and horizon of our projects. At this level we deliberate and act in relation to matters which we take to have practical import. We pursue the fulfillment of our needs using the means which both circumstance and capacity afford us. Given that we are a being ontologically characterised as a caring-about-others as well as a self-project, this pragmatic and self-conscious level of existence will be cognisant of others and will be marked by ways of life involving pragmatic cooperation and competition with others. As such, this level of our being will be highly relevant to my exploration of the emergence of ethics at the four levels of our being.

However, given the reflexivity of our active lives at this level, we will need to re-examine our notion of what ethics is. When I described ethics as comprising those action-guiding norms which tend to bring people's actions into line with social and interpersonal requirements, I did not distinguish between patterns of response and behaviour which have been inculcated in us causally and processes which require self-consciousness and deliberation. Our affections, feelings of responsibility, and the priorities that arise between them are more than operative elements in our motivational sets. They are open to reflection and questioning. If we were to confine ourselves to the first three levels of our being, we would engage in this

questioning in light of our biological needs, inculcated desires, and consciously recognised worldly interests. If we were to acknowledge the fourth
level of our being, we would take our ideals, our faith, and our ultimate
aspirations into account as well. In either case, we would be deliberating
and acting in light of determinable interests or aspirations of which we can
be reflexively aware. At the third level of our being, we would be engaging
in such deliberation in order to facilitate the achievement of our interests,
and perhaps to reconcile the pursuit of those interests with the need for
social harmony. It seems that at this level of our being, ethical thinking will
be pragmatic and prudential.

Now, there are many thinkers who argue that ethics and morality constitute a category of practical thinking which is not prudential in its very
nature. They follow Kant in arguing that morality imposes obligations
which apply to us irrespective of our goals and aspirations rather than being
imperative because of those goals and aspirations. In terms of my thesis, this
would mean that morality exists for us only on the fourth level of our being
and that this level would have to be conceived of as separable from the rest
of our being. This view of morality requires that the levels of our being from
which our inclinations, affections, and practical concerns arise are not relevant to our moral lives.

My problem with this view is not only that it partitions human being in
a way that does not do justice to the wholeness of our being, but also that it
fails to explain how our moral lives can be grounded in, and expressive of,
our deep caring, where the latter is understood as comprising our caring-
about-others and our self-project. This would leave morality without a point.
One terminological way of dealing with this problem is to distinguish ethics
from morality. Let me suggest that ethics be understood in the Aristotelian
sense, in which it pertains to anything which is conducive to living life successfully and well, whereas morality be understood in the Kantian sense of a
set of imperatives which is universal, objective, and independent of the first
three levels of our ontological being. I will return to this distinction between
ethics and morality in Chapter 8. For the moment, I will only say that prudential thinking would be a part of ethics in Aristotle's sense, because living
life successfully and well is a project which elicits our deep caring at all four
levels of our being. Prudential thinking might also be placed into my model
of human being by relating it more centrally to our being as self-project; ethical thinking is more strongly related to our being as caring-about-others.
However, in this form the distinction cannot be sharp either, because self-

project and caring-about-others are simply two forms of the same deep caring which grounds all of our motivations.

These points can be supported by drawing on arguments by Alasdair MacIntyre,[1] who develops a historically based critique of morality in his book *After Virtue*. MacIntyre divides the history of moral theory roughly into three phases. The current phase, that of modernism, is one that has had bequeathed to it the failures of the preceding phase, resulting in the confused appeals to emotivism which characterise moral discourse in our time. This preceding phase, which MacIntyre calls the Enlightenment project, consists of the attempt to ground the morality which was bequeathed to it by the pre-Enlightenment phase, which embraced both the ancient Greeks and the medieval Scholastics. His thesis is that the language of morality and of moral debate amongst philosophers today is an anachronistic relic of a time when morality had a foundation in the commands of God or in a teleological metaphysics of humanity which those commands expressed.

The fundamental point about the first historical phase of moral thinking is that it was teleological and holistic. It embraced a unitary conception of a human being's function in relation to the cosmos, to society, and to itself. Aristotle's notion of *Eudaimonia* provides a striking model of this conception by proposing a notion of human happiness as a goal of all human striving, constituted by the excellent functioning of all aspects of the human soul, from the appetitive to the contemplative. Given such a notion, the task of moral theory was simply to set out advice and principles whereby this telos of human beings could be realised. According to MacIntyre, the theological reformulation of this tradition, whether in the hands of Christian or non-Christian thinkers, left the basic structure of moral theory unaffected. As he puts it, "the threefold structure of untutored human-nature-as-it-happens-to-be, human-nature-as-it-could-be-if-it-realised-its-telos, and the precepts of rational ethics as the means for the transition from one to the other remains central to the theistic standing of evaluative thought and judgment."[2]

Given that this earlier structure of moral thought came to be perceived as religious and teleological, the new secular age of the Enlightenment required that the duties and commands of morality should be grounded in such a way that no teleological thinking was involved. Thus began a process of thought which resulted in the rejection of metaphysics in favour of an empirical approach to ethics. The divine law which provided the deontological character of morality (so that morality was seen as an expression of obligation and command) was tied to the mysterious purposes of God. Once God was rejected, therefore, the obligations of morality needed to be grounded in new ways.

Accordingly, what the Enlightenment phase sought to achieve was to replace the implied hypothetical structure of the imperatives flowing from such moralities with categorical imperatives — commands which do not depend on any telos or purposes on the part of the humanity subject to that command. The deep quandary which MacIntyre identifies in this project is that the commands of morality which previously obtained their legitimation from a teleological conception of humankind now required that legitimation to be based on the conception of human nature as it is. The three terms MacIntyre uses to define the structure of moral theory are therefore reduced to two, and moral precepts are to be derived simply from human nature as it exists empirically, rather than as it is metaphysically understood.

MacIntyre traces the Enlightenment project through Diderot and Hume, who would found morality on desire and the passions; through Kant, who would found it on reason; to its culmination in Kierkegaard, for whom the basis would have to be blind choice itself. The inevitable failure of this project is manifest in Kant, for whom morality could not be grounded in an empirical understanding of human life. This meant that a metaphysical foundation remained necessary in that God had to be postulated as the one who guaranteed that morality would still have a point. I will discuss Kant more thoroughly in Chapter 8.

MacIntyre applauds Nietzsche for fearlessly announcing the beginning of the modern phase but rejects his honest conclusion that a new self-assertive amoralism should replace the entire empty historical edifice of moral theory, which he viewed as merely a mask for the will to power. In place of this unwelcome conclusion, MacIntyre would revive an Aristotelian conception of virtue based on a teleological view of human life. Such a modern teleological view will focus not on a metaphysical notion of the telos of humanity, as it did for Aristotle, or of the *summum bonum,* as it did for Kant, but rather on an empirical and naturalistic notion of a general object of any human volition.

In an attempt to give substance to such a notion, MacIntyre suggests that every human life strives to be integrated and whole just as a narrative must be. In literature, there are demands of an aesthetic kind which will secure the integrated totality of a narrative; in the same way, a life as lived will generate demands within itself which, if followed, will secure the integrity and wholeness of that life. The virtues, in this conception, become those practices which are conducive to the integrity of a life. This is a naturalistic conception of the good which, though shaped by cultures, will be instantiated in the lives of individuals and which is therefore empirical rather than metaphysical. For all its banality, the word *happiness* can still be used to capture it.

It would seem, then, that the minimal requirement for any morality — even one that wishes to be free of metaphysics — is a teleology of human aspirations. To be free of metaphysics, such a teleology must be grounded naturalistically, as it would be for MacIntyre, in the biography of individuals and cultures. And insofar as it is our aspirations and fundamental motivations which provide this grounding, ethical thinking will be pragmatic and prudential in the sense that it will be directed towards the attainment of those aspirations and thus expressive of our deep caring.

The Nature of Ethics

I understand the word *ethics* in light of its ancient Greek etymological source: *ethos*. The ethos of a social group or of society at large (if it can be said that there is but one ethos for complex modern societies) is that vague and underdetermined set of standards of behaviour, characteristic modes of feeling, and shared practical attitudes by way of which people recognise one another as belonging to the same group. In preceding chapters, I have used the term *culture* in much the same sense. People's self-projects and their being as a caring-about-others are given concrete historical form by the cultures in which they are situated. Hegel used the term *sittlichkeit* to express this idea.[3] This term refers to the shared worldview of a people, especially as it pertains to practical concerns.

What a social group regards as important to do and to achieve, and the proper styles of behaviour that operate in that group, are elements of its ethos. The ethos of a social group concerns not only what individuals are required to do in order to remain recognisable as a part of that group, but also how they are required to feel about matters that the group regards as important. A native of the Amazonian jungles who does not feel a respect and love for the rain forest would be failing to participate in the ethos of his people, even if he actually did all those things which are required of him in his community. It is, of course, obvious that such a person in the Amazon region who was overtly careless in his behaviour towards the environment would be even more quickly exorcised from his people.

At the third pragmatic level of our being, ethics is understood as a society's ethos issuing in an open-ended set of action-guiding arrangements and attitudes, some of which may be implicit in forms of social life, others of which are explicitly expressed as social and interpersonal rules. The component elements of ethics understood as the ethos of a people are quite various and wide-ranging. They include customs such as characteristic ways of dressing; the annual round of festivals and celebrations; the way in which significant events in life such as births, deaths, marriages, and other rites of passage are celebrated; and the ways in which domestic and private life are ordered. They include also etiquette, which I understand to mean table manners, proper dress for various occasions, and the many subtle ways in which social interactions are structured. For example, how to greet an acquaintance in the street is a subtle matter of etiquette. If the acquaintance is a close friend, one should stop and chat if time permits or apologise for not doing so if it does not; if the acquaintance is merely a colleague from work, then a friendly greeting will suffice. That such action-guiding rules exist and are deeply ingrained is indicated by the embarrassment that follows from mistakes that might be made in this area. If one person in such an exchange stops and extends a hand in greeting while the other walks on and merely greets the other with a wave, there will be hesitation and hurt on one side or the other. Implicit norms of etiquette will have been flouted. Niceties of mutual recognition will not have been observed. In these areas of life, there do exist subtle action-guiding rules of behaviour.

To a great extent, a society's ethics also consists of the practical attitudes which are taken for granted regarding such things as our relations to others, sexuality, money, and the objects and practices a society finds important. These matters are often thought to constitute an ethics because they dictate what people feel obliged to do. I do not mean that people always think of such matters as falling under explicit rules or norms, though they sometimes do, but rather that to treat them in untypical ways is either unthinkable or socially unacceptable. Failure to behave appropriately in a given situation or failure to express the appropriate attitude in one's actions elicits forms of social disapproval which include derision, moral condemnation, disapproval, ostracism, or merely being the object of dislike. In this conception of ethics, the social dimension is paramount, and the role of ethics is to secure both the harmony and cohesion of a society and the status and roles of individuals within it.

The dominant ethos of a society can also come to expression in various action-guiding arrangements which are present in that society. I use the word *arrangement* here to convey the idea that ethics considered at the third level of our being is a human and social product. It may not be possible to know whether any particular person or social group initiated the arrangement, and it may not exist in the formal manner of a social institution, but it is part of the social reality which individual agents must deal with. Of course, we must not conclude that this means that ethics is nothing more than a social imposition. Insofar as agents are fully formed members of a culture, that culture's ethical demands will be the historically available form given to an agent's primordial caring or the inchoate motivations of sociability of which Darwin spoke. This shows how my conception of ethics is linked to caring. Culturally formed persons will tend to care about the things that their cultures posit as important, and therefore caring and ethics will tend to coincide.

A society typically contains a number of action-guiding arrangements and institutions which are more formal than its ethos (given the multicultural nature of many societies, there will also often be more than one ethos). The most obvious and palpable example is the law. In the form of criminal law, a society's laws forbid a number of actions and dictate sanctions for transgressions. Additionally, in its other forms, the law establishes rights, allocates responsibilities and obligations, and enables a large number of formal social and commercial transactions. The ordering of social and personal life in a modern society owes a great deal to the law, and an individual's actions are frequently and appropriately guided by that law. In this sense, the law is an important action-guiding social arrangement.

It is clear, therefore, that the law is of ethical significance. Law, like other formalised expressions of a society's action-guiding arrangements, should accord with and partly constitute the ethos of a community. There would be conflict in a community where the expectations and norms arising from the implicit requirements of social living were at variance with the officially enunciated norms. A law could become unenforceable if the majority of people did not find it to be in accordance with that society's ethos.

The problem with this, of course, is that no modern society is sufficiently coherent in terms of its ethos for this ideal to obtain. It is for this reason that what is legally enjoined or forbidden is only contingently related to what a society holds up as morally required or condemned. I oppose the view that what is considered immoral should be made illegal, a view called legal moralism. Although some provisions of the criminal law might have been instituted in the past simply because the relevant behaviour was thought to be immoral, the contemporary mood is that this is not appropriate. Thus, for example, sodomy between consenting adults was illegal in many places until recently for the simple reason that it was thought to be immoral, but in societies where liberal principles have become dominant, this is no longer an adequate justification. Whether it is prejudice or moral condemnation which motivates those legislators who would still seek to criminalise homosexual practices, the justifications for such legislation make reference to social goods such as hygiene or the protection of the young. Moralistic reasons by themselves are no longer acceptable in societies which take themselves to be enlightened.

This example depends on my distinction between ethics and morality. If the condemnation which nonconformist practices often attract is a function of the fact that such behaviour falls outside the ethos of that society's dominant groups, then it is clear that criminalising such practices constitutes an illiberal imposition of the ethos of the majority on an aberrant minority. To avoid this impression, the dominant group in a society — from whom the legislators are usually drawn — will often enhance their disapproval with a rhetoric which calls the behaviour immoral. It will not seem adequate to say that the behaviour is wrong because most people ostracise it; the disapproval or disgust which is felt will be so strenuous and will seem so necessary and natural that it gives rise to the claim that the behaviour in question is immoral.

An alternative to this appeal to morality is the appeal to the society's ethos itself. It might be argued, for example, that a practice which most find disgusting should be outlawed because of the offence and the threat which such behaviours pose to the wider ethos of the community and thus to its solidarity. The problem with this approach, of course, is that in modern societies it is simply not true that any one ethos holds sway to such an extent that the cohesion of those societies depends upon it. Modern societies are unified by the apparatus of the state, of which law is a crucial part. The moralities which exist in a given society are not crucial to this apparatus.

Perhaps one final explanation for the continuing appeal of legal moralism might be that if the law is an obligatory action-guiding social arrangement (in that it is backed by sanctions) which is formalised and equally applicable to all members of a state, then it offers itself as a perfect model and medium for the imposition of the idea and content of a universal, objective, and impartial morality.

I will return to the notion of morality in Chapter 8, but it is interesting to note at this point that in distinguishing between law as an action-guiding arrangement and law as an enactment of morality, I have implied that morality is more than an action-guiding arrangement. If we understand most action-guiding arrangements as rational in the sense that they can be justified with reference to benefits and goods to be attained by their observance (some customs and rules of etiquette would not be rational in this sense), then we understand them in a purely prudential way. Therefore, we might say that the prohibition under criminal law of murder is a prudential arrangement which secures a degree of security and safety within society. Regarding murder as morally wrong is quite a different matter, one which introduces the notion of morality as a source of obligation or prohibition independent of social and cultural prudential arrangements. It is because this difference exists that we can ask whether what the law enjoins coincides with what morality enjoins.

Professional ethics is another example of an action-guiding arrangement which embodies an ethos. It differs from law in the extent of its formal articulation and scope and in the nature of the sanctions applied for transgression. Many professional organisations enunciate a set of guidelines for their members, offering guidance as to how those members should behave in difficult or ambiguous situations. Moreover, they do this in order to preserve and enhance the reputation of the profession and to increase public trust in the standards of behaviour of the professionals. Thus, for example, the professions of nursing, medicine, accounting, and many others have set out what they regard as the proper standards of professional behaviour. For individual members of these professions, these charters or statements of professional ethics will be useful as action-guiding principles. Of course, as with any action-guiding principle, the individual will still need to judge when it is appropriate or necessary to apply the standards.

The professions usually police their ethics with a variety of sanctions. Doctors and lawyers can be prevented from practising if their behaviour is found to fall short of the desired standards. It is for this reason that I consider professional ethics to be akin to law. It is an institutional arrangement for ordering certain social relations, backed up by sanctions. Again, it bears only a contingent relation, I would suggest, to those standards which are traditionally referred to as morality. It is because the public expects its doctors and lawyers to appear moral in their professional practice that professional standards are instituted which accord with the demands of morality.

Following Alasdair MacIntyre's arguments, I should again mention ·actical and prudential reasoning when I list action-guiding arrange-
ıts. Not only is such reasoning ethical in the context of the overarching
that people pursue, whether for unity and coherence in their lives or

for a specifiable kind of happiness, it is also ethical in the context of their more immediate goals. It expresses their caring in the sense of their self-project and their caring-about-others. Insofar as individuals pursue a number of specifiable goals, and insofar as society offers people, as part of the ethos inherent in its cultures and subcultures and as part of the historical possibilities available at a given time, certain goals, projects, and aspirations, so the practical and prudential deliberations of individuals will be both action guiding and socially structured.

These deliberations will be action guiding because people will feel constrained to act in certain ways in order to achieve the goals that they have, and they will be socially structured because the goals that people have are social and historical possibilities. It is not possible for a modern person to aim to be a village chief, and it is not possible for a villager in an undeveloped region to aim to be a company executive. Not only is it not possible to achieve these aims, it is not possible even to have them. They are not available as roles within the ethos of those societies. As a result of social and political struggle, it has only recently become possible for women in our society to aim to be business executives, although it is still more difficult than it ought to be to achieve this aim.

Prudential thinking and practical reason are action-guiding elements in the historical ethos of a people in three senses, then: firstly in the sense that individuals will guide their actions in light of their aims and their knowledge of available means, secondly in the sense that the availability of means is a social and historical matter, and thirdly in the sense that the possibility of even entertaining certain aims is a function of the ethos of that social group.

There are still other ways in which the ethos of a given community is expressed in the form of action-guiding norms and constraints. One of these is through role models. Every society holds up to its younger members role models and ideal forms of life which they are implicitly encouraged to follow. In many hunter-gatherer societies, the young men are urged to be warriors. This urging is not explicit, though it might sometimes be, but implicit in the forms of social life which accord to successful warriors the highest status, the spoils of their efforts, and access to other rewards such as women and food. To give certain social roles a higher status and greater rewards is the most common means for inculcating a desire in the young to fulfill those roles.

Conversely, to accord only a low status to certain occupations guarantees that those occupations will be followed only grudgingly or under duress.

The traditional role of women in our own society demonstrates this and also demonstrates the possibility of a countermovement whereby the occupants of the devalued roles can themselves accord a higher status to that role, in opposition to the ethos of the surrounding society. However, this countermovement is never deemed fully successful until the valuation which the outsider group gives to itself is accepted and acknowledged by the society at large. In a society such as ours, the role of the private entrepreneur is valued more highly than that of the professional caregiver, a fact not unconnected to our preconceptions about which role is more suited to men and which to women, and to the variation in status accorded to men and women as such. All of these subtle and shifting elements in the ethos of a society will have an action-guiding influence on such decisions asthe career choices of members of that society.

In addition to the different valuations given to various roles in a society, there are also varying valuations given to the character traits that traditionally accompany those roles. For example, in societies that value the warrior role, the virtue of courage will also be valued, whereas in societies that expect women to be domestic servants, the virtues of service and caring will be accorded praise when displayed by women in the home. The virtues associated with the role of the entrepreneur are enterprise, energy, and competitiveness, virtues that are also found and developed in the sports arena. Virtues and character traits are variously stressed and praised in different historical periods and in different forms of society. Humility, for instance, is not a virtue that is much praised or stressed in a society such as ours. These character valuations are a part of the particular and various ethics of a community.

Nevertheless, there may be some virtues that are useful in most social and historical settings, and these will be likely to form part of the wisdom of humankind as a whole. It is hard to imagine social contexts in which patience and generosity would not be deemed virtues. Yet even here we can counter the suggestion that these virtues are universally valued by noting that they are not always applied or valued in every context. One need only think of certain aristocratic or samurai traditions to see cases where it would have been deemed ignoble to display patience or generosity towards peasants, although these virtues might have been required when dealing with other nobles or samurai.

The final form of action-guiding arrangement which I want to discuss is possibly the most important: language itself. As I noted in Chapter 5, communication contains ethical commitments. In communicating with others, I accord them certain forms of respect. I typically assume, for example, that they are telling the truth and presenting themselves honestly. Moreover, I must typically want to tell the truth. If interlocutors did not standardly intend to tell the truth, then discourse as such would be threatened. If everyone typically thought that everyone else was lying, then no communication would be taken seriously.

Further, the forms of communication include differing role definitions for interlocutors in relation to their varying degrees of authority to speak, their various needs in relation to the communication situation, and their various rights to initiate or steer the communication in different directions. The pragmatics of any speech situation constitute an action-guiding arrangement in my sense. Speech situations require interlocutors to adopt certain stances. Parties to a communication must be open, responsive, and truthful, and they must contribute in ways appropriate to their roles. Indeed, interlocutors are typically defined by the communication situations in which history and circumstances insert them.

One might think that the deliberations and actions of an individual agent in a given society conform to the ethos of that society because, insofar as that individual is formed within that society, they are caused to do so. However, my argument maintains that this conformity is a function of the individual's deep caring in the twin forms of self-project and caring-about-others. We seek to realise ourselves by means of that which is most readily available — namely, our social formation — and we seek to establish and maintain solidarity with others through conformity to that formation which has shaped us. Our deep caring gives rise to a primordial and prereflexive existential commitment to the ethoses of our society.

Nevertheless, as the phenomenon of social and moral reform demonstrates, there is room for the individual to adopt practical stances which are opposed to those of the society's dominant ethos. This would seem to imply an irreducible element of practical freedom, or what has traditionally been called *free will*. Proponents of this concept who also acknowledge our social context will often speak of a dialectical relationship between individuals' social formation and their free will, such that individuals contribute to the development of society even while they are subject to its forces. These contributions are then said to arise from the irreducible freedom at the core of these individuals. But this notion is viciously dualistic and appeals to a problematic metaphysical view of human nature.

To understand the phenomenon of ethical nonconformism and reformism, it might be easier to remind ourselves that no modern society has only one ethos. That is why I have just now started using the rather clumsy plural *ethoses*. I would expect to find, on reading a relevant history or biography, that any moral reformer or ethical nonconformist was formed within the ethos of a smaller subculture. The pacifist in a bellicose society might be a member of a Quaker group. In such a case, the origin of the alternative thinking lies not in an individual's freedom but in an oppositional social ethos.

Nevertheless, the notion of freedom, or more specifically, the notions of originality and creativity in the ethical sphere, do seem to find purchase in history. Just as there is creativity in art, theoretical innovation in science, and theological refinement in religion, so there seems to be the possibility of the emergence of new ethical views. The ethical dynamism evidenced by history seems not to be merely a case of varying the mixtures of pre-existing ethoses. There does seem to be such a phenomenon as ethical freedom.

To explicate this freedom in nonmetaphysical terms, without positing a uniquely human faculty called free will, I will need to explore how the action-guiding arrangements which I have been describing actually guide action. There would seem to be two alternatives. Action-guiding arrangements might provide what Bernard Williams calls "external reasons" for action, or they might provide "internal reasons."[4] The former alternative means that by virtue of such factors as the sanctions which come in their train, it is objectively the case that acting in accordance with these arrangements is in the interest of the agent. Williams suggests that the characteristic linguistic formulation for ascribing an external reason occurs when we say that there *is* a reason for Jones to do something, as opposed to saying that Jones *has* a reason to do it. When we can ascribe an external reason to Jones's action, there is no implication that Jones is entertaining that reason as a mental state or that he even knows about it. There might be a reason for me to run to the railway station: my train is running early. But this is true even when I am unaware of it and consequently can entertain no such reason for acting.

In contrast, internal reasons are reasons that agents actually have for acting in a certain way. For me to have a reason in the internal sense requires that I have the relevant beliefs and desires. These reasons may be either mental dispositions or mental states with phenomenological content. Either way, such reasons must be understood as being actualised when agents are motivated to act. When acting, agents either express prereflexive inclinations and drives or realise plans, aspirations, and commitments which are conscious elements in their motivational sets. To have and act upon internal reasons in this sense is to exercise *phronesis* as I described it in Chapter 6. Our behaviour can be internally rational whether or not we consciously deliberate about it, but it can only be deemed rational in this way if we actually have reasons for so acting, whether these reasons be prereflexive or conscious.

Even where action-guiding arrangements for ordering people's lives exist which render it externally reasonable to follow those arrangements, I would argue that ethical agents follow those arrangements for internal reasons. Ethical agents are agents who care. They are motivated to follow action-guiding arrangements. The ordering of social relations might be achieved by laying down rules, regulations, and laws and backing these up with sanctions ranging from peer disapproval to legal punishment, but no imposition of rules backed by sanctions can ever be effective by itself. When people do not want to obey the law, a community becomes ungovernable. When a professional ethics is widely flouted, no amount of policing will put a stop to the corruption. The majority of people must want to obey the rules (even if only to avoid sanctions) if those rules are to be effective. It remains possible that reasons exist for agents to act in accordance with action-guiding arrangements in Williams's external sense even when those agents have no internally held reason for, or motivational stance towards, so acting, but such external reasons are not ethically relevant. To speak of them is to think sociologically.

The relevance of the distinction between external and internal reasons to our question about freedom is ironic. It seems that it is the existence of external reasons which leaves agents free. One might think that if there is a reason for the agent to act, then that agent is less free than if there were not such a reason. But the existence of an external reason for a particular action does not by itself impinge upon the agent and therefore leaves that agent free to act in light of that reason or not. Even if agents do act in accordance with such reasons, they do so unwittingly, unless that reason has somehow been turned into a motivation. Without an internal motivational element, external reasons mean nothing to us, except insofar as unfortunate consequences may flow from our not having acted in accordance with them.

In this way, there being reasons for all of us to act in accordance with our society's action-guiding arrangements is certainly a circumstance that leaves us free. But this fact is hardly of much interest if it is based simply on those reasons' not entering into our motivational sets through our beliefs or desires. The more interesting question is whether we can describe ourselves as free in the context of having internal reasons, especially if these reasons are seen to include those elements of *phronesis* that arise at the lower levels of our being, including the biological level at which causality reigns.

Internal reasons may correspond to external reasons, as when the former consist in a recognition and acknowledgment of the latter, or they might be of a different order altogether. For example, altruism might be thought of as comprising actions performed for internal reasons in the absence of external reasons, because, by definition, it is not in the interest of the agent to act altruistically. In this case, one's reason for acting is internal because it arises out of one's being as a caring-about-others. On the other hand, acting in this way also arises, as does all action marked by integrity, out of one's own self-project. So even when there is no external reason to perform the altruistic action, in the sense that it is not in the interest of the agent at the first three levels of his or her being to do so, it might be in that agent's interest at the fourth level. The agent's self-project may move towards fulfillment by acting in this pragmatically selfless way.

Returning to our adherence to action-guiding arrangements, we can readily see that agents will willingly obey rules and conform to ethoses when those rules or ethoses enable them to pursue their pragmatic projects. These agents' external reasons are readily internalised. But agents might also internalise rules which are not in their pragmatic interests, if such rules enable them to pursue the most fundamental ideals arising from their being as self-project and caring-about-others. For example, people drive on the required side of the road to the extent that they are committed to the value of safety on the roads, not only for themselves but also for others. People obey the laws relating to property because they respect the property of others or fear the breakdown of respect for their own. They see their interests being served by the laws relating to property, and they also find these laws congenial to their concern for the property rights of others.

It would seem that the terms *motivation* and *internal reasons* are both underdetermined in the sense that they can refer to prereflexive desires, drives, and even reflexes, as well as to consciously acknowledged practical needs and plans, fear of sanctions resulting from transgression, and ethical ideals. Action-guiding arrangements can be either prudential means for achieving one's goals or means for furthering one's commitments or both. Given a characteristic motivational set which includes both a concern for self and a desire to contribute to sociability, and given that we are, ontologically, both a self-project and a caring-about-others, agents will accept a society's ethics if these ethics are seen as rules of thumb whereby these agents will better be able to express their primordial caring. The internalisation of these external reasons can thus be understood as an expression of our whole being leading to integrity. And should this not be seen as an instance of freedom?

When people obey rules because they agree with them, they do so with internal reasons, and this is often described as a free adherence to those rules. This means that whether or not there are external reasons for them to obey in the sense that it is in their objective interest, people are motivated to do so. Insofar as such adherence is adopted as a conscious policy, we are clearly dealing with a case of freedom of action, as that term is standardly understood.

However, what of the prereflexive levels of our motivational sets, those that arise from the lower levels of our being? Do we not normally theorise these motivations in causal terms and thereby deny our freedom? It is my claim that we should interpret these prereflexive motivations rather than explain them. We should see them as instances of primordial caring. They are determinable inclinations towards acting in a certain way that are activated and focused by specific circumstances in which we find ourselves. The action-guiding arrangements of our society are form-giving contexts which determine our comportment towards sociability to the extent that the ethoses that enliven those arrangements accord with commitments to which our own caring has given rise.

At this point it is relevant to remind ourselves of the holistic nature of our model of what it is to be as a human being. It would be an artificial restriction of our discussion if we left out the fourth level of our existence. Our faith, our ultimate concerns and aspirations, and our fundamental commitments are also involved. If the ethoses of the various social groupings we identify with and the explicit rules of those groupings are consistent with all of these, we will be inclined to follow them; if not, then we owe it to ourselves to disobey them. If a society's action-guiding arrangements fail to reflect the commitments of members of that society, then pressures to change them will arise, or they will be reduced to a merely rhetorical set of standards and ideals used to provide a veneer of acceptability for actions which are actually unethical in that society's terms. If our primary commitment was to obey the laws, there could be no martyrs and moral reformers. Such a commitment would express only the first three levels of our being. Ethical innovation and freedom arise from our self-project and caring-about-others at the fourth level of our being, the level at which our deepest commitments are grounded and at which our highest ideals come to expression.

But does it follow that agents can adopt or reject social action-guiding arrangements more or less freely? I seem to be suggesting that if such arrangements are seen to accord with one's commitments, one will accept them, but if they are not, one will seek to change them. However, as we noted earlier, the processes of socialisation are more subtle than this suggestion would imply; ethical norms and standards are apt to be internalised before we realise it.

This is especially true in the case of role models and character ideals. These are culturally available forms of identity by which we are shaped and which provide, along with apparently "natural" ways of doing things and attitudes to a wide range of everyday projects, the specific acculturation through which I exercise my caring-about-others and my self-project. It would require deliberate reflection to scrutinise and then possibly change the way in which I have been shaped by such an action-guiding arrangement as my very identity. Whether such a process comes upon one suddenly, as it sometimes reportedly does in conversion experiences, or whether one undergoes a lengthy period of possibly anguished thought, or, indeed, whether one merely finds oneself in tune with the prevailing ethos, some such reflective process is necessary if we are to develop into fully autonomous and mature ethical agents. And what this process inevitably brings to our attention is our faith, our ideals, and our deepest commitments. These not only provide the motivational basis and possibility for such reflection, they also provide its content.

It seems, then, that the question of freedom in relation to internal reasons inevitably leads our discussion towards the fourth level of our being, as if the basis of reflexive judgment upon our own ethical formation could be found here. But do not think that I am positing an existential core of our being which arises at this level and which is the ultimate source of our motivations and the ultimate standard against which the ethoses and practices of our society must be judged. Even if the content and articulation of such judgments were found at this level, the basis of our disquiet about the social ethoses that form us is our deep caring.

Even the fourth level of our being is subject to social formation, and my highest ideals are as much a product of my culture as are my practical projects. My freedom and possible ethical nonconformism do not depend upon there being an untouchable self which transcends the world and which comes to articulation in the self-affirmation of the fourth level of my being. Our freedom for ethical nonconformism consists in the possibility of a clash between the ethos of an action-guiding arrangement and that deep caring expressed as self-project or caring-about-others which is the deepest motivational level of our being. That this primordial caring can be distinct from the ethos which would shape it into conformity is demonstrated by noting that it is always determinable rather than determined, open-ended rather than formed, infinite rather than caused. Although our being as caring needs historical formation so that we can have an identity and so that we can have ideals to appeal to when we stand apart from the ethos of our society, our being as deep caring always eludes this formation and this identity. It is not a self.

Ethical Discourse and Caring

Before developing in Chapter 8 a proper understanding of the importance to our freedom of the fourth level of our being, we should explore the connection between this freedom and ethical discourse. By ethical discourse, I mean debate and discussion about what should be done, about whether what was done merited praise or blame, and about the values and goals of various activities. Traditionally, ethical discourse (I do not include moral theory understood as metaethics in these points) was seen as an exercise of practical reason in light of divine commands, categorical imperatives, or utility. That we reason about our actions at all in this way was seen as evidence for our freedom. There would be no point in deliberation if we had no choice. Further, we would have no need of divine or categorical imperatives if our motivational sets were not capable of waywardness, where this waywardness was itself taken as evidence of our freedom. The faculty of reason as exercised in ethical discourse, then, was seen as evidence for our freedom in two ways: firstly, because acting in light of practical reason was seen as an expression of freedom and, secondly, because our freedom, allegedly experienced by agents as waywardness, required the control that reason could provide.

The idea that individuals were subject to waywardness was based on the two quite different phenomena of weakness of will on the one hand and ethical nonconformism on the other. Weakness of will is the reflexive experience of not doing what one knows one should do or what one has decided to do. Ethical nonconformism, for its part, is the perceived departure from accepted and dominant standards of behaviour on the part of an individual or small group. As I indicated earlier, it can be recognised as evidence of freedom in the form of ethical innovation and heroism. But it can also be seen, especially by those in the dominant group, as evidence of freedom in the form of waywardness.

This points to a further role for ethical discourse. Moral nonconformists are considered by their communities not to be following the accepted social norms, whether these are understood as divine commands, as categorical imperatives, or in terms of other theoretical formulations. As I have argued, it is they who most radically demonstrate freedom in the ethical sphere. It is also they who, if they do not wish to be ostracised, most need to be able to explain and justify their actions to their communities. If our acting ethically — in accordance with our community's ethos and action-guiding arrangements — is motivated from within by our caring, and if our caring is largely formed in us by our community, then our acting ethically will seem natural to us and without need of justification. But in the case where our caring is genuinely expressed in commitments which are at variance with the social norms, we will struggle with ourselves and, perhaps as a consequence of acting, with others. This latter struggle will often take the form of ethical debate.

Peter Singer has suggested that the justificatory discourse of ethics might have evolved as early human beings saw the need to justify or excuse their actions in the face of social disapproval.[5] This suggests that ethical discourse is rational in its very nature and justificatory in its intent. It is not so much expressed in deliberation before an action as in justification after it. For my part, I have argued that because ethics should be understood as a combination of the action-guiding arrangements and the ethoses of a society understood as forms of life by which agents are shaped and to which they are typically committed, the ethical decisions of such agents are generally made prereflexively. It is their socially formed caring-about-others and their self-projects which provide the motivational source of the commitments of ethical agents. Characteristically, therefore, ethical discourse will only arise in the context of social disharmony when individuals or groups find themselves unable to be committed to the predominant ethics. This shows that ethical discourse is a second-order practice which arises out of ethical nonconformism or reformism. Aberrant behaviour needs to be justified rationally in a way that conforming behaviour does not.

Of course, it would be erroneous to see an agent's arguments in favour of his or her nonconformist action as typically a cynical attempt to be excused for transgression. Rather, such an exercise of reason could be the expression of the very same caring-about-others and self-project that the aberrant behaviour is. Indeed, the stress here should be on caring-about-others. Ethical discourse might be a form of the kind of deep communication we explored in Chapter 5.

What might the motivation behind such ethical arguments be, if we do not think that they are merely cynical self-justifications? Perhaps it is the preservation of community despite transgression. It is genuine caring-about-others which seeks to help others in the community see that the unacceptable action was, in fact, an expression of a valid commitment. And this commitment might be considered valid because the discourse shows that it is already implicit in the community's forms of caring. It might also be considered valid because the discourse moves the community to care in a way that it previously did not. This would be a case of genuine ethical reform.

This advocacy of one's own commitments is present not only in formal ethical discourse, but also in ethical action itself. It was Sartre who famously argued that when we act authentically, we act for all others.[6] This means that when we express our commitment, we also implicitly advocate that commitment to others. I believe Sartre was drawing on Kant's idea that acting morally involves implicitly legislating the moral law for all other rational human beings, because Sartre implies that we implicitly address all others in this way. If he had been more faithful to the phenomenological method at this point, Sartre would have argued that we do indeed prereflexively urge others to act as we do but that this urging does not have universal scope. It is more reasonable to suppose that our advocacy is directed more fully towards those others for whom we care — the others who are of our community, who are the objects of our caring-about-others. Some degree of open-endedness might be involved here, but we would consciously acknowledge the function of advocacy implicit in our enacted commitments only in relation to others who are in some degree significant to us. On this point I differ from Singer also. He regards ethical discourse as being addressed universally to all humankind simply because it is rational and should therefore appeal to anyone.

Given that my being as a human being involves both a self-project and a caring-about-others, my authentic action cannot but be responsive to, and formative of, the ethos of my community. There is a will to communicate

159

not only in my discourse but also in my actions. And this will to communicate is not simply the will to convey or receive information, it is an expression of my caring-about-others. It is not simply a matter of enacting alternative ethical values or roles and justifying them with reasons, it is a matter of establishing community actively and discursively and thereby defining myself in relation to that community. If it is not simply a matter of saving one's own skin, the justificatory ethical discourse which Singer takes to be the origin of ethics is an attempt to maintain community in the face of either transgressions against action-guiding arrangements or a breakdown in the ethos of that community. I would add that the effort is not merely one of maintaining the community. Insofar as my identity depends on that of the community, it is also an effort to maintain myself. My self-project is also implicated. In this way, my deep caring as self-project and as caring-about-others is the foundation of ethical discourse.

Of course, this statement applies most obviously to traditional and closed societies in which there is a homogeneity of community and in which the only conflicts that can arise are conflicts between the individual and a single set of social norms. Modern societies reveal conflicts between different communities within them. When the ethos of one community or subculture comes into conflict with the ethos of another within a given society, we have a somewhat different scenario. The behaviour of an individual may be deemed unacceptable by a given group, even when that individual acts in ways that he or she believes accord with arrangements and norms arising within that individual's subcommunity. It is simply that this agent is now in a different context. The agent might be with a different ethnic group, or in a different place of work, or in a different suburb.

Whatever the reason, there is now a disharmony between the ethos in which the agent was formed and that which is present in the new context. If the agent engages in justificatory discourse, he or she might explain apologetically that the transgression was due to not understanding the new context, or the agent might appeal to norms and standards which he or she claims should apply to all contexts and in light of which the action was acceptable. This latter strategy might also give rise to the traditional ethical discourse with which we are familiar. But my point is that such discourse will still be grounded in a concern to re-establish communication with others at a deep level and to re-establish the integrity of one's own being. The ethos of a community is the generalised and formed expression of the caring of its members.

The deep communicative aspect of ethical discourse and of ethical behaviour has a negative as well as a positive aspect. The positive aspect of a discourse that arises from our caring, both in the form of our caring-about-others and our self-project, is that the coherence of a community might be maintained despite deviations from that community's ethos; the negative aspect is intolerance and moral bullying. We are all familiar with the phenomenon of ethically committed persons who seek to use the law, or any other means of social pressure, to impose their own ethical views and practices upon others. Whatever our reaction to this, we can now see that this might be a genuine expression both of their self-projects and their caring-about-others. If ethical commitment is in its very nature communicative, if it stems from our very ontological being that we would want others to do as we do, then it is at least understandable that moral intolerance could arise. Legal moralism is a further social consequence of this deeply ambiguous communicative aspect of ethical commitment. Moral theory, or ethics understood as the philosophical discourse which seeks to ground norms rationally, may also be implicated in the illiberal quest for ethical uniformity. It is here that the universality of ethical views is posited. Given that ethics expresses our self-project, our caring-about-others, and our desire for community, it is not a matter which we can take lightly.

The four levels of our being, taken together, are both ethically ambiguous and ethically imperious. It is a difficult question to decide whether our caring-about-others is best expressed by forcing others to do what we consider morally right or allowing them authentically to do what we might disapprove of. One of the classic arguments for legal moralism appeals to the desire for social cohesion.[7] The countermovement to these various forms of moralism — tolerance of differing ethical practices and views — is a virtue that must also arise from our caring-about-others and our self-projects.

In Chapter 8, I will argue that ethical discourse need not be understood as an imposition of or an appeal to ultimate norms and standards of behaviour which are objectively and universally true, though, especially in traditional societies, they may be thought to be. For the moment, I will conclude by saying that among the interests humans pursue through practical projects at the third level of their being are not only interests related to survival and well-being, but also interests relating to conviviality and sociability. Each of us is a caring-about-others as well as a self-project. It follows that ethical discourse need not be understood simply as a discourse which seeks to justify one's actions so as to defend oneself against social disapproval. Rather, it can be understood as an expression of deep caring which seeks to advocate one's own commitments to others so as to preserve the cohesion of a social group even as its ethos changes.

Such advocacy cannot be an imposition if I recognise others as infinite and as unable to be contained within the ethoses that form them. This brings us back to Levinas's claim that expression and speech are forms of infinite ethical commitment to others. In discourse, interlocutors allow one another to be in their infinite dimensions. Indeed, as with the human face, the meanings of utterances, insofar as they arise from the speakers' infinity, are themselves transcendent realities which break out of the functions that they might serve in the context of practical discourse. The deepest ethical responsibility — to accord respect to the other — is grounded in discourse. For Levinas, language is "a response to the being who in a face speaks to the subject and tolerates only a personal response, that is, an ethical act."[8] The ethos of a language community is a communicative ethos in which, like Harré's moral orders, participants accord one another the right to be.

But Levinas's view takes us beyond that of Harré. Moral orders are primarily the social contexts in which praise, blame, respect, critical gossip, and social identity are established and maintained. The centering points of these contexts are persons who would accord respect, rights of action, or symbiotic enhancement to others. But there is nothing in Harré's exposition that removes us from the third level of our being, from an essentially pragmatic framework of solidarity. Levinas adds the fourth level of our being.

Discourse, as Levinas understands it, calls us to the ethical responsibility of coexisting with infinities, of allowing the individuality and transcendent being of the other to share my world. In this framework, ethics is more than an action-guiding arrangement which constrains my action and calls me to responsibility. It is a form of interhuman solidarity through which my being can come to fulfillment at all four levels and in which I am called to permit the being of the other to also come to such fulfillment. In this communicative context, the centering points are infinities calling each other to be infinite. It follows that discourse not only entails certain ethical stances on the part of interlocutors, it also shows us to be communicative in our ontological and ethical being. Discourse establishes and maintains the infinity or transcendence of my being, and insofar as I am ethical, insofar as I am a caring-about-others, I will express my being in communication, and I will be enhanced in my being through communication. This explains why I will seek to communicate my ethical stances to others and that others will seek to communicate theirs to me; ethics is social and communicative in its very nature. And this is not simply a matter of the formation and maintenance of social identity and approval as arising from moral orders. It is an ontological expression of my being as caring in the twin forms of self-project and caring-about-others.

8

MORALITY AND INTEGRITY

In Chapter 7, I distinguished ethics from morality in the following terms: ethics is that set of action-guiding arrangements expressive of the ethoses of a society, or of subcultures within it, which leads to behaviour, thinking, and discourse which guide us in living life well at all four levels of our being so as to fulfill our being as a self-project and a caring-about-others. As such, ethics can be interpreted as prudential. I also noted, towards the end of Chapter 7, an ethical discourse focused upon justifying aberrant behaviour, a discourse which had the aims of restoring ethical community and expanding its ethos. This discourse extends the aim, implicit in all ethics, of expressing our being as self-project and caring-about-others.

In this way, ethics and its discourses are grounded in our caring. Insofar as our being as self-project and as caring-about-others — of which ethical actions are expressions — is socially formed, most everyday actions will flow naturally within a framework of practical necessity which we hardly ever need call into question. It will seem as if most of the actions we perform are simply there to be performed without reflection. They are things that, given our situation, we "must" do, in the sense that it simply would not occur to us not to do them.

However, reflexivity does make a difference. People do sometimes ask themselves why they do what they do and whether what they do is worthwhile or correct, especially in situations of crisis or dilemma. In this new context of reflection, the motivations and reasons that lead to an action can become the object of scrutiny and assessment along with the actions — and their consequences — themselves. This mode of reflection takes people out of the practical world which is the context of the third level of our being. At this third level, we pursue historically given objects of action, thinking only of the means required to achieve those goals. The meanings and values of the actions themselves are taken for granted. Insofar as such actions fit into the ethos of that culture, and insofar as the agent does also, both the objects of such actions and their ontologically grounded aims are fulfilled with hardly any thought given to them at all.

The enactment of our ontological being as caring in the twin forms of self-project and caring-about-others is an aim implicit in the pursuit of the object of our actions. And most often the objects of our actions are implicit in the social meanings of those actions. It follows that if reflexive thinking about the objects and the worth of our actions is action guiding, it is so in a new and different sense from the justificatory and socially oriented ethical discourse which arises in connection with action-guiding arrangements and social ethoses.

Our cultural tradition has developed an action-guiding discourse in this new sense which helps us unravel the interconnections between deep caring, our faith as that positive attitude towards life which aims to seek and establish the meaningfulness of that life, our commitment to do whatever is necessary in order to achieve this and to be consistent with that faith, and the many things and persons we come to care about as an expression of these commitments or this faith, and thus of the primordial deep caring which is their ground. The name of this discourse is morality.[1]

In the Introduction, I reported approvingly on a sustained attack on the pretensions of traditional morality and moral theory. In my terms, the object of this attack is an action-guiding arrangement, expressed as imperatives and norms of character, which is taken to be of universal application and therefore independent of any specific social ethos; rationally and reflexively grounded and thus independent of at least the first two levels of our being; objective or realist and therefore independent of the relational contexts in which we exist; and nonprudential and thus independent of the aims we each have as a self-project and caring-about-others. For reasons made clear in previous chapters, I share the rejection of morality as a transcendentally founded rationalist, universal, objectivist discourse which would ground obligations as external reasons. Nevertheless, the discourses and practices of morality can be understood as profoundly meaningful for human existence.

Like theoretical science, art, myth, and religion, morality is a human cultural creation that gives expression to the fourth level of our being.

Morality and the Fourth Level of Our Being

Morality concerns the guidance of action. Questions ranging from the particular — What am I to do now? — to the general — How should I live my life? — can be moral questions. Admittedly, particular deliberations of small scope may not often strike us as being of moral import. I may simply be asking myself what should be the next step in an ongoing project or routine. However, as the traditional Aristotelian view would have it, any project in which I am engaged, no matter how limited or routine, will be open to support by reasons. And the reasons or principles which such support appeals to will themselves warrant a grounding in broader reasons or principles, and so on, until we reach a reason or goal for action which can have no further justification or which justifies itself. This will be an ultimate goal which is not justifiable by any further reasons.

But if questions ranging from, What am I to do next? to, How should I live my life? cannot be ultimately answered on the basis of reasons, then how are they answered? Aristotle appeals to an unquestionable telos inherent in our natures as human beings for this basis. Contemplation and the intuition of fundamental principles are the intellectual abilities needed to apprehend this telos so as to constitute the wisdom in light of which practical or prudential reason can make specific judgments.

My view is that such questions are answered by reference to an individual's commitments or to what an individual cares about. An ultimate goal will be one which appeals to us simply because it accords with the faith we have, in light of which we can affirm our lives as meaningful. It will be one through which we can express our primordial caring in a way mediated by the ethos of our society. If the specific action or project can be seen to accord with this faith, then it is worth doing. However, it is not our faith which is the ultimate court of appeal. Faith is a culturally mediated articulation of our deep caring specific to the fourth level of our being rather than to our whole being. Rather, it is deep primordial caring which is the basis for the meaningfulness of our lives and which makes our actions worthwhile.

Nevertheless, as we reflect on our lives and articulate our deep caring, our reasoning leads, both in Aristotle's thinking and in mine, to the fourth level of our being. I might say that I am motivated to do my best in my teaching duties because I am committed both to the improvement of the lives of my students and to the enhancement of my own career. In turn, I might say that I care for my students in this way because I see that it is through them that society will improve and because their own lives will be enhanced by their studies. I will be identifying broader concerns when I say this, concerns for society and for other human beings. As for my own career, I might say that I care about it because of the income it provides me and that this income, in turn, is important because of my love of consumer goods or of the family I support. But the objects that I acknowledge myself to be pursuing will be particular expressions of the fundamental aim of my caring in the twin forms of self-project and caring-about-others.

My use of *because* in the preceding sentences may be seen as identifying either a motivational causal sequence or rational justification, or a horizon of intelligibility. I may indeed be able to order my commitments in a sequence that echoes that of my practical reasons, but it is those commitments which motivate my actions while my reasons merely serve to explicate them. Insofar as I am committed to my project, I may owe it to myself or to others to have a reason for being engaged in it, but insofar as the project is important to me, it will be of little practical significance whether I can articulate that reason or not.

Just as the end point of Aristotle's rationalising sequence is that project that needs no justification — being fulfilled and without regret for the way one has lived one's life — so the end point of my interrogation of the sequence of commitments is primordial caring. When no more wide-ranging commitment can be articulated, I might say, "I simply care about that, that's all." The aim that needs no justification is not some external goal or object towards which I strive, but the fulfillment of my being as a self-project and a caring-about-others. The important difference between this way of understanding the matter and Aristotle's is that Aristotle needs a specific object for the whole of a human being's striving to be focused upon. *Eudaimonia* might be a very formal concept, but it still needs to be specific enough to attract the allegiance of human beings if Aristotle's claims are to be accepted.

To claim that there is one goal in life which everyone universally pursues must be seen as conducive to the universalist tendency of traditional moral thinking. We can escape this tendency while still speaking in general terms about humanity if we adopt a hermeneutic model for interpreting the great variety of historical forms which human striving has taken. With such a hermeneutic model, we can postulate a fundamental aim which is not specifiable in advance of my effort to realise it. Rather, it will be pre-intentional, ever determinable, and open-ended.

We should note the logical structure of the Aristotelian argument. It moves from a specific goal to an overarching goal of which all mediate goals are determinate expressions. There is an assumption on Aristotle's part that without an ultimate justification, all human action would be meaningless. I will call this the argument towards ultimacy. It is striking how many examples of this argument there are. It seems that philosophers are prone to this argument whenever they turn to the question of what makes human living meaningful. So we might suggest that human life is meaningful to the extent that we have loving relationships with others. But we would add that to have such a relationship only with one other is not enough. We must also have a meaningful relationship with a larger whole, be it our families, our ethnic or cultural group, our social class, or our national identity.

But even these ever larger contexts for relationship and formation of identity are not enough. One must also have a relationship with, or find one's identity through, an ultimate Other. This "Thou" to which "I" am related may be an all-encompassing Reality, an all-embracing History, or a personal Other of transcendent worth. But whatever its metaphysical articulation, it will be an ultimate Other without which my merely worldly relationships will be only a temporary consolation for the meaninglessness of my existence.

Again, it might be suggested that my life can be meaningful insofar as I have realisable hopes. It certainly seems true that if I have nothing to hope for, then my life will not seem worth living. My hopes must be realisable and motivational. In this way, I might hope for my next meal, or I might hope for a promotion at work. But are these rich enough hopes to give my life meaning? Surely not. I also hope for the fulfillment of my larger projects. I hope that my family will prosper, that my social group will flourish, that there will be peace on earth and a sustainable future on this planet. But is even this enough? For the advocates of ultimacy, it is not. There must be a transcendent hope which will embrace all others and be their fulfillment. Some call it Heaven; others call it Nirvana. Millenarians will seek its fulfillment on earth while others pursue it in transcendent realms.

So it is with ethics. The ethos of a community, its action-guiding arrangements, and its standards of character and behaviour will be sufficient for many as a matrix for practical reason. Even when a crisis or a dilemma forces people to reflect on their goals and objectives, the ethical customs and expectations current in that society will provide enough guidance for them.

But for the advocates of ultimacy, the practical aims which are inherent in our self-projects and our caring-about-others and which are mediated by specific cultural formations will not be sufficient. For an action to be a good one or the right one to perform, there must be an ultimate justification for it or an ultimate requirement to which it responds. It is this thinking which gives rise to the discourses of morality.

In my view, traditional morality understood in this way is a human cultural discourse marked by features which are to be explained as hypostatised expressions of our being as caring. The traditional discourse of morality and the metaphysical beliefs inherent in it grow out of the human tendency to render as ultimate, objective, and metaphysically grounded as possible the expectations which arise out of those social arrangements whose purpose is social cohesion and expression of ethos, those arrangements which are adhered to with deep commitment arising from our being as self-project and caring-about-others. Morality in the tradition of Plato and Kant is the development into an unacceptably absolutist form of a legitimate form of reflection and questioning centred on the question of what I should do in a given situation or what I feel others should do in certain situations.

Once we see this tradition for what it is, we are free to seek to understand the human concerns that have sustained it and to reinterpret the notion of morality in light of those concerns. There are at least two such concerns. One is that of resolving one's own crises and practical dilemmas in matters of importance, and the other is that of preserving communication with others in relation to those matters which are communally felt to be of the greatest importance. The first concern involves our deep caring as self-project; the second involves our deep caring as caring-about-others.

I suggested earlier that it is in situations of crisis or dilemma that we are apt to engage in that form of reflection which our tradition has formalised into moral discourse. Situations of crisis are ones where the everyday flow of activities and decisions, along with the implicit values, aims, and objects of those activities, are suspended. This might happen when an agent suffers a deep grief or disappointment, when our expectations of others are frustrated, when trust is betrayed, or simply when the agent is very tired or bored. It is at times like these that people are apt to ask themselves what in their lives is really important. Answering this question involves conferring a degree of determination to one's deep caring by identifying the things or people that one cares about. It involves defining one's identity in terms of one's commitments and involvements with others. For this reason, such reflection primarily expresses deep caring as self-project, although it cannot fail to implicate caring-about-others as well. Errors in such reflection lead to bad faith and self-deception.

Deliberative dilemmas constitute the other context in which the kind of reflection that leads to moral discourse frequently arises. Dilemmas occur when we are subject to conflicting internal motivations or reasons — when we care about or are committed to projects that conflict with each other or cannot be realised consistently with each other. Given my complex model of what it is to be a whole person, there are several ways in which I could theorise such dilemmas. Firstly, there will be conflicts within one level of our being. Perhaps the least interesting of these will be conflicts which occur only at the third level of our being, as when I need to place my everyday tasks into an order of priority. Secondly, there will be conflicts between lower and higher levels of our being. (I use *higher* and *lower* without any moral connotations. They refer simply to the levels of our existence. There is no reason to accord more respect to one level of our existence than to another.) I will not develop all the possible variations on this, although I will propose a few examples. There can be conflict between the lower levels of our being and the third level. There will be occasions when the activities we need to perform in pursuit of our everyday projects place us into conflict with our inclinations. There will be mornings when I prefer to sleep in rather than get up to go to work. Or I might be on a diet and be offered a piece of cheesecake.

More interesting for my interpretation of morality will be cases where we feel that we must act in a way that is contrary to our inclinations because of our commitment to values which arise at the fourth level of our being. For instance, I am about to make a donation to the Wilderness Society when I see a bargain price on a stereo component I have wanted for a long time, or I am married and meet an attractive unattached person at a party. Suppose that I "do the right thing" in each case. Kantians would analyse this by suggesting that I obeyed a universal moral imperative and acted despite my baser inclinations. And they would suggest that this showed that moral imperatives or duties do exist as objective realities external to me.

My analysis, in contrast, maintains that doing the right thing stems from our own highest ideals and commitments as these express our primordial caring. If there is a conflict with baser inclinations, it is an internal conflict rather than a conflict with some external reason arising from objective moral demands. My four-level model of what it is to be a human being might tempt me to account for this conflict in terms of inclinations stemming from the lower levels coming into conflict with inclinations or commitments stemming from the higher. However, this account would be much too reminiscent of the traditional moralistic model of conflict between unruly desires and impartial reason.

Part of the burden of my alternative model is to insert reason into all the levels of our being and to present a model which is holistic even as it allows us to discriminate between various modes of being. All four of these modes or levels of being are rational and appetitive in some form, and our being as a whole person embraces and unifies these levels. Thus, my using these levels to account for conflict should not be read as a re-creation of the reason-versus-desire model. What we seek in our moral lives is not the control of desire through reason, but the coherence of reason and desire at all four levels of our being. There must be harmony within and between all four levels of our being. And this unifying of our being is an existential project rather than an inevitable ontological process. Our self-project has our integrity and cohesion as its aim, just as our caring-about-others has our sociability and communication with others as its aim.

That moral dilemmas are not always conflicts between desire and reason is demonstrated most clearly when we note that there may be conflicts which seem to occur within the fourth level of our being, the level which traditional thinking would see as the pre-eminent locus of reason, especially in its transcendent form. In my view, such fourth-level conflict will be reflected upon as a conflict between our ideals, commitments, and aspirations. There may be conflict between inherent values such as preserving the wilderness and making the beauty of that wilderness more widely available by putting a tourist road through it. Another example might be where a nurse experiences conflict between his or her caring for an elderly, suffering, and terminally ill patient and his or her caring for the value of life. This is the kind of dilemma which is almost paradigmatic of those which generate moral reflection and debate.

But the apparent intractability of such dilemmas as these stems from their being discussed as nothing more than conflicts within the fourth level of our being, conflicts between ideals or moral obligations. Such dilemmas would not seem so intractable if we remembered that they occur at the fourth level of a whole person's being as a caring-about-others and a self-project. What this means is that they are not theoretical problems which belong solely to that mode of thinking and reflection that occurs at the fourth level of our being. They are practical problems. A person must make a decision, and this decision is not simply a thoughtful resolution of a dilemma, but a decision about what to do. What the person does will be the expression and determination of his or her caring and commitment, not the expression of his or her having solved a problem in moral theory. The decision may be experienced as an attempt to "do the right thing" in that situation of dilemma, but prereflexively it will have the aim of maintaining the integrity of one's self-project and caring-about-others at all four levels of one's being and of communicating to the world how this might be done in a similar situation.

Our integration and fulfillment as a self-project and caring-about-others is the aim of all our authentic ethical actions. This integration is within and between the levels of our being, and this fulfillment is at once the fulfillment of our self-project and of our caring-about-others. In situations that involve no dilemma, this aim or project need give rise to no anguish or even reflection. But where dilemmas do arise, they threaten this primordial aim of our caring. Dilemmas are not simply theoretical moral puzzles but threats to our very integrity. It is for this reason that our whole being is engaged by them and that an air of importance, urgency, and even anguish attaches to them. And it is for this reason, in turn, that they are the stuff of traditional morality. Moral theory is important to us and is charged with helping us to resolve moral dilemmas because our integrity and fulfillment as persons is important to us. But we should not make the mistake of thinking that moral theory can resolve dilemmas by offering us generalised guidelines or norms. Moral dilemmas can only be resolved by action and commitment, because it is only these that can integrate our being.

One might object that if both sides of a practical dilemma originate in me, then there is a sense in which it is true that I always do what I want to do, whether I "do the right thing" or not. But if the person who eats the cheesecake does what he wants to do and the person who does not eat it also does what she wants to do, albeit that she responds to a more creditable want, then how do we explain the difference? And why do we accord more respect to the person who does "the right thing"? And how do we explain the sense of obligation which that person feels which leads her to act in that way?

As I have indicated, one way to explain this is in terms of the levels of our being. We desire many different and incompatible things, and we have goals and objectives at a number of different levels of our existence. Our bodily needs and desires may conflict with our ideals and with one another, and the various ideals we hold dear may be incompatible. Of course, it is true that whenever we act freely (as opposed to acting under hypnotic suggestion, for example), we act on the basis of some motivation that we actually have. In other words, we do what we want to do. (Remember that wants are not simply blind desires or drives but expressions of *phronesis*. They are desires shaped by reason.)

But in situations where we are inclined towards both of two options which a situation offers us, we must choose. Traditional moral theory would introduce practical reason as the arbiter at this point. But as Kant has shown, the only value in light of which pure reason can decide is pure consistency. In my view, the choice will have to arise from our motivations or commitments. But it would be an error to suppose that such commitments operate at a level of our existence which allows them to adjudicate between the conflicting wants.

A model of human being which comprises a number of discrete levels can explain the conflicts which give rise to dilemmas, but not the resolution. I must be able to decide which of my wants is more important, and if this decision were to arise from a specific level of my being, then that level would be in control of the others, and this would deny the holism which is central to my model. Rather, in making such a decision, I either make one option more important or declare that I have discovered it to be so. This constitutes making a commitment. Such a commitment cannot arise from any one of the levels unless we think that this one level controls the others. Rather, such a commitment arises through the levels of my being from my primordial caring. The twin aspects of this caring, my self-project and my caring-about-others, are fulfilled when I commit myself to act and when this action is authentically mine, as opposed to being an instance of self-deception. Yet having said all this, I must acknowledge that the fourth level of our being is of special significance. It is the level at which we express the culturally formed reflexive articulation of our aim towards fulfillment as a self-project and a caring-about-others.

The notion of my being as caring points to an ontological comportment towards the world which leads us to act. It is a dynamism in our whole being which is more foundational even than our internal reasons. Bernard Williams is right to question the role of external reasons by pointing to the inner life of the agent as the proper locus of our practical reasons,[2] but he does not say enough about the motivations and action-initiating factors in an agent's character. Being ethical does not consist of obeying rules or following maxims and reasons, even internal reasons; it consists of having commitments which lead one to action (even in the cases where their actual enactment is frustrated by circumstances). This is not to deny, of course, that internal reasons are not of importance to agents. One must articulate what one is committed to and what one cares about so as to make one's behaviour consistent in the pursuit of those goals over time.

This is the role of the fourth level of our being and, more specifically, of moral thinking. Given that we are reflexive beings and given that we are sometimes troubled by crises or dilemmas, we must be able to see that we are acting consistently with our faith and our commitments. Giving oneself maxims or reasons to act and creating for oneself ideals of character which one seeks to realise, and doing so with appropriate regard to one's social ethos, are methods for achieving this consistency. In these ways one's actions can be made to deliberately express one's commitments. In these ways, one will have internal reasons to actor internal rules to follow. But the motivational force behind these reasons or rules will be one's caring.

Yet we do sometimes have the feeling that the higher levels of our existence are foreign to us in some way, that they are not as intimately owned by us as our more imperious and lower desires. Our ideals sometimes seem to be impositions from which we would shake ourselves free, especially when we become aware of them in the form of moral norms. The explanation for this impression is that our ideals and commitments are formed in us as part of our upbringing, whereas many of our more immediate desires belong to our biological natures. And we feel we own our biological natures more fully and intimately than we own our socialisation. We might want to be independent of the latter, but we normally cannot separate ourselves from the former.

This is a peculiarity of the modern condition for human beings. Most of the Western tradition from Plato to roughly the nineteenth century felt decidedly uncomfortable with the lower levels of human being. The subjugation of the body and its desires was felt to be the first step towards moral maturity, and sainthood was defined in terms of the degree to which persons could elevate themselves (sometimes literally) above their worldly existence. Perhaps the modern suspicion of high ideals and the celebration of physicality is a reaction to all this.

Crises and dilemmas give rise to moral thinking because they lead us to question ourselves at the spiritual level of our being. If we accept the view that morality is primarily concerned with interpersonal harmony and the requirements of sociability, then the modality of our being that is centrally involved in morality would be our caring-about-others. However, insofar as it is our ethical self-image and our faith which we enact when we act ethically, we are also expressing our self-project. When we fulfill our so-called moral obligations, we are fulfilling our demands upon ourselves and putting into effect our self-grounded commitments. We are pursuing what is important to us and living out our faith. We are pursuing our integrity. Even when a great many of the projects we pursue are directed towards the welfare and benefit of others, it is our own sense of self and of what is most important to us that provides the prereflexive aim and motivational impetus.

It follows that rather than supposing that it is solely our caring-about-others which grounds morality, it is also our self-project. We should recall the Aristotelian insight that ethics is centrally concerned with the fulfillment of the agent's own life. Although Aristotle is not unmindful of social harmony and the requirements of sociability, his primary focus in his *Ethics* is upon the individual agent. His understanding of ethics is that it is a discourse focused upon guidelines for effective living. Social harmony is a consequence of the fulfillment that individuals achieve if they live their lives effectively and wisely.

Other moral ideals may similarly be interpreted as expressions of our deep caring as self-project. A great part of the European tradition of moral thought has concerned itself with how individual agents stand in relation to the judgment of God upon their actions. Again, talk of the rights of individual conscience implies a recognition of the self-referential nature of much of our moral discourse. Phrases such as "being true to oneself" or "owing it to oneself to do X" give expression to this self-directed orientation in our practical lives.

However much trouble philosophers seem to have with the notion of our having duties towards ourselves, popular sentiment certainly recognises the idea that we can impose standards and expectations upon ourselves. This accounts for the difference between shame and guilt. Shame is the feeling that may be aroused in me by others when public expectations or norms are flouted, whereas guilt is the feeling that is aroused in me by myself when I feel myself to have failed to live up to my own expectations. The co-presence of shame and guilt in our lives reflects the duality of our deep caring as a caring-about-others and as a self-project.

Freedom and Integrity

In Chapter 7, I raised the question of freedom by asking how ethical innovation or nonconformism was possible on the part of individuals or groups if those individuals or groups are formed by their cultures and their attitudes are set by the ethoses of those cultures. I suggested that one's internalised social ethos and one's primordial caring are not coextensive. Being as an infinity cannot be confined in its necessary historical form. I can now add that there is at least one overwhelming piece of evidence for the reality of our freedom. This is the phenomenon of moral dilemma. Moral dilemmas are not possible for agents whose paths are unequivocally laid out before them. Perhaps this phenomenon might also give us a further clue to the nature of our freedom.

I take a hermeneutic approach to understanding human freedom. This approach accepts that the ascription of freedom is an interpretation of human phenomena, whatever the causes of these phenomena at a physical, biological, or even psychological level. Like most interpretations, ascriptions of freedom will be based on judgments which are learned in the context of a specific culture and which may differ between cultures. Certain bureaucratic social work cultures may regard the indigent as having freely chosen their lifestyles (and therefore as deserving of the discomforts which these entail), whereas the needy themselves understand their actions as falling under the rule of necessity and ill fortune.

To overcome the conflicts of interpretation which my approach engenders, I add to it a phenomenological perspective. This approach seeks the criteria for ascribing freedom not in an observational mode, as when we ask of an action not our own whether it was voluntary or when we ask of an agent other than ourselves whether he or she was responsible, but rather in a reflexive mode, as when we ask these questions of ourselves. And we do not normally ask these questions of ourselves in quite these terms.

I do not typically ask whether I acted voluntarily or whether I was responsible for what I did. In most cases when I do not act voluntarily or was not responsible, I have no reason to ask myself these questions at all. I already know. If someone bumps me at a party and I spill my drink on the new carpet, others (especially those who had not noticed the bump) might ask whether I acted voluntarily, but I have no need to ask this of myself. I would know that spilling the drink was something that I was caused to do and that it was not an action of mine. I would not need to own this action as an action at all. In more formal language, I would know that this action was not an intentional action on my part.[3]

And my owning an action, or acknowledging it as my intentional action in reflection, is not only something that I do retrospectively. I might be in a situation which calls out to me for a response. I might be near that burning building with Fenelon inside and be the only person present. I might be near the cheesecake and be feeling hungry. I will know, in such situations, that it is up to me to act. I cannot say that the matter does not pertain to me. I must own the situation in the sense that I must act in it, and I must subsequently own the action I perform. And this means that if I do not act, I must own that too. To own an action or a call-to-action is to interpret it as genuinely mine. It is to accept responsibility for it. It is to acknowledge it as being apposite to my caring.

The traditional approach to freedom understands the word *freedom* as a noun: it is a faculty or a power that we have. In keeping with my earlier methodological suggestions, I propose that we understand freedom by using a verb. *Freedom,* unfortunately, does not easily translate into a verb. It does, however, translate into an adverb, and we can speak of "acting freely" in a given situation. This phrase might turn out to be coextensive with other phrases that I use, such as "acting ethically" and "acting authentically" or "acting with integrity." But there is a word which better approximates the nonexistent verb I am seeking. This is the verb *to own.* As I have already indicated, I propose that we explicate our freedom through a phenomenology of "owning" an action or a call-to-action that arises in a practical situation. I can argue for this negatively by saying that if I were literally caused to act, whether by external forces such as a bump on my arm or by internal forces such as an overwhelming desire for cheesecake, then I would not need to own my action, and this would show that I had not acted voluntarily or freely.

But the cheesecake example might leave one in doubt. Could I refuse to own this action and excuse myself from the blame or shame attached to eating that cheesecake on the grounds that overwhelming appetite caused me to eat it? To do so would be a classic case of bad faith. It is a consequence of my four-level model in which our feelings of hunger belong to us at the first level of our being that these feelings should be acknowledged as part of our wholeness as persons and therefore a constitutive part of our integrity. We should acknowledge these desires as aspects of our being, even if we agree that they run counter to our acknowledged intentions. As I indicated earlier, perhaps the only internal force which would genuinely allow us to excuse ourselves from responsibility is the internalised force of hypnosis. (And even here there are limits to what hypnotised agents can be made to do.) It follows that owning our actions is an ethical gesture expressive of our being as a self-project and constitutive of our integrity.

But we should be wary of this somewhat existential stress on our integrity, lest it seem like a stress on the individual and on the adherence of that individual to ideals, models of character, and moral imperatives. This would favour our being as self-project over our being as caring-about-others, and this would, in turn, give rise to a distorted notion of freedom. In traditional societies, one's most intimate identity was formed by the tribe, the village, or the clan of which one was a member. One could not have conceived of wanting to exist independently of this social formation. All one's wants were those dictated by the traditional social group. All one's aspirations and ideals were simply those of the group, and solidarity with the group was unquestionable. One could not but own the ideals and morals of one's society because they formed part of one's very identity. And, of course, one would not feel that they were imposed upon one either.

Today things are different. Due to the multifarious cultural and subcultural formations and the various ideals and ideologies that operate in our much larger societies, and due to the much more relaxed approach to pleasure, we are pulled in many directions. There is no longer a homogeneous set of norms and ideals which shapes each one of us, and there is no longer a single ideal character type displaying the right ordering of the levels of our being. Insofar as we seem able to choose our goals and ideals, we no longer feel as intimately bound to them, and our identities are not formed by them.

The fact that our identities are not entirely the product of our cultural formations leaves space for the idea of a self or a kernel of our being which would be the referee in this tug-of-war between conflicting values. Through the various cultural pressures and ideals to which I am subject, I begin to gain a new and modern sense of myself as the master of my own destiny, as the arbiter between the various and incommensurable ideals and values that I am constantly being taught to adopt. As a result, many of the ideals that I do adopt, and many of the commitments that I do make, will seem either to be the product of free choices on the part of this true self which resides somehow at the core of my being or to be external impositions upon this self. In the latter case, when I enact my deepest commitments, I will seem to be exercising free will by answering the call of duty or obeying an externally imposed command, whereas in the former, I will seem to be exercising free will by giving expression to my true self.

As we have already seen, I reject the moral realism in the notion of external commands, and my response to the notion of a true self existing at the core of my being is that it is yet another metaphysical postulate. My alternative thesis is that our selves are formed by our cultures on the basis of our biological and cognitive beings. Cultural formation envelops and transforms the first three levels of our existence and offers us ideals and aspirations by way of which we can enhance that formation through faith. At all levels of our existence, therefore, what we are is not something which we have as an essence but something which is formed in relation to our historical and cultural environment and which I can own in affirmation.

But this social formation involves more than simply having a fixed identity. That our identities are a function of social roles and situations is obvious. Our fundamental project of living life in a meaningful way, under the guidance of some leading ideals or aspirations, is made possible by the historical formation through which the four levels of our being are expressed. But these self-projects of ours must include a reflexive stance of either owning or not owning that very formation.

The idea of infinity which I have borrowed from Levinas captures this idea well. At the first three levels of our being, we are dialectically related to the causal influences of biology, sensibility, and acculturation. But we are not merely a projection towards, and a formation by, this causality. This realm of causality or facticity constitutes only my past and present. As I explained in Chapter 3, we also have a future. That towards which we project our being and that from which we receive our being is an infinite extension of facticity. It is the limitlessness of my horizons and the transcendence of the other, and it is the call to own and affirm these relationships at all the levels of my being.

One concrete form that this call takes is moral self-appraisal. We judge ourselves. We sometimes need to ask ourselves whether we would own what we have done or whether a situation calls us to our responsibility. Can we excuse ourselves from what we have done or from the responsibility of acting in a situation that confronts us? Although I have suggested that we know ourselves better than anyone else, so that we can easily know whether we intentionally spilled our drink or not, there will be morally complex actions and situations in which owning an action or call-to-action will be difficult for us. It depends on my ethical judgment of the action whether I approve of it. One may assume that it would be more difficult for me to own an action which I did not approve of. This shows that approving of an action of mine and owning it are two different acts. This also shows that if owning an action or a call-to-action is a way of interpreting ourselves as free, then the notion of freedom is not understood as a metaphysical or essential precondition for being and acting in a human way, but as an ethical challenge.

This links my interpretation of the notion of freedom to that of integrity. Traditionally, the question of free will has not been raised as a purely theoretical one in philosophical anthropology. Rather, it has been raised in the context of moral thinking as it pertains to the ascription of responsibility and the attribution of praise or blame. Kant was right when he said that moral thinking would have no point if we were not free, and Aristotle was right when he said that it would not be appropriate to praise or blame people for their actions if they did not act voluntarily. Freedom is not only postulated as an a priori condition for moral decision making; it has import for my self-project and ethical self-image. This freedom would need to be denied if I wanted to escape from moral blame.

Moral choice and moral guilt are the twin phenomenological sources of the discourse of freedom. I have already suggested that dilemmas and crises are the twin phenomenological sources of moral thinking. One can see the parallel here. Freedom and morality belong together in a discourse arising from the limitations of action-guiding arrangements as they operate at the first three levels of our being.

It would seem, then, that acknowledging an action or a call-to-action as mine is itself a moral stance through which I emerge into the fourth level of my being. Accepting responsibility in the sense of accepting the aptness of praise, blame, or guilt and in the sense of accepting that it is up to me to act in a given situation no matter what the pragmatic dangers or moral ambiguities is a moral stance which expresses my primordial caring in the twin forms of caring-about-others and self-project. Consequently, we need to ask under what conditions I would own an action or a call-to-action as mine. And what does it mean, morally speaking, when I do so? In what way does owning an action or a call-to-action express my caring and my commitments? And how does my owning actions in this way arise from the integrity of my being?

To answer these questions requires a discussion of the dialectic through which my identity is bound up with that of others, because it is this dialectic which displays the integrity of my being as a self-project and a caring-about-others and which I affirm in owning my life. If our social formation were complete, I could not but own those actions of mine performed consistently with that formation. In that case, the only actions I might not be inclined to own would be those which depart from the ethos and action-guiding arrangements of my social groupings and of which I myself had come to disapprove. This scenario would also deny the possibility of those cases where I depart from the social ethos but do so in the spirit of ethical innovation and with self-approval in light of my highest ideals. My owning my actions cannot be coextensive with social approval of my actions. But how can I move from the social formation that defines my identity at the four levels of my being if there is not some irreducible real self at the core of my being which would be the origin of such transcendence?

One way of answering this question is to advert to the fact that the social processes of person formation are processes that expand rather than constrain the possibilities of that person. This is consistent with widely held views on the value of education. Mere training develops functional reactions at the second level of our being. Education in particular and social person formation in general give people skills and knowledge which expand their pragmatic possibilities at the third level of their being. But education is also part of that higher cultural formation through which persons develop mature ideals, sound judgment, the ability to weigh competing claims arising from calls-to-action, and the faith that permits them to affirm life and stand by their commitments. It also allows them to reflect critically upon their societies and cultures and to develop alternative ethoses from which oppositional and innovative stances might be taken. All this is standard humanist doctrine.

What is not so often noted is that education in this rich and multilevel sense is necessarily conveyed by persons. Some people would describe the preceding passage as a process upon which individuals embark at their own initiative or into which they are inserted by history, without noticing that other persons are involved. Rats can be trained in mazes by the mere impersonal correlation of stimuli. But the education which the rhetoric of the previous paragraph describes must be imparted by other persons. I take it to be obvious that what is crucial to these educative processes is personal interaction. Even when we read an educative book, we are in contact with the thinking of another person. Essential to educative processes at all the four levels is the inspiration and example that one's teachers convey, even if indirectly through a text. It seems that personal formation in specific cultural and social contexts is always dependent on personal interaction.

Being sequestered with tribal elders was an important part of initiation in traditional societies. Even the highest ideals and deepest commitments through which we express our caring are elicited in us by others. Of course, the influence of inspirational others upon us may be indirect or mediated by tradition. Except in the case of immediate disciples, adherence to great moral teachings such as those of the Buddha, of Jesus, or of more recent sages is inspired without any physical personal contact.

It is striking how often people who come under the influence of great teachers — and even people who have merely undergone a mainstream educational experience — describe themselves as liberated by it. Indeed, we have already seen an explanation for this at a very early stage of a person's life. We noted that a young child's maturation depends on a psychological symbiosis or a moral order involving the acknowledgment of the autonomy of that child by significant adults. This constitutes a liberation for that child, mediated by other persons. At the more mature stage of a person's life, when the higher-level educative processes which I am alluding to take place, the influence of the educator on that person is likewise a development of freedom for that person.

Our ability to own our situations is not only the product of an individualistic existential self-project but of our relational and communicative being as a caring-about-others. Our ability to transcend our acculturation is not based on an irreducible self at the core of our being but on the liberation accorded by contact with others. Though the ontological basis for this is the duality of our being as caring-about-others and as self-project, it is the reality of the other which draws me to this freedom. As Levinas has argued, the infinity of the other makes me infinite.

Those who hold a solipsistic model of education in which relatively mature individuals embark on a journey of self-formation and make use of formal and informal educational opportunities to expand the dimensions of their being might object that such a project is pre-eminently the expression of our caring in the form of self-project. But that such an educative journey cannot be taken without the stimulus, inspiration, and acknowledgment of significant others shows that our caring in the form of caring-about-others is equally implicated. The presence of another person in my life is as educative and formative of my caring in my mature years as it was when I was a child. My relationship with significant others is an expansion of my being and, as such, a formation of my being.

But what is the argument for the claim that education as mediated by significant others is an expansion of my being and a source of freedom for me?

This argument is simply Levinas's point that the other is infinity and that the relationship between the other and me is one of communication and speech.[4] The infinity of the other calls me to my infinity; the transcendence of the other opens me to my infinite horizons. Education is but the most formal of the many social processes and interactions in which this call is heard. It is a form of that dialectic through which I have both my identity and the possibility of owning that identity.

This notion of infinity also gives us an alternative explication for the concept of freedom. The term that Levinas contrasts with infinity is *totality*, a term he borrows from Hegel, with whose philosophical anthropology he strongly disagrees. For Hegel, the processes of person making which I have been describing are to be understood as expressions of the self-development of Reason in history such that individuals find and fulfill their destiny to the extent that they take their proper place in History and the State. I do not have room here to render this view plausible, nor do I need to. It is enough to note, as Kierkegaard has so famously done,[5] that this view renders the individual subservient to history and without any but a spurious autonomy. The individual is inserted into, and subject to, a historical and rational totality. It is also interesting to speculate that Hegel's position is the most elaborate working out of the moralistic rationalism inherent in Kant, in which freedom consists precisely in a rational subservience to a universal Law.

However this might be, Levinas argues against this Hegelian conception by proposing that persons partake of a quality of infinity. Persons are not to be limited to the totality which would embrace them. Human beings can live with limitless horizons. Though this may be thought to be a reformulation of the familiar Kantian thesis that individuals have a dimension which transcends their facticity and allows them to participate in a Kingdom of Ends, it differs from this in being a phenomenological thesis rather than a transcendental one. Whereas Kant's doctrine of freedom depends on a transcendental argument in which reason postulates the reality of freedom in order to render intelligible the phenomenon of morality, Levinas claims the experiences of the face of the other and of speech as phenomenological evidence for his view.[6]

Infinity is freedom. It is as if the four-level model I have been developing could be seen as a building with four stories but no roof. If to be as a human being can be understood as a striving through and in the four levels of our being towards our own self-realisation and towards our solidarity with others, and if we use the notion of height to say that this striving is upwards, then our infinity means that this striving has no upper limit. And insofar as it has no upper limit, it is free.

By saying this, I do not mean that our striving meets with no frustration. Daily life is fraught with disappointments and hindrances. A great many of our projects fail or are thwarted. Freedom does not mean omnipotence. Our infinity does not deny our finitude. There is no denying that my death will bring my pursuit of infinite aims and my caring about the infinity in others to an end and that this is a finitude that negates infinity. However, I do not characteristically intend that death. I am called to be resolute in the face of its inevitability, as Heidegger says,[7] and I live my life beyond it.

This does not mean that we ignore death and falsely live as if it were not our terminus. It means that our primordial caring is expressed as a faith that life is to be affirmed despite the negation of death. Our lives ignore death only in the sense that we pursue goals and values greater and more lasting than ourselves. Our deaths would only be problematic and negative for us if we were preoccupied solely with ourselves as isolated individual self-projects. But the infinity of our self-project and our caring-about-others is our projective reach beyond this limit. The traditional concern for immortality was not simply an extension of our first-level concern for survival or a fantasy of denial, but a fourth-level concern for transcendence and infinity. This is the limitless extension of my self-project which I must embrace if I am to be true to myself as infinite, and true to those others who have made me so; it is also the limitless extension of my caring-about-others which I must embrace if I am to be true to the call to responsibility which the infinity of others directs towards me. Our faiths and our ethical commitments are expressions of our deep primordial caring.

Levinas's concepts have allowed us to see that these faiths and commitments are expressions of our infinite horizons and of our freedom. But does this mean that the explication of freedom should be offered in terms of the open-endedness and limitlessness of my being, where this is an ontological interpretation of my being as caring? Such an analysis would be more adjectival than verbal. In pursuit of a concept of freedom that characterises a mode of my being, I have suggested that our freedom should be understood as owning our actions and the calls-to-action that are directed towards us in given situations.

Can we now understand our willingness to own our actions and responsibilities to be grounded in our seeing these actions and these calls-to-action as according with our faiths and commitments? I will doubtlessly own any action or call-to-action which accords with my caring in this way. But this suggestion grounds our freedom on judgment. It would be akin to seeing an action as falling under a moral principle. What we are seeking to describe is not a judgment but a feeling of harmony, of integrity, or of peace with ourselves which accompanies our action. It would be the experience of the fulfillment of our being as self-project and caring-about-others, the opposite of guilt.

I suggest that we can own those actions and calls-to-action which express our caring as self-project and caring-about-others at all four levels of our being. The key term here is *express*. The experience I seek to describe is not the result of reflection and self-appraisal. It is the phenomenological accompaniment of the direct flow of our practical lives from our commitments and caring. Our freedom is to be understood as our ability to situate our projects within the openness and infinity of our determinable caring so as to focus and form it historically. It is not a matter of judging that our projects accord with an already formed caring; it is a matter of forming that care through our projects in a way that constitutes the integrity of that caring through time.

But this view does present a difficulty. The primordial disposition of caring is determinable by any action I perform and any commitment I make. In this view, freedom has become authenticity in the sense that I can own any action which flows from my whole being. The only difference between this and classic existentialism is that this whole being includes both the first three levels of my being, where facticity has influence, and the caring-about-others upon which my affections, responsibilities, and will to communicate are based.

Many people have argued that there is no basis in classical existentialism for moral discrimination and therefore anything is permissible. The only solution I can offer to this problem is that whereas classical existentialism sees choice as springing from a sheer nondeterminate subjectivity which provides no basis or direction for that choice, I posit a whole being which includes the first three levels as well as the fourth. The social formation and purposes of the ethical agent provide an agenda which shapes the primordial caring of that agent in light of historical exigencies. The matrix of affections and responsibilities which the cultural formation of all persons establishes on the ground of their caring comes to expression in those actions which answer the call of those affections and responsibilities. Those actions which do not are deviant or pathological. The fourth level of our being is that sphere of reflection which gives agents a basis for discriminating between those culturally available actions which express their deep caring as self-project and caring-about-others and those which do not. Such discriminations will be articulated in light of the agent's ideals, faiths, and moral commitments.

But even these are cultural products. It is because our deep caring is ever underdetermined by our acculturation, because we are infinite, that we remain free despite this formation. But this transcendent quality of deep caring is effectively different from the nothingness which is the origin of authenticity in existentialist doctrine only in that it is situated within facticity.

To those who find the absence of objective moral guidelines disturbing here, I would reply that I do not consider it to be the task of philosophy to stipulate what is right and what is wrong on the basis of moral theory. However, I can indicate that my view does not imply a complete moral anarchy by finally offering a solution to our problem of moral dilemma. Moral dilemmas of the sort that inhibit action are usually thought to arise when our reasons clash. We consider ourselves to have reasons to act in one way and also to have reasons to act in a different and incompatible way. The discourse of moral theory then seeks to give us a set of higher-order reasons, or a set of principles, in light of which an agent can adjudicate between the competing reasons. But if these higher-order principles do not accord with the agent's commitments, then they will be an external imposition, which my arguments have already rejected. The discourse of reasons and principles seems not to assist agents in dilemma.

The reason for this is now plain. I argue that moral dilemmas arise when our commitments clash. Our reflection on such situations may establish reasons as the articulation of these conflicting commitments so that the dilemma is described as a clash of reasons, but these reasons will be the internal expressions of my caring just as they are in nonconflictual situations. But if my caring and the given situation create for me two mutually exclusive calls-to-action both of which fully accord with my ultimate commitments and infinite strivings, then how could my commitments also ground a reason which might adjudicate between them? Would not such a metareason simply be another reason to add to one side of the dilemma or the other? If my operative reasons are owned by me as authentically mine, then what higher status could an adjudicating reason have?

The answer, of course, is that it is not a reason but choice which is needed. I simply have to opt for one horn of the dilemma rather than the other. But when I do so, does this show that I care about the persons relevant to that horn of the dilemma more than I care about the persons implicated in the other, or that I care more about the moral identity that would come to expression in one course of action than that which I would realise for myself in the other? No. Neither my caring-about-others nor my self-project are static and determinate bases for my choice and my action in this way. These two aspects of my being as caring are constantly dynamic, constantly being realised in the way I live.

A dilemma is a fork in the road of life's journey which might give me pause, but I must travel on, and I both express and further specify my caring by choosing to take one road rather than another. I do not act in one way rather than the other because I see that action as according more fully with my commitments and caring, as if my commitments were given facts about me to which I must be true. My action directly expresses and enacts that commitment and caring.

And what is this deep caring apart from my action? It is not a fact about me but an ever determinable orientation of my being. It is the way I face the world, the way I strive, as well as an orientation towards what I strive for. It is realised in action. It is not a predetermined mental state or disposition against which I must measure my action or into harmony with which I must bring it. It is open-ended. It is aptly described by Wollheim as instinct,[8] if by this we understand not a biological determination but an open and ever determinable prereflexive disposition. In nonambiguous situations, my actions and commitments simply flow from this disposition and are determined by the situation. In situations of dilemma, the determinations that would shape my caring are ambiguous. I must choose.

But my choice is just as much an expression of my being in all its levels and in both of its orientations as would be a free-flowing action. In either case, in doing what I do, I express my caring as self-project and as caring-about-others. But only in cases of dilemma do I also create my being. All my actions express and form my caring, but only my actions in situations of dilemma present me with the need to own and acknowledge this, because only these actions ask me to add a new direction to the formation of my being through time. Only dilemmas call for explicit commitment.

That this new element is present is ironically shown by the air of crisis and regret which attaches to dilemmas. If only one responsibility can be met and the other must be rejected, I will have regret. But I will have no cause for guilt, because only one thing could be done. I advanced my self-project and answered the call of my caring-about-others. But I could commit myself to only one horn of the dilemma. I was not true to my self or to a preformed commitment in a way that I would not have been if I had followed the other horn of the dilemma. A dilemma is a scale with equal weights. In that situation, I must express my caring in choice rather than in that action that seems natural and obvious. I cannot accede to all the responsibilities that I own and still act. I can only create.

This also allows us to solve our problem of ethical innovation. It follows from what I have said about choice that morality is frequently creative. Moral creativity and innovation are the most striking expressions of my being as freedom. Insofar as I genuinely create my being when I act in dilemmas, I can neither explain nor justify what I have done. I can only discover in yet greater detail the infinity and openness of my caring. After all, if I can explain and justify the action with reasons, then I could have acted in the light of those reasons in the first place, and there would not have been a dilemma. Unless, of course, I justify the action in light of the outcome. But this would be an appeal to good fortune rather than moral discrimination.

When two others who are equally important to me and who are in situations of equal urgency call out to my responsibility, my caring must respond out of its own infinity. One of those others must become more important to me and one of those situations more urgent. I am called upon to exercise ethical creativity. Many would understand freedom as being precisely the possibility of this creativity. But this begs the question of whether such creativity has a basis in the instinct and cultural formation which constitute the four levels of my being. Both this creativity and this formation are necessary, given that the basic aims of my being as deep caring are ever determinable. My claim is that freedom will consist in my ability, despite regret for the option not taken, to own the option that was. This constitutes my freedom and integrity. The phenomenological reflexive evidence of this ability will include self-esteem and commitment. One will believe in one's choice, and one will want to exhort others to it.

If commitment is the reflexive expression of caring as self-project and caring-about-others, then it involves integrity, because integrity is a reflexive acknowledgment of the subjective unity of that commitment and that caring. Perhaps this is what Nietzsche means by the notion of self-overcoming. We must acknowledge what we are in terms of our cultural formation, and yet we must be prepared to go beyond this by way of ethical innovation when our caring and situations demand this of us.

My commitment and freedom have communicative meaning. My infinity calls up the infinity of the other. In my integrity, I send out a mute example for others to follow. But we should not confuse that communicative and hortatory dimension of commitment with the moral self-righteousness of those who would impose their moral beliefs on others or be intolerant of ethical difference. Moral self-righteousness does not arise from a fulfillment of caring through ethical creativity but from a determination to bring one's own behaviour and choice into line with a fixed and predetermined faith. It would be akin to the judgment which I rejected earlier that one's actions conformed to one's caring, where this caring was forced to adopt the form of a standard of behaviour or character. To adhere to and protect a moral self-image which is a concretised historical expression of my self-project is to deny my infinity and freedom. This would be fanaticism. It is this stance, the protection of my own moral purity, which is rightly criticised as moral insensitivity.

There is an argument against pacifism which holds that it fails to take seriously the need to protect from aggression those who are bound to one by ties of affection or responsibility, and that this failure arises from an excessive and egotistical preoccupation on the part of pacifists with their own moral commitments and integrity.[9] But pacifism is not important because pacifists want to retain a pure conscience by not fighting, but because even in the face of urgent and important calls upon their responsibility, they want to deliver a moral message — that peaceful means must continue to be sought even in the face of unforgivable aggression. This would be a stance of moral creativity and caring-about-others, rather than a self-centred and fanatical protection of the moral self-image which might be thought to express one's self-project.

The pacifist faces a dilemma and solves it by choosing, just as a soldier faces the same dilemma and solves it by choosing differently. Neither is more right than the other. Both are moral and free. To be moral is to be free because it is to choose creatively and with commitment. Such a choice expresses one's caring. Either choice is also communicative in intent. Indeed, this is the basis of the importance of the pacifist's position, as it is of any authentic moral nonconformism. These commitments display the possibility of moral creativity and therefore of the infinity and freedom which are manifest at the spiritual levels of human being.

Such ethical creativity is also displayed when I choose differently from one situation to the next. It is a consequence of the objectivist, universalist, rationalist, and impartial moral stances of the Kantian tradition that like situations should fall under general moral principles in like ways and should thereby elicit like actions. If it is wrong to procure an abortion in one case, then it is wrong to procure an abortion in any other case. Or, to put it in a more familiar form, if it is wrong in itself to procure an abortion, then it is always wrong, no matter what the distinguishing circumstances of a specific case. The latter formula makes the stronger statement, because the earlier statement could be countered by the quite valid observation that no two circumstances are ever exactly alike. Each person who might be seeking an abortion has a distinct biography and a unique set of circumstances. What applies to one need not apply to another. It is because of this that the Kantian tradition and the earlier natural law tradition sought to articulate general principles under which all relevant cases should be judged.

But the person who cares approaches the matter differently. It is the particular and unique features of a case to which such a person will be sensitive. Such a person will attend to the needs of the other and seek to respond to their own caring as self-project and caring-about-others. This may produce dilemmas, especially if the caregiver also adheres to moral guidelines and culturally approved ideals. But if an ethical choice is inherently creative and expressive of the infinity of the agent, then there will be no reason to expect that caring persons will feel bound either by ethical expectations, perceived moral rules, or even their own moral self-understandings and consciences as established in previous cases. What caring motivates is a creative and caring response to what is important and urgent in the particular situation.

So, do I create myself in harmony with what I already am when my action arises from my caring? If so, I would not be creative. How, then, can I own the action as mine? But I have not argued that this owning is based on such harmony. Rather, it must create it. My self-project and my caring-about-others are dynamic. I own what I do when what I do continues and expresses that dynamism. If I am in harmony with any being, it is with the being that I am not yet. This being is a being which I project. It is my unformed future. My search for integrity, which is the determinable aim constituting the infinitely deep foundation of our being, is not simply an attempt to coordinate my past into a meaningful biographical narrative. It also projects forward in time and consequently must always include a creative dimension.

But because my integrity includes the continuity of my life as project from the past into the future, this creativity is not radical. Those existentialists who argue that we choose out of a radical nothingness are both right and wrong. We choose out of our infinity. Logically, there is much in common between choosing out of open-endedness and choosing out of nothing. But nothing contains nothing out of which one can choose, whereas open-endedness is the open-endedness of a full four-level being embracing the biological drives and needs, the cultural upbringing, the right to autonomy, and the sharing of practical projects. This is still freedom, but it has a basis. We live our lives as moral and ethical beings in expression of what we are. But when we choose, we express the creativity of an infinite and ever determinable being. Only situations of dilemma can demonstrate this to us, as Sartre himself saw with his example of the student who had to choose between going to war or looking after his mother.[10] It is when the other or the situation calls me to it that I create moral innovation. We freely express our self-project and our caring-about-others as we act ethically within the infinitude of our moral horizons.

Notes

Introduction

1. See, for example, Alasdair MacIntyre, *After Virtue: A Study in Moral Theory*, London, Duckworth, 1981, and Bernard Williams, *Ethics and the Limits of Philosophy*, London, Collins, 1985.

2. See, for example, Bernard Williams, *Morality: An Introduction to Ethics*, Cambridge, England, Cambridge University Press, 1972, Chapter 1.

3. For example, Peter Singer, *Practical Ethics*, Cambridge, England, Cambridge University Press, 1979, pp. 219ff.

4. For a seminal work in this new tradition, see Carol Gilligan, *In a Different Voice: Psychological Theory and Women's Development*, Cambridge, Mass., Harvard University Press, 1982. Also relevant is Nell Noddings, *Caring: A Feminine Approach to Ethics and Moral Education*, Berkeley, University of California Press, 1984.

5. Aristotle, *The Nicomachean Ethics*, Book 6, 1139b22–1139b26.

6. Bernard Williams, *Ethics and the Limits of Philosophy*, Chapter 10.

7. I have discussed this issue in the context of Williams's theses in Stan van Hooft, "Obligation, Character, and Commitment," *Philosophy* 63 (1988), pp. 345–362.

8. Williams, *Ethics and the Limits of Philosophy*, p. 188, is concerned with "a 'must' that is unconditional and *goes all the way down*." (The italics are Williams's own.)

9. Jeffrey Blustein, *Caring and Commitment: Taking the Personal Point of View*, New York, Oxford University Press, 1991.

10. Ibid., p. 141.

11. Ibid., p. 134 (my emphasis).

12. Ibid., p. 91.

13. Ibid., p. 48.

14. Ibid., p. 49 (emphasis in the original).

15. Ibid., p. 52.

16. Ibid., p. 75.

17. Ibid., pp. 126ff.

18. Ibid., p. 127.

19. Ibid., p. 129.

Chapter 1: Commitment

1. Kai Nielsen, "Morality and Commitment," *Ideal Studies* 7 (1977), pp. 94–107, p. 97.

2. Leszek Kolakowski, *Religion,* Oxford, England, Oxford University Press, 1982, p. 203.

3. Ibid., p. 218.

4. Stuart Hampshire, "Public and Private Morality," in Stuart Hampshire (ed.), *Public and Private Morality,* Cambridge, England, Cambridge University Press, 1978, p. 44.

5. Ibid., p. 47.

6. Ibid.

7. Gabriele Taylor, "Integrity," *Proceedings of the Aristotelian Society (Supp.)* 55 (1981), pp. 143–159, p. 156.

8. Hampshire, "Morality and Pessimism," *Public and Private Morality.*

9. Peter Singer offers a similar answer in Chapter 10 of his *Practical Ethics,* Cambridge, England, Cambridge University Press, 1979.

10. Jean-Paul Sartre, "Existentialism Is a Humanism," reprinted in W. Kaufmann (ed.), *Existentialism From Dostoevsky to Sartre,* rev. and exp. ed., New York: World Publishing, 1956.

11. Basil Mitchell, *Morality: Religious and Secular,* Oxford, England, Oxford University Press, 1980, p. 10.

12. Taylor, "Integrity," p. 144.

13. I discuss the issue of weakness of will in Stan van Hooft, "Weakness of Will," *The Southern Journal of Philosophy* 26, no. 3 (1988), pp. 403–421.

14. Hampshire, "Morality and Pessimism," *Public and Private Morality,* p. 15.

Chapter 2: Caring

1. Nell Noddings, *Caring: A Feminine Approach to Ethics and Moral Education,* Berkeley, University of California Press, 1984, p. 25.

2. Examples include Simone M. Roach, "The Act of Caring as Expressed in a Code of Ethics," *Canadian Nurse* 78 (June 1982), pp. 30–32; J. Watson, *Nursing: Human Science and Human Care: A Theory of Nursing,* Norwalk, Conn., Appleton-Century-Crofts, 1985; Barbara A. Carper, "The Ethics of Caring," *Advances in Nursing Science* 1 (April 1979), pp. 11–20; Doris J. Riemen, "The Essential Structure of a Caring Interaction: A

Phenomenological Study," Ph.D. diss., Texas Women's University, Ann Arbor, Michigan, University Microfilms International, 1983; B. Blattner, *Holistic Nursing*, Englewood Cliffs, N.J., Prentice-Hall, 1981; M. Leininger, *Caring: An Essential Human Need, Proceedings of Three National Caring Conferences*, Thorofare, N.J., Charles B. Slack, 1981, and *Care: The Essence of Nursing and Health*, Thorofare, N.J., Charles B. Slack, 1984; Anne P. Griffin, "A Philosophical Analysis of Caring in Nursing," *Journal of Advanced Nursing* 8 (1983), pp. 289-295.

3. For example, Eike-Henner W. Kluge, "Nursing: Vocation or Profession," *Canadian Nurse* 78 (February 1982), pp. 34-36; Peter Nokes, *The Professional Task in Welfare Practice*, London, Routledge and Kegan Paul, 1967; George J. Agich, "Professionalism and Ethics in Health Care," *Journal of Medicine and Philosophy* 5 (September 1980), pp. 186-199; W. Gustafson, "Motivational and Historical Aspects of Care and Nursing," in Leininger, *Caring*. I discuss these issues in Stan van Hooft, "Caring and Professional Commitment," *The Australian Journal of Advanced Nursing* 4, no. 4 (June-August 1987), pp. 29-38.

4. Milton Mayeroff, *On Caring*, New York, Harper & Row, 1971.

5. Ibid., p. 48.

6. Noddings, *Caring*.

7. Robert C. Solomon stresses the cognitive element in emotions in *The Passions: The Myth and Nature of Human Emotion*, Notre Dame, Ind., University of Notre Dame Press, 1983, especially Chapter 3.

8. Harry Frankfurt, "The Importance of What We Care About," *Synthèse* 53, no. 2 (1982), pp. 257-272.

9. Ibid., p. 260.

10. Bernard Williams, *Ethics and the Limits of Philosophy*, London, Collins, 1985, p. 183.

11. Frankfurt, "The Importance of What We Care About," pp. 260-261.

12. It is for this reason that some of the literature concerned with professional caring makes use (I think inappropriately) of Martin Buber's description of "I-Thou" relationships.

13. Richard Wollheim, *The Thread of Life*, Cambridge, England, Cambridge University Press, 1984, Chapter 2.

14. Ibid., p. 60.

15. Ludwig Wittgenstein, *Philosophical Investigations*, Oxford, England, Basil Blackwell, 1963, (I, 620).

Chapter 3: On Being Human

1. The central text supporting my hypothesis is Martin Heidegger, *Being and Time,* John Macquarrie and Edward Robinson (trans.), Oxford, England, Basil Blackwell, 1973, Sections 64–65.

2. Aristotle, *The Nicomachean Ethics,* Book 1, 1102a5–1103a4.

3. My model also owes some inspiration to Karl Jaspers, who, although he does not speak of caring, develops a four-level model of human existence by saying, "In every form of his being man is related to something other than himself: as a being to his world, as consciousness to object, as spirit to the idea of whatever constitutes totality, as Existenz to Transcendence" ("On My Philosophy," Felix Kaufmann [trans.], in Walter Kaufmann [ed.], *Existentialism From Dostoevsky to Sartre,* rev. and exp. ed., New York, New American Library, 1975, p. 168).

4. Edward O. Wilson, *Sociobiology: The New Synthesis,* Cambridge, Mass., Harvard University Press, 1966. For further uncompromising statements, see David P. Barash, *Sociobiology: The Whisperings Within,* London, Collins, 1979, and Richard D. Alexander, *Darwinism and Human Affairs,* Washington, D.C., University of Washington Press, 1979.

5. Sociobiology Study Group of Science for the People, "Sociobiology — Another Biological Determinism," in Arthur L. Caplan (ed.), *The Sociobiology Debate,* New York, Harper & Row, 1978. *The New York Review of Books* also carried a number of vehement reviews of Wilson's work, such as Stuart Hampshire's review of Wilson's *On Human Nature* in the October 12, 1978, edition.

6. E. O. Wilson and C. J. Lumsden, *Genes, Mind, and Culture: The Coevolutionary Process,* Cambridge, Mass., Harvard University Press, 1981.

7. For example, Michael Ruse, *Sociobiology: Sense or Nonsense?* Dordrecht, Netherlands, D. Reidel Publishing, 1979; Roger Trigg, *The Shaping of Man: Philosophical Aspects of Sociobiology,* Oxford, England, Basil Blackwell, 1982; Gunther S. Stent (ed.), *Morality as a Biological Phenomenon,* Berkeley, University of California Press, 1978; Neil Tennant, "Evolutionary Versus Evolved Ethics," *Philosophy* 58 (1983), pp. 289–302; and Michael Ruse, "The Morality of the Gene," *Monist* 67 (1984), pp. 167–199.

8. Joseph S. Alper, "Facts, Values, and Biology," *The Philosophical Forum* 13, nos. 2–3 (1981–1982), pp. 85–108.

9. J. P. Chaplin's *Dictionary of Psychology,* New York, Dell Publishing, 1968, defines a trait as "a relatively persistent and consistent behaviour pattern manifested in a wide range of circumstances, or a biological characteristic."

10. John R. Searle, "Sociobiology and the Explanation of Behavior," in M. S. Gregory, A. Silvers, and D. Sutch (eds.), *Sociobiology and Human Nature,* San Francisco, Jossey-Bass, 1978, pp. 164–182.

11. This thesis contradicts the central premises of the empiricist tradition. It is most fully elaborated by Maurice Merleau-Ponty in his *Phenomenology of Perception,* Colin Smith (trans.), London, Routledge and Kegan Paul, 1962.

12. Heidegger, *Being and Time*, Section 16.

13. This point is thoroughly argued by Robert C. Solomon in his *The Passions: The Myth and Nature of Human Emotion*, Notre Dame, Ind., University of Notre Dame Press, 1983.

14. Merleau-Ponty, *Phenomenology of Perception*, p. 156.

15. Abraham Maslow, "A Theory of Metamotivation: The Biological Rooting of the Value-Life," *The Journal of Humanistic Psychology* 7, no. 2 (Fall 1967), pp. 93–127.

16. In his *Nietzsche: Life as Literature*, Cambridge, Mass., Harvard University Press, 1985, Chapter 6, Alexander Nehamas argues that Nietzsche has a position like this one.

17. Aristotle suggests that a fulfilled life is one where we can, in looking back over life in old age, judge it to be so. *Nicomachean Ethics*, Book 1, 1098a18.

18. Heidegger, *Being and Time*, Sections 50ff.

19. Apart from Heidegger's *Being and Time*, the most notable example is Jean-Paul Sartre, *Being and Nothingness: A Phenomenological Essay on Ontology*, Hazel Barnes (trans.), New York, Philosophical Library, 1956. Arguably the originator of this way of thinking was Nietzsche, with his dictum that we should "become who we are" (*The Gay Science*, Walter Kaufmann [trans.] New York, Random House, 1974, paragraph 270).

20. Even Nietzsche still spoke in these terms in his essay "Schopenhauer as Educator."

21. Rom Harré, *Personal Being: A Theory for Individual Psychology*, Oxford, England, Basil Blackwell, 1983, Chapter 9.

22. Plato, *The Republic*, Part 5, Section 2.

23. Aristotle, *Nichomachean Ethics*, Book 1.

Chapter 4: Caring-About-Others

1. Jean-Paul Sartre, *Being and Nothingness: A Phenomenological Essay on Ontology*, Hazel Barnes (trans.), New York, Philosophical Library, 1956, Part 3, Chapter 1, Section 4: "The Look."

2. Immanuel Kant made this claim in his *Lectures on Ethics*, Louis Infield (trans.), New York, Harper & Row, 1963, p. 164. Modern versions of this view have been put by Thomas Nagel in his "Sexual Perversion," *The Journal of Philosophy* 66, no. 1 (1969), pp. 5–17, and Robert Solomon in his "Sex and Perversion," in R. Baker and F. Elliston (eds.), *Philosophy and Sex*, Buffalo, N.Y., Prometheus Books, 1975. Their views have been criticised by Alan Goldman's "Plain Sex" in Alan Soble (ed.), *The Philosophy of Sex: Contemporary Readings*, Totowa, N.J., Rowman and Littlefield, 1980. However, Goldman's apparently liberating stress on sex as a purely physical activity creates difficulties for correctly understanding the expressiveness of the body. Goldman seems to speak dualistically of physical acts which can be used to communicate emotions or not. My view of communication, developed in Chapter 5, would rule this out.

3. Kant, *Lectures on Ethics*, p. 167.

4. Martin Buber uses an example like this in *The Knowledge of Man: A Philosophy of the Inter-human*, Maurice Friedman (ed.), New York, Harper & Row, 1965, p. 74.

5. This model is loosely based on one developed by Peter Singer in *The Expanding Circle: Ethics and Sociobiology*, Oxford, England, Clarendon Press, 1981, pp. 111ff.

6. Aristotle, *Nicomachean Ethics*, Book 8.

7. For a fuller discussion of this distinction, see Irving Singer, "The Sensuous and the Passionate," in Alan Soble (ed.), *The Philosophy of Sex*, pp. 209–231.

8. This is a thesis fully developed by Emmanuel Levinas in *Totality and Infinity: An Essay on Exteriority*, Alphonso Lingis (trans.), Pittsburgh, Pa., Duquesne University Press, 1969; see especially p. 204.

9. Paul Ricoeur, *Fallible Man*, Charles A. Kelbley (trans.), New York, Fordham University Press, 1986, pass.

10. Immanuel Kant, *Groundwork of the Metaphysics of Morals*, 2nd ed., H. J. Paton (trans.), London, Hutchinson University Library, 1948, p. 75.

11. Jean-Paul Sartre, *Being and Nothingness*, Part 3, Chapter 3.

12. Levinas, *Totality and Infinity*, p. 200.

Chapter 5: Communication

1. Maurice Merleau-Ponty, *The Phenomenology of Perception*, Colin Smith (trans.), London, Routledge and Kegan Paul, 1962, especially Chapter 6.

2. My thinking on language has been especially influenced by two articles by Charles Taylor published in the first volume of his *Philosophical Papers: Human Agency and Language*, Cambridge, England, Cambridge University Press, 1985, entitled "Language and Human Nature" and "Theories of Meaning."

3. This example has been made famous by Ludwig Wittgenstein in his *Philosophical Investigations*, Oxford, England, Basil Blackwell, Part 1, Section 19.

4. This is one of the major points made by George Steiner in his *After Babel: Aspects of Language and Translation*, London, Oxford University Press, 1975, especially Chapter 2.

5. Sartre argues that a shared human condition is the basis for communication in his "Existentialism Is a Humanism," reprinted in W. Kaufmann (ed.), *Existentialism From Dostoevsky to Sartre*, rev. and exp. ed., New York, New American Library, 1975, p. 362. A more sophisticated argument for this position is put by Karl Jaspers in "On My Philosophy," Felix Kaufmann (trans.), in W. Kaufmann, pp. 158ff.

6. With these points, Levinas shows himself opposed to those poststructuralist theories that would assert that language speaks the subject. Levinas is still sufficiently in the existentialist tradition to want to give ontological priority to the speaker over language. On these points, see Adriaan Peperzak, "From Intentionality to Responsibility: On Levinas' Philosophy of Language" in Arleen B. Dallery and Charles E. Scott (eds.), *The Question of*

the Other: Essays in Contemporary Continental Philosophy, New York, State University of New York Press, 1989, pp. 3-22.

7. Jürgen Habermas developed his views on communicative ethics in a number of articles, including "On Systematically Distorted Communication," *Inquiry* 13 (1970), pp. 205-218; "Towards a Theory of Communicative Competence," *Inquiry* 13 (1970), pp. 360-375; "Moral Development and Ego Identity," *Telos* 24 (1975), pp. 41-55; "Some Distinctions in Universal Pragmatics," *Theory and Society* 3, no. 2 (1976), pp. 155-167; and *Legitimation Crisis*, Boston, Beacon Press, 1975, pp. 100ff. Some of these ideas and papers are gathered together in his *Communication and the Evolution of Society*, Thomas McCarthy (trans.), Boston, Beacon Press, 1979. For an early commentary, see Stan van Hooft, "Habermas' Communicative Ethics," *Social Praxis* 4, nos. 1-2 (1977), pp. 147-175.

8. Emmanuel Levinas, *Totality and Infinity: An Essay on Exteriority*, Alphonso Lingis (trans.), Pittsburgh, Pa., Duquesne University Press, 1969, p. 200.

9. See Sections 26-27 of Martin Heidegger, *Being and Time*, John Macquarrie and Edward Robinson (trans.), Oxford, England, Basil Blackwell, 1973.

10. This thesis is fully developed by Sabina Lovibond in *Realism and Imagination in Ethics*, Oxford, England, Basil Blackwell, 1983.

11. I should mention one other famous "internalist" theory of moral motivation at this point: that of Freud. For Freud, moral norms are internalised paternal demands which one becomes locked into through the operation of the Oedipus complex. If there are ideals, aspirations, and other "spiritual" values in Freud's system, they arise by sublimation from these psychic mechanisms. Given that the Oedipus complex arises from sexual desire, Freud's view is reductionist in the sense that it reduces the higher levels of our being to the first, biological level. However, my own theory does not counter Freud's. It does not operate within the same theoretical framework as his. Whereas he needs to work within a single-level biological ontology in order to pursue his scientific, explanatory project, my descriptive and interpretive project allows me to use four ontological levels, without needing to explain the higher levels in terms of the lower. I should also note that unlike Freud, I take the ideals and aspirations which we articulate at the fourth level of our being at face value as a genuine aspect of our whole being. For a classic study of Freud's views on moral development, see J. C. Flugel, *Man, Morals, and Society: A Psycho-Analytical Study*, New York, International Universities Press, 1945.

12. I am not using these terms the way that Sartre did in Part 1, Chapter 2 of his *Being and Nothingness: A Phenomenological Essay on Ontology*, Hazel Barnes (trans.), New York, Philosophical Library, 1956. For Sartre, these states were inevitable and indicative of a profound contradictoriness at the core of our being. My usage is more naive. I use these terms to designate the opposite of self-knowledge. The old adage that we should know ourselves urges us to overcome self-deception and fantasy in our self-image. It must be possible to achieve this to a satisfactory degree for ordinary living, even if Sartre's thesis is also true.

Chapter 6: Prereflexive Ethics

1. Mary Midgley, *Beast and Man: The Roots of Human Nature*, New York, Cornell University Press, 1978.

2. See, for example, Mary Midgley, "Gene Juggling," *Philosophy* 54 (1979), pp. 439–458. See also my discussion of sociobiology in the first section of Chapter 2.

3. Midgley, *Beast and Man*, pp. 256ff.

4. Jürgen Habermas, "Knowledge and Human Interests: A General Perspective," in Jeremy J. Shapiro (trans.), *Knowledge and Human Interests*, London, Heinemann, 1972.

5. Aristotle, *The Nicomachean Ethics*, Book 2, 1103a18–1103a25. His argument is based on the assumption that whatever is caused by nature is fully determined.

6. Midgley, *Beast and Man*, pp. 169, 190.

7. Ibid., pp. 52, 53.

8. Ibid., p. 332.

9. Ibid., p. 75.

10. Ibid., p. 193. Emphasis in the original.

11. Jeffrie G. Murphy, *Evolution, Morality, and the Meaning of Life*, Totowa, N.J., Rowman and Littlefield, 1982.

12. Such views were soundly criticised by Anthony Flew in his *Evolutionary Ethics*, London, Macmillan, 1967.

13. Murphy, *Evolution, Morality, and the Meaning of Life*, p. 71.

14. Ibid., p. 76.

15. For a very thorough discussion of this notion, see Agnes Heller, "The Power of Shame," in *The Power of Shame: A Rational Perspective*, London, Routledge and Kegan Paul, 1985.

16. Murphy, *Evolution, Morality, and the Meaning of Life*, p. 78. Emphasis in the original.

17. Ibid., pp. 78, 79.

18. Ibid., p. 83.

19. Ibid., p. 99. It is worth noting the similarity between this definition and that definition of moral commitment offered by Bernard Williams described in Chapter 1.

20. Ibid., p. 101.

21. These points constitute a fairly orthodox position in psychology. For as good an account as any, see David Elkind and Irving B. Weiner, *Development of the Child*, New York, John Wiley & Sons, 1978, especially pp. 130ff.

22. Freud first developed the notion of the superego in his 1923 work *The Ego and the Id*. For a classic study of Freud's views on moral development, see J. C. Flugel, *Man, Morals, and Society: A Psycho-Analytical Study*, New York, International Universities Press, 1945.

23. Richard Wollheim, *The Thread of Life*, Cambridge, England, Cambridge University Press, 1984, Chapter 7.

24. Rom Harré, *Personal Being: A Theory for Individual Psychology*, Oxford, England, Basil Blackwell, 1983, pp. 248ff.

25. Ibid., p. 106.

26. This is the central thesis of that movement of thought called Deep Ecology. For an example, see Arne Naess, *Ecology, Community, and Lifestyle*, David Rothenberg (trans., ed.), Cambridge, England, Cambridge University Press, 1989.

27. Peter Singer, *The Expanding Circle: Ethics and Sociobiology*, Oxford, England, Clarendon Press, 1981, p. 151.

28. Ibid., p. 159.

Chapter 7: Ethics and Prudence

1. Alasdair MacIntyre, *After Virtue: A Study in Moral Theory*, London, Duckworth, 1981.

2. Ibid., p. 51.

3. For a good discussion of the concept of *sittlichkeit* as used by Hegel, see Charles Taylor, *Hegel and Modern Society*, Cambridge, England, Cambridge University Press, 1979.

4. Bernard Williams, "Internal and External Reasons," in *Moral Luck*, Cambridge, England, Cambridge University Press, 1981.

5. This is argued by Peter Singer, *The Expanding Circle: Ethics and Sociobiology*, Oxford, England, Clarendon Press, 1981.

6. Jean-Paul Sartre, "Existentialism Is a Humanism," reprinted in W. Kaufmann (ed.), *Existentialism From Dostoevsky to Sartre*, rev. and exp. ed., New York, New American Library, 1975, p. 350.

7. I refer to the argument of Lord Patrick Devlin published as *The Enforcement of Morals*, Oxford, England, Oxford University Press, 1965.

8. Emmanuel Levinas, *Totality and Infinity: An Essay on Exteriority*, Alphonso Lingis (trans.), Pittsburgh, Pa., Duquesne University Press, 1969, p. 219.

Chapter 8: Morality and Integrity

1. The word *ethics* is used very widely and ambiguously in the literature, including as a name for the discourse which I am calling *morality*. However, my distinction between ethics and morality does serve to quarantine valid action-guiding arrangements from the critique that I offer of the traditional Platonic/Kantian discourse of morality.

2. Bernard Williams, "Internal and External Reasons," in his *Moral Luck*, Cambridge, England, Cambridge University Press, 1981.

3. Anscombe's intentionality test relies on agents' own superior knowledge of whether their actions are their own. Anscombe suggests that if the question Why did you do that? (whether it receives an answer or not) is accepted as applicable, then we have a case of an intentional action. Whenever agents accept such a question as applying to them, it shows that those agents own those actions as their own. See G.E.M. Anscombe, *Intention,* Oxford, England, Basil Blackwell, 1957, Section 5.

4. Emmanuel Levinas, *Totality and Infinity: An Essay on Exteriority,* Alphonso Lingis (trans.), Pittsburgh, Pa., Duquesne University Press, 1969, Section 3.

5. For a good exposition of Kierkegaard's relationship to Hegel, see Robert C. Solomon, *From Rationalism to Existentialism: The Existentialists and Their Nineteenth-Century Backgrounds,* New York, Harper & Row, 1972, Chapter 3.

6. For a discussion of the question whether Levinas's argument is empiricist or transcendental, see Robert Bernasconi, "Rereading Totality and Infinity," in Arleen B. Dallery and Charles E. Scott (eds.), *The Question of the Other,* Albany, State University of New York Press, 1989.

7. Martin Heidegger, *Being and Time,* John Macquarrie and Edward Robinson (trans.), Oxford, Basil Blackwell, 1973, Sections 46-53.

8. Wollheim on instinct was discussed in Chapter 1.

9. I refer to Jan Narveson's chapter "Violence and War," in Tom Regan (ed.), *Matters of Life and Death: New Introductory Essays in Moral Philosophy,* New York, Random House, 1980, pp. 109-147. Jeffrey Blustein, in his *Caring and Commitment: Taking the Personal Point of View,* New York, Oxford University Press, 1991, pp. 86, 87, also discusses this issue. Blustein sees the duty to maintain one's own integrity as a second-order duty which gives added importance to one's core commitments, rather than as a separate commitment capable of competing with core commitments. He does not see it as likely that agents could refuse to do what their core commitments demanded simply to preserve their integrity. Rather, their concern for their integrity gives a greater steadfastness to their moral commitments.

   My own view would be that integrity would not be a second-order concern because our self-project, of which the self-image which integrity would seek to preserve is an expression, is equiprimordial with the caring-about-others which is the basis of the moral core commitments Blustein talks about. In this way integrity is implicated in all moral actions rather than being a further principle in light of which we might or might not act. My distinction between the aim of an action and the object of the action will help solve the problem. My integrity can be the aim of my ethical actions while utility is their object. Given the duality of my deep caring, there is nothing egotistical in being concerned for integrity even while my intentions focus beyond me toward others.

10. Jean-Paul Sartre, "Existentialism Is a Humanism," reprinted in W. Kaufmann (ed.), *Existentialism From Dostoevsky to Sartre* (rev. and exp. ed.), New York, New American Library, 1975, p. 354.

Bibliography

Agich, George J. "Professionalism and Ethics in Health Care," *Journal of Medicine and Philosophy* 5 (September 1980), pp. 186–199.

Alexander, Richard D. *Darwinism and Human Affairs*, Washington, D.C., University of Washington Press, 1979.

Alper, Joseph S. "Facts, Values, and Biology," *The Philosophical Forum* 13, nos. 2-3 (1981-1982), pp. 85–108.

Anscombe, G.E.M. *Intention*, Oxford, England, Basil Blackwell, 1957.

Aristotle, *The Nicomachean Ethics*, J.A.K. Thomson (trans.), Harmondsworth, England, Penguin Books, 1955.

Barash, David P. *Sociobiology: The Whisperings Within*, London, Collins, 1979.

Bernasconi, Robert. "Rereading Totality and Infinity," in Arleen B. Dallery and Charles E. Scott (eds.), *The Question of the Other*, Albany, State University of New York Press, 1989.

Blattner, B. *Holistic Nursing*, Englewood Cliffs, N. J., Prentice-Hall, 1981.

Blustein, Jeffrey. *Caring and Commitment: Taking the Personal Point of View*, New York, Oxford University Press, 1991.

Buber, Martin. *The Knowledge of Man: A Philosophy of the Interhuman*, Maurice Friedman (ed.), New York, Harper & Row, 1965.

Carper, Barbara A. "The Ethics of Caring," *Advances in Nursing Science* 1 (April 1979), pp. 11–20.

Devlin, Lord Patrick. *The Enforcement of Morals*, Oxford, England, Oxford University Press, 1965.

Elkind, David, and Irving B. Weiner. *Development of the Child*, New York, John Wiley & Sons, 1978.

Flew, Anthony. *Evolutionary Ethics*, London, Macmillan, 1967.

Flugel, J. C. *Man, Morals, and Society: A Psycho-Analytical Study*, New York, International Universities Press, 1945.

Frankfurt, Harry. "The Importance of What We Care About," *Synthèse* 53, no. 2 (1982), pp. 257–272.

Gilligan, Carol. *In a Different Voice: Psychological Theory and Women's Development*, Cambridge, Mass., Harvard University Press, 1982.

BIBLIOGRAPHY

Goldman, Alan. "Plain Sex," in Alan Soble (ed.), *The Philosophy of Sex: Contemporary Readings,* Totowa, N.J., Rowman and Littlefield, 1980.

Griffin, Anne P. "A Philosophical Analysis of Caring in Nursing," *Journal of Advanced Nursing* 8 (1983), pp. 289–295.

Gustafson, W. "Motivational and Historical Aspects of Care and Nursing," in M. Leininger (ed.), *Caring: An Essential Human Need, Proceedings of Three National Caring Conferences,* Thorofare, N.J., Charles B. Slack, 1981.

Habermas, Jürgen. "Knowledge and Human Interests: A General Perspective," in Jeremy J. Shapiro (trans.), *Knowledge and Human Interests,* London, Heinemann, 1972.

——. *Legitimation Crisis,* Boston, Beacon Press, 1975.

——. *Communication and the Evolution of Society,* Thomas McCarthy (trans.), Boston, Beacon Press, 1979.

Hampshire, Stuart. *Public and Private Morality,* Cambridge, England, Cambridge University Press, 1978.

Harré, Rom. *Personal Being: A Theory for Individual Psychology,* Oxford, England, Basil Blackwell, 1983.

Heidegger, Martin. *Being and Time,* John Macquarrie and Edward Robinson (trans.), Oxford, England, Basil Blackwell, 1973.

Heller, Agnes. "The Power of Shame," in *The Power of Shame: A Rational Perspective,* London, Routledge and Kegan Paul, 1985.

Jaspers, Karl. "On My Philosophy," Felix Kaufmann (trans.), in Walter Kaufmann (ed.), *Existentialism From Dostoevsky to Sartre,* New York, World Publishing, 1965.

Kant, Immanuel, *Groundwork of the Metaphysics of Morals,* 2nd ed., H. J. Paton (trans.), London, Hutchinson University Library, 1948.

——. *Lectures on Ethics,* Louis Infield (trans.), New York, Harper & Row, 1963.

Kaufmann, Walter (ed.). *Existentialism From Dostoevsky to Sartre,* rev. and exp. ed., New York, New American Library, 1975.

Kluge, Eike-Henner W. "Nursing: Vocation or Profession," *Canadian Nurse* 78 (February 1982), pp. 34–36.

Kolakowski, Leszek. *Religion,* Oxford, England, Oxford University Press, 1982.

Leininger, M. (ed.). *Caring: An Essential Human Need, Proceedings of Three National Caring Conferences,* Thorofare, N.J., Charles B. Slack, 1981.

——. *Care: The Essence of Nursing and Health,* Thorofare, N.J., Charles B. Slack, 1984.

Levinas, Emmanuel. *Totality and Infinity: An Essay on Exteriority,* Alphonso Lingis (trans.), Pittsburgh, Pa., Duquesne University Press, 1969.

Lovibond, Sabina. *Realism and Imagination in Ethics,* Oxford, England, Basil Blackwell, 1983.

MacIntyre, Alasdair. *After Virtue: A Study in Moral Theory,* London, Duckworth, 1981.

Maslow, Abraham. "A Theory of Metamotivation: The Biological Rooting of the Value-Life," *The Journal of Humanistic Psychology* 7, no. 2 (Fall 1967), pp. 93–127.

Mayeroff, Milton. *On Caring,* New York, Harper & Row, 1971.

BIBLIOGRAPHY

Merleau-Ponty, Maurice. *Phenomenology of Perception,* Colin Smith (trans.), London, Routledge and Kegan Paul, 1962.

Midgley, Mary. *Beast and Man: The Roots of Human Nature,* New York, Cornell University Press, 1978.

———. "Gene Juggling," *Philosophy* 54 (1979), pp. 439–458.

Mitchell, Basil. *Morality: Religious and Secular,* Oxford, England, Oxford University Press, 1980.

Murphy, Jeffrie G. *Evolution, Morality, and the Meaning of Life,* Totowa, N.J., Rowman and Littlefield, 1982.

Naess, Arne. *Ecology, Community, and Lifestyle,* David Rothenberg (trans., ed.), Cambridge, England, Cambridge University Press, 1989.

Nagel, Thomas. "Sexual Perversion," *The Journal of Philosophy* 66, no. 1 (1969), pp. 5–17.

Narveson, Jan. "Violence in War," in Tom Regan (ed.), *Matters of Life and Death: New Introductory Essays in Moral Philosophy,* New York, Random House, 1980.

Nehamas, Alexander. *Nietzsche: Life as Literature,* Cambridge, Mass., Harvard University Press, 1985.

Nielsen, Kai. "Morality and Commitment," *Ideal Studies* 7 (1977), pp. 94–107.

Noddings, Nell. *Caring: A Feminine Approach to Ethics and Moral Education,* Berkeley, University of California Press, 1984.

Nokes, Peter. *The Professional Task in Welfare Practice,* London, Routledge and Kegan Paul, 1967.

Peperzak, Adriaan. "From Intentionality to Responsibility: On Levinas' Philosophy of Language," in Arleen B. Dallery and Charles E. Scott (eds.), *The Question of the Other: Essays in Contemporary Continental Philosophy,* New York, State University of New York Press, 1989.

Plato. *The Symposium,* Walter Hamilton (trans.), Harmondsworth, England, Penguin Books, 1951.

———. *The Republic,* H.D.P. Lee (trans.), Harmondsworth, England, Penguin Books, 1955.

Ricoeur, Paul. *Fallible Man,* Charles A. Kelbley (trans.), New York, Fordham University Press, 1986.

Riemen, Doris J. "The Essential Structure of a Caring Interaction: A Phenomenological Study," Ph.D. diss., Texas Women's University, Ann Arbor, Michigan, University Microfilms International, 1983.

Roach, Simone M. "The Act of Caring as Expressed in a Code of Ethics," *Canadian Nurse* 78 (June 1982), pp. 30–32.

Ruse, Michael. *Sociobiology: Sense or Nonsense?* Dordrecht, Netherlands, D. Reidel Publishing, 1979.

———. "The Morality of the Gene," *Monist* 67 (1984), pp. 167–199.

Sartre, Jean-Paul. "Existentialism Is a Humanism," reprinted in W. Kaufmann (ed.), *Existentialism From Dostoevsky to Sartre,* rev. and exp. ed., New York, New American Library, 1975.

——. *Being and Nothingness: A Phenomenological Essay on Ontology*, Hazel Barnes (trans.), New York, Philosophical Library, 1956.

Searle, John R. "Sociobiology and the Explanation of Behavior," in M. S. Gregory, A. Silvers, and D. Sutch (eds.), *Sociobiology and Human Nature*, San Francisco, Jossey-Bass, 1978.

Singer, Irving. "The Sensuous and the Passionate," in Alan Soble (ed.), *The Philosophy of Sex: Contemporary Readings*, Totowa, N.J., Rowman and Littlefield, 1980.

Singer, Peter. *Practical Ethics*, Cambridge, England, Cambridge University Press, 1979.

——. *The Expanding Circle: Ethics and Sociobiology*, Oxford, England, Clarendon Press, 1981.

Sociobiology Study Group of Science for the People. "Sociobiology — Another Biological Determinism," in Arthur L. Caplan (ed.), *The Sociobiology Debate*, New York, Harper & Row, 1978.

Solomon, Robert C. *From Rationalism to Existentialism: The Existentialists and Their Nineteenth-Century Backgrounds*, New York, Harper & Row, 1972.

——. "Sex and Perversion" in R. Baker and F. Elliston (eds.), *Philosophy and Sex*, Buffalo, N.Y., Prometheus Books, 1975.

——. *The Passions: The Myth and Nature of Human Emotion*, Notre Dame, Ind., University of Notre Dame Press, 1983.

Steiner, George. *After Babel: Aspects of Language and Translation*, Oxford, England, Oxford University Press, 1975.

Stent, Gunther S. (ed.), *Morality as a Biological Phenomenon*, Berkeley, University of California Press, 1978.

Taylor, Charles. *Hegel and Modern Society*, Cambridge, England, Cambridge University Press, 1979.

——. *Philosophical Papers: Human Agency and Language*, Cambridge, England, Cambridge University Press, 1985.

Taylor, Gabriele. "Integrity," *Proceedings of the Aristotelian Society (Supp.)* 55 (1981), pp. 143–159.

Tennant, Neil. "Evolutionary Versus Evolved Ethics," *Philosophy* 58 (1983), pp. 289–302.

Trigg, Roger. *The Shaping of Man: Philosophical Aspects of Sociobiology*, Oxford, England, Basil Blackwell, 1982.

van Hooft, Stan. "Habermas' Communicative Ethics," *Social Praxis* 4, nos. 1-2 (1977), pp. 147–175.

——. "Caring and Professional Commitment," *The Australian Journal of Advanced Nursing* 4, no. 4 (June-August 1987), pp. 29–38.

——. "Weakness of Will," *The Southern Journal of Philosophy* 26, no. 3 (1988), pp. 403–421.

——. "Obligation, Character, and Commitment," *Philosophy* 63 (1988), pp. 345–362.

Watson, J. *Nursing: Human Science and Human Care: A Theory of Nursing*, Norwalk, Conn., Appleton-Century-Crofts, 1985.

Williams, Bernard. *Morality: An Introduction to Ethics*, Cambridge, England, Cambridge University Press, 1972.

BIBLIOGRAPHY

——. "Internal and External Reasons," in *Moral Luck*, Cambridge, England, Cambridge University Press, 1981.

——. *Ethics and the Limits of Philosophy*, London, Collins, 1985.

Wilson, E. O., and C. J. Lumsden. *Genes, Mind, and Culture: The Coevolutionary Process*, Cambridge, Mass., Harvard University Press, 1981.

Wilson, Edward O. *Sociobiology: The New Synthesis*, Cambridge, Mass., Harvard University Press, 1966.

Wittgenstein, Ludwig. *Philosophical Investigations*, Oxford, England, Basil Blackwell, 1963.

Wollheim, Richard. *The Thread of Life*, Cambridge, England, Cambridge University Press, 1984.

Index

Abandonment, 78

Absolutism, 168

Acculturation: and attitudes, 67-69, 86; as cultural formation, 54, 77; and involuntary expression, 99; and passivity, 114; and role models, 156

Action-guiding arrangements, 145, 158

Action-guiding norms, 140

Advocacy, 159-61

Affection, 77

Aims: distinguished from objects, 200(n9)

Alienation, 64, 69

Allowing others to be, 94

Altruism. 77, 134, 154

Animals, 122, 130

Anomie, 69-70

Anscombe, G.E.M., 202(n3)

Aristophanes, 90

Aristotle: on *Eudaimonia*, 57, 72, 142, 166-67; on feeling rightly, 2, 39; on friendship, 88, 135; on goals for life, 119, 143, 165; on habits, 130; on the nature of ethics, 141, 175; on *phronesis*, 122; on practical reason, 126; on the soul, 4, 49; on voluntariness, 180

Art, 74, 76, 87, 118

Artists, 59

Attention, 38

Attitudes: as evaluative preconscious structures, 56; as a form of determinable caring, 58, 76; and ideals, 67; required by language, 103, 105; shared, 86

Authenticity, 46, 111, 185

Autonomy, 134-35

Bad faith, 116, 170, 177

Behaviourism, 101-02, 130

Being, 7, 48

Being-for-others, 75

Belief, 40, 56-57

Blustein, Jeffrey, 9ff, 202(n9)

Body, 49, 65, 174

Bond: of affection, 131, 136; of love, 79

Buber, Martin, 195(n12), 198(n4)

Call-to-action, 16, 95, 110, 137, 180; defined, 138, 177

Carelessness, 30

Caring: as adjective, 30; as adverb, 44; as a burden, 29; cognitive element in, 35; and commitment, 27, 28, 139; contrasted with desire, 42; contrasted with rule-bound, 31; failures of, 38; and importance, 36; indicated by action, 37; as motivation, 29-39; about oneself, 34

Caring about: contrasted with caring for, 32, 35, 119

Caring-about-others: defined, 75ff; equiprimordial with self-project, 76; structure of, 138

Caring for: contrasted with caring about, 32, 35, 119

Caring professions, 31

Character: Hampshire on, 14-15; ideals of, 156; moral significance of, 83; related to commitment, 16-17, 18; and roles, 150; Williams on, 4

Charity, 92

Childhood, 133

Choice, 18, 172, 186, 190

Circle, as map of our relationships, 81, 91, 137

Commitment: and attitudes, 58; basis of faith, 69-71; contrasted to *a* commitment, 26; defined, 13; and fulfillment, 162; making or having, 18; objects of, 17ff; to persons, 19-20; related to caring, 27, 28, 139; related to freedom, 23; related to obligation, 26; related to reason, 71-72; to a way of life, 17-18; Wolheim applied to, 43

Communication: and conflict, 87; and ethical discourse, 159; defined, 96; on the Biological Level, 99-100; universal dimension, 109

Communicative ethics, 111, 150, 162

Communicative gestures, 78, 97

Community, 74, 95, 159

Conflict, 86

Connotation, 104

Conscience, 125, 131-33

Cooperation, 84

Creativity, 188. *See also* Moral creativity

Crisis, 169

Cultural formation. *See* Acculturation

Culture, 7, 144

Customs, 145

Darwin, Charles, 124–27, 131, 146

Death, 53, 61–63, 101, 104, 184

Decision, 171. *See also* Choice

Deep caring: defined, 4, 8; distinguished from the biological level, 50; distinguished from determinable caring, 57; as meaning-giving, 55, 67; not intentional, 39, 44; related to commitment, 28; related to ethics, 165; and self-image, 64

Deliberation, 140

Denotation, 104

Dependence, 77

Deontology, 142

Desire, 41ff, 56; contrasted with reason, 121ff, 171

Dialogue, 111

Diderot, 143

Dilemma, 170, 176, 186–87

Dispositions, 51, 58. *See also* Mental dispositions

Discourse ethics. *See* Communicative ethics

Dualism, 1

Duty, 178

Dyad: mother-child, 133

Education, 181

Ego ideal, 116

Einstein, Albert, 61

Embarrassment, 98

Embodiment, 78, 100, 136

Emotion, 55

Emotivism, 142

Encounter, 93, 109

Enlightenment, 142

Enthusiasm, 69, 89

Environment, 76. *See also* Nature

Ergon, 120

Ethical agents, 153

Ethical discourse: founded in deep caring, 160; functions of, 157–58

Ethical feelings, 124–29

Ethical freedom, 152

Ethical ideals. *See* Ideals

Ethical innovation, 155, 176, 188

Ethical nonconformism, 152, 156–57, 176, 189. *See also* Moral reform

Ethical project: self as, 116

Ethics: basis for, 76, 112, 115–118; and community, 95; defined, 120, 140; distinguished from morality, 141, 147, 199(n1); distinguished from prudence, 141; and *ethos,* 144; and law, 146; Levina's theory of, 94, 110; professional, 148; as theory of morality, 113; sociological theories of, 114

Ethos, 86, 144

Etiquette, 111, 145

Eudaimonia, 57, 120, 142, 167–68. *See also* Fulfillment; Happiness

Evolutionary theory, 77, 100, 124–29

Executive virtues, 26

Existentialism, 46, 63, 66, 116, 178, 185

Expression, 98, 109, 162, 185

Expressive intentions, 105

External reasons, 152–55

Face: of the other, 92

Facticity, 53, 179

Faith, 68ff, 87, 156, 166, 175

Fanaticism, 28

Fear, 77, 132

Feminism, 2, 29

Fenelon, Archbishop, 137, 177

First-person description, 66

Flew, Anthony, 198(n12)

Fondness, 33

Form of the Good, 24

Frankfurt, Harry, 36

Freedom: as authenticity, 185; and commitment, 23; and dilemmas, 176–180; as an ethical challenge, 180; and ethics, 157; and external reasons, 153–55; and instincts, 123; as a noun, 177; as owning our actions, 184, 188; Sartre on, 22, 76, 94; and sex, 89

Free will, 7, 151

Freud, Sigmund, 45, 121, 125, 132, 197(n11). *See also* Psychoanalysis

Friendship, 88, 135

Fulfillment, 62, 85, 173, 185. *See also Eudaimonia*

Gender, 63

general principles, 190

Genotype, 51

God, 1, 92, 175

Goldman, Alan, 195(n2)

Guilt, 117, 175

Habermas, Jürgen, 111, 122
Habits, 123, 130
Hampshire, Stuart, 14, 17, 26
Happiness, 72, 144. *See also Eudaimonia*
Harré, Rom, 133, 162
Health, 101
Hegel, G.W.F., 144, 183
Heidegger, Martin, 48, 55, 76; on death, 63, 184; on social chitchat, 111
Hermeneutics, 7, 45, 155, 167, 176
Hiddenness: of attitudes, 88
Holism. *See* Whole person
Hope, 168
Horizon, 45, 57, 63, 86, 119, 120, 167
Human condition, 108
Hume, David, 76, 112, 128, 143
Hunting: as example of caring-about-others, 79
Huxley, J. S., 124

Ideals: bonds with, 136; and ethical innovation, 156; as expressions of deep caring, 66ff; as objects of commitment, 70; and persons, 21; at the spiritual level, 87, 107
Identity, 82, 90. *See also* Integrity
Immortality, 183
Importance: and caring, 36; and deliberation, 169, 172; and instincts, 124; as a mark of the moral, 4, 10, 58, 116, 137; and meaning, 70; self-project, 117
Individuality, 73, 90-1
Infancy, 77
Infinity, 92, 109, 162
Information theory, 97
Instinct, 42, 44, 50, 51, 80, 121, 125, 187; open and closed distinguished, 123
Integrity: and authenticity, 47; Blustein on, 9, 11; and creativity, 190; and dilemmas, 172; and ethical discourse, 160; and external reasons, 154-55; and freedom, 180; as owning our actions, 188; and pacifism, 189, 200(n9); related "to integrate," 60, 71, 73; and self-project, 63, 68, 154, 171; and sex, 89; Taylor on, 15, 24; and virtues, 144. *See also* Whole person
Intentional actions, 176
Intentionality, 42, 99, 200(n3)
Intentions, 37
Interests, 58, 60, 86, 161
Internal reasons, 152-55
Intimacy, 85, 90-1

Intolerance, 161
Involuntary expressions, 97
Isolation, 38

Jaspers, Karl, 196(n3), 198(n5)

Kant: as absolutist, 169, 183; on ethics, 1, 141; on freedom, 180; on Kingdom of Ends, 93; on legislating the moral law, 159; on practical reason, 172; and objectivism, 113; on sexuality, 78
Kierkegaard, Søren, 143, 183
Kingdom of Ends, 93
Kohlberg, Lawrence, 134
Kolakowski, Leszek, 14

Language: as action-guiding arrangement, 150; established sociability, 106; needed for praxis, 101; referential view of, 113; and self-expression, 106, 110; and shared attitudes, 105; and the world, 104
Law, 146
Legal moralism, 146, 161
Levinas, Emmanuel; on encounter, 109, 134; on ethics, 94, 110; on expression, 162; on infinity, 92-5, 179, 182-84; on language, 196(n6)
Lexicon, 103
Life plan, 61, 64
Love: family, 135; and identity, 91; and infinity, 92; romantic, 87; sexual, 78, 89-90, 100; and shared faith, 87-91
Lumsden, C. J., 51

MacIntyre, Alasdair, 142-44, 148
Marriage, 19
Marx, Karl, 58
Maslow, Abraham, 59, 85
Mayeroff, Milton, 33
Meaning, 54, 63, 99; of life, 7, 62, 69
Mental activities, 39ff
Mental dispositions, 39ff, 119; applied to motivation, 52
Mental state, 39ff
Merleu-Ponty, Maurice, 55, 100
Metaphysics: of the self, 63ff; and ethics, 142
Methodology, 6. *See also* Hermeutics; Phenomenology
Midgley, Mary, 121
Mitchell, Basil, 22
Modernism, 142

Moral creativity, 188–89
Moral crisis, 169
Moral development, 130–35
Moral dilemma, 169. *See also* Dilemma
Moral obligation, 117
Moral order, 133
Moral psychology, 126
Moral realism, 113, 128, 179. *See also* Objectivism
Moral reform, 151, 159. *See also* Ethical noncon-
    formism
Moral self-appraisal, 179
Moral theory, 1, 157, 172–74
Moralism. *See* Intolerance
Morality: and deliberation, 83; as discourse, 165;
    distinguished from ethics, 141, 147; distin-
    guished from prudence, 141; and religion,
    68, 112
Mothering, 131
Motivation, 52, 29–39, 115, 154
Murphy, Jeffrey G., 124-29

Naming, 102
Narrative, 143
Natural selection. *See* Evolutionary theory
Nature, 136. *See also* Environment
Needs, 50, 59–60
Nielson, Kai, 13, 17
Nietzsche, Friedrich, 46, 64, 127, 143, 188,
    197(n19)
Nihilism, 1, 64
Noddings, Nell, 34, 46
Norms: distinguished from habits, 130
Nouns: replaced by verbs, 6, 48, 60, 64, 121, 177.
    See also Verbs

Objectification, 93
Objectivism, 10, 113, 128. *See also* Moral realism
Obligation: and ethics, 1; and law, 146; to self, 23
Obsession, 28
Oedipus complex, 125, 132, 199(n11)
Ontology, 8, 48, 75, 83, 92, 173
Others, 93, 109
Owning: an action, 98, 176; as autonomy, 134;
    as freedom, 184; and integrity, 180; invol-
    untary expressions, 97-8; my life, 73; our
    biological level, 174; our self-image, 65,
    116, 179

Pacifism, 189
Pain, 97, 101, 102

Particularism, 93, 190
Passion, 69, 89
Pavlov. *See* Behaviourism
Paying attention, 30
Personality, 132
Phenomenology: as infinity, 110; inner experi-
    ence, 45, 50; methodology, 6, 8, 159, 176,
    183
Phenotype, 51
Philosophy, 61, 74
Phronesis, 122–29, 153–54, 172. *See also* Practical
    reason; Prudence
Plato: as absolutist, 169; on the body, 174;
    on morality, 3; on social contract, 84;
    Symposium, 90; Theory of Forms, 61;
    on *thumos,* 70
Pluralism, 71, 73
Postmodernism, 67, 73, 113, 178; and moral
    theory, 1–3
Poststructuralism, 198–199(n6)
Practical necessity, 3, 36
Practical reason: Darwin on, 126; and dilemmas,
    173; distinguished from theoretical
    reason, 122; relation to desire, 123
Practical syllogism, 122
Praxis, 56, 83
Prejudice, 82–83
Profession: and commitment, 16
Professional ethics, 148
Prudence, 123–29, 141, 148. *See also Phronesis*
Psychoanalysis, 131. *See also* Freud
Psychological symbiosis, 133-4

Racism, 82
Rapport: basis for love, 88
Reaction, 54
Reason: in animals, 122; and commitment,
    13–17; and conscience, 125; contrasted
    with desire, 121, 171; as control, 157; and
    faith, 69; implicit, 168; practical, 15, 148;
    practical and theoretical distinguished,
    122
Reflection, 69, 73, 117
Reflexivity, 52, 56, 102, 122, 129, 164
Relational being, 135. *See also* Psychological
    symbiosis
Relativism, 114, 127
Religion, 14, 68, 74, 87, 112, 118; and moral
    sanctions, 175
Responsibility, 77, 82, 131; bonds of, 136–38

Ricoeur, Paul, 92
Rights, 133, 146
Role models, 136, 149, 151, 156
Romantic thought, 74
Rousseau, Jean-Jacques, 84
Rules, 31

Sartre, Jean-Paul: on acting for others, 159; on bad
    faith, 199(n12); on being-for-others, 75, 76,
    94; on choice, 21–22, 37, 191
Schopenhauer, Arthur, 61
Science, 61, 118
Self, 63, 81, 156, 178
Self-authentication, 59, 85
Self-consciousness, 52
Self-deception, 116, 170
Self-image, 64, 66, 87, 116; ethical, 174
Self-project: defined, 63, 66; equiprimordial with
    caring-about-others, 76; ground for ethics,
    116; and life-world, 55; Sartre on, 76; and
    survival, 53
Self-realisation, 66. *See also Eudaimonia*
Self-righteousness, 189
Selfishness, 46, 77, 134
Sensitivity, 67
Sex, 78, 89, 90
Sexism, 82
Sexual love. *See* Love
Shakespeare, William, 64
Shame, 125, 175
Signals: as behavioural triggers, 101
Singer, Peter, 137, 158, 159
Sittlichkeit, 144
Sociability, 77, 81, 86, 146, 161; Darwin on, 124–27;
    and language, 106. *See also* Solidarity
Social contract, 84
Social chitchat, 111
Society, 84
Sociobiology, 50, 61, 125, 127–29
Socrates, 24–27
Solidarity, 75, 77, 80, 85–86, 95, 135; established
    through language, 110; as function of ethics,
    115. *See also* Sociability
Solomon, Robert C., 197(n13)

Spinoza, Baruch, 61
Summum bonum, 143
Superego, 132, 199(n11)
Sympathy, 92, 102, 105

Taylor, Gabriele, 24
Teleology, 143
Telos, 127, 166
Ten Commandments, 113
Theoretical reason: distinguished from practical
    reason, 122
Third-person description, 66
Thumos, 70
Totality, 183
Traditional morality, 169
Traits, 51, 123, 150
Trust, 85ff

Ultimacy, 3, 70, 73, 168
Ultimate concern, 89
Universalism, 167
Utilitarianism, 1, 11, 17

Verbs: preferred to nouns, 6, 48, 60, 64, 108, 121.
    See also Nouns
Virtue, 1, 34, 116, 143, 150
Vocation, 16
Vulnerability, 36

Waddington, C. H., 124
Weakness of will, 24, 157
Whole person, 10, 48, 54, 56, 61, 172, 176. *See also*
    Integrity
Wholeness, *See* Whole person
Williams, Bernard: on external reasons, 152–53,
    173; on practical necessity, 3–4, 36, 124
Will to Power, 46
Wilson, E. O., 51, 127
Wollheim, Richard: applied to commitment, 43;
    on instinct, 44, 50, 121, 125, 187; on the
    mental, 39–45, 52, 58
Women, 150

Xenophobia, 82